Relationships in Counseling

and the Counselor's Life

Jeffrey A. Kottler and Richard S. Balkin

AMERICAN COUNSELING
ASSOCIATION
6101 Stevenson Avenue, Suite 600
Alexandria, VA 22304
www.counseling.org

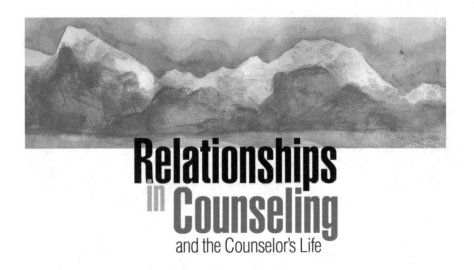

Relationships
in Counseling
and the Counselor's Life

American Counseling Association
6101 Stevenson Avenue, Suite 600 | Alexandria, VA 22304

Associate Publisher	Carolyn C. Baker
Digital and Print Development Editor	Nancy Driver
Senior Production Manager	Bonny E. Gaston
Production Coordinator	Karen Thompson
Copy Editor	Kay Mikel

Cover and text design by Bonny E. Gaston

Library of Congress Cataloging-in-Publication Data

Names: Kottler, Jeffrey A., author. | Balkin, Richard S., author.
Title: Relationships in counseling—and the counselor's life / Jeffrey A. Kottler, Richard S. Balkin.
Description: Alexandria, VA : American Counseling Association, [2017] | Includes bibliographical references and index.
Identifiers: LCCN 2016035471 | ISBN 9781556203602 (pbk. : alk. paper)
Subjects: LCSH: Counseling psychologist and client. | Counseling psychologists. | Counseling psychology—Practice.
Classification: LCC BF636.6 .K685 2017 | DDC 158.3—dc23 LC record available at https://lccn.loc.gov/2016035471

Table of Contents

Preface

What is truly special about human beings as a species? Is it that we have invented tools to increase our proficiency at gathering food and managing daily life? Is it our development of language? Perhaps it is our complex social behavior? Although we have developed these abilities to an extraordinary degree, at least compared to other inhabitants of the planet, they are hardly unique. After all, chimpanzees have been known to use tools to hunt for food or to defend themselves. Ants and termites are far better organized in their social networks, and dolphins and whales rely on their own verbal language system to communicate regularly.

What distinguishes us from other creatures is that we have developed the capacity for empathy: We are mind readers! Evolution has equipped us with the ability to reliably and accurately sense what others are feeling and to place ourselves in their shoes (or sandals). This has permitted us to decode others' body language, facial expressions, and verbal subtleties in such a way that we can usually assess whether someone is an ally and friend or a potential threat. This has made it possible for us to function more cooperatively within our social groups and to respond sensitively to members of our "tribe" who need support, reassurance, or assistance. The empathic mind is also what makes counseling work, in all its forms and permutations.

With respect to the practice of counseling relationships, we are talking about a subject so complex and challenging that it defies any simple explanation or easy answers. Dozens of models reflect their own particular emphasis or theoretical orientation, whether in the form of transference, working alliance, real relationship, empathic resonance, collaborative stance, attuned responsiveness, attachment interactions, corrective emotional experience, or immediacy, to mention only a few. Each relational conception attempts to explain, or at least to describe, the mechanisms of change that take place during the time counselors and clients spend together.

In spite of the emphasis on empirically supported treatments (or ESTs), manualized strategies, and evidence-based practice (or EBP), relatively little attention is paid to the results of the studies upon which most models are based. A consensus in the field has emerged that many specific interventions and strategies have limited impact on counseling outcomes compared to the so-called common factors, which include client and counselor characteristics and, especially, the helping relationship. In addition, counselors feel undue pressure to incorporate particular strategies that may actually act as a barrier to more successful helping efforts. We all hunger for new techniques, novel interventions, and revolutionary advances in theory development, sometimes forgetting that the power of the relationship strengthens everything else we do to help people.

This book integrates the evidence supporting relational factors in counseling in a way that is both accessible and clinically useful. In addition, we focus on the reciprocal impact of the counseling alliance—how practitioners, as well as clients, are affected as a result of the intimate encounter, for better or worse.

An Unusual Collaboration and an Improbable Partnership

This is a book about relationships. It is also a story about our own relationship, which began 15 years ago when Rick was a doctoral student, taking an advanced group course that used one of Jeffrey's texts as a primary source. It was the first book in the field in which the author felt "real" to Rick, so much so that he was determined to meet Jeffrey at the next professional conference. Their first meeting was one of unequal power, with Rick as the deferential student and Jeffrey an established academic. There were other brief meetings at subsequent conferences, but mostly polite encounters. They would not have another conversation for more than 12 years.

Meanwhile, Rick worked hard to establish his own professional identity and reputation as a scholar and counselor educator. While Jeffrey continued writing two or three books each year about relationship issues, Rick mostly concentrated on his own research agenda and teaching, specializing in inferential statistics and assessment instruments (we warned you this was an unusual partnership).

In his wisdom (or audacity), the president of the American Counseling Association, who was a long-standing friend to both of us, as well as being Rick's mentor, invited us to team up to keynote the national conference. Jeffrey's first thought—and the first words out of his mouth during the keynote speech—was, "What the heck was he thinking?" It seemed ridiculous, first of all, to invite two people to deliver a speech together about relationships in counseling but particularly so considering that their styles were so completely different, their interests almost in opposite domains, and they hardly knew one another, much less ever collaborated on anything before.

Rick and Jeffrey tried to negotiate their differing opinions about the best format and structure for this speech, which represented one of the highlights of the careers of both men. Jeffrey was far more experienced in this area, having delivered similar keynotes at other international and national conferences in the past, but that didn't mean that Rick was any less opinionated about what they should do and how they should do it. In their dialogue with one another, they eventually settled on the idea of emphasizing process as well as content, which, after all, is what counseling is all about. What can one really do in 40 minutes that makes any kind of difference to an audience of several thousand people crowded in a hot room? They decided they would try to model the kind of relationship that they wished to profile in their talk, one that was collaborative, genuine, warm, engaging, and empowering. You know, the usual.

Jeffrey was quite comfortable with this format and was used to improvising and winging it, depending on his mood and the audience responses, but Rick much preferred a clear structure. As a quantitative researcher, he was far more familiar with presenting findings supported by numbers. He loved the idea that they could write out a script ahead of time and basically get to read it on the teleprompter on stage. However, Jeffrey was insistent that the experience would be more lively, entertaining, and interesting if they tried to *be* with one another in such a way that it reflected what they were actually talking about.

It was when they were about to walk out on stage that Jeffrey informed Rick that he made a few changes to the slides and not to be surprised if he "went off script a little bit." This doesn't sound exactly collaborative, but Jeffrey's intent was to help Rick loosen up a bit so they might capitalize on the strengths of their own relationship to support and empower one another. Rick was trying to calm his nerves and practicing deep breathing, so he barely registered what Jeffrey had just told him. It all became quite clear when they landed on stage and Jeffrey proceeded to ignore their prepared slides altogether and walked to the edge to talk directly to the audience. He told them that Robert Smith must have been a little crazy to pair two such radically different professionals together and then give them a little more than half an hour to talk about the most complex, multifaceted, confusing, and significant feature of what we do—forming relational connections with clients.

Then, something magical happened. Jeffrey, the consummate storyteller, launched into a tale about his latest adventures working in Nepal with at-risk girls, highlighting how this was essentially a relational intervention. He finished with a flourish, leaving the audience practically in tears, and then turned to Rick and said, "Over to you, Partner." Rick responded with a horrified look on his face as the next slide came on the screen profiling him with the words, "I love statistics!" The audience laughed uproariously at the awkward transition, wondering how Rick would recover.

What happened next sometimes occurs in rich, collaborative partnerships when the participants decide to just trust one another and go with the flow. Rick told his own story, also off script and spontaneously created, and they both knew at that exact moment that they were going to be okay, that this would indeed work. They weren't certain what the association's president imagined would ever happen in this shotgun marriage, but it turned out just fine.

Jeffrey and Rick began their relationship in the customary and familiar configuration of unequal power that eventually was negotiated into one of mutual trust and optimal functioning, and this is what led them to coauthor this book together as a much more detailed and deep investigation of the most important subject in our profession—the most effective relationships that counselors develop and nurture with their clients, as well as with their loved ones.

Overview of What (Mostly) Follows

In this book, we address common misconceptions about what works in counseling and present strategies for further developing the counseling relationship and enhancing our own expertise and outcomes. Representing the strengths of the two coauthors—one, an empirical researcher and editor of the flagship journal in the field, and the other, a noted storyteller and writer—key facets of the counseling relationship are supported by engaging examples and stories that are integrated with existing research on counseling outcomes.

Part 1 introduces and reviews some of the basic assumptions that counselors, therapists, and researchers hold about the nature of helping relationships, including some of the discrepancies and debates in the field regarding how and why they empower change efforts. Part 2 describes some of the more practical ways relationships are used both as leverage and to facilitate trust and growth. We include chapters on some of the standard relationship interventions and also explain how relationships are embedded in a cultural and environmental context. We discuss how relationally based counseling is used to treat trauma, and how it uses storytelling structures, and we address some creative and innovative ways to enhance relational power. Part 3 moves to a discussion of how relationships operate in a counselor's personal life, such as how we are affected and influenced by our work, how we process disappointments and failures, how we deal with our own personal conflicts, and the ways we model in our lives what we teach to others.

Because of the focus on core factors that lead to successful outcomes, this book is appropriate as a textbook for a variety of courses in the curriculum including Introduction to Counseling, Theories of Counseling, Counseling Skills and Strategies, and more advanced Practicum courses. Although we have infused research and examples related to diversity throughout the book, Chapter 5, "Customized Relationships," provides an opportunity for us to address issues of diversity with respect to the counseling relationship more directly. After all, it is the ways that we adapt and individually personalize our relationships that make them optimally potent and responsive.

Acknowledgments

First of all, we thank Robert Smith, former president of the American Counseling Association, for the rather unusual idea of pairing us together as partners to explore the nature of counseling relationships. Although we were initially hesitant, if not downright reluctant, to consider such an idea, we are grateful for his support and encouragement. We are also appreciative of Carolyn Baker, Associate Publisher of ACA's publications, for her help in putting this massive project together, and to Quentin Hunter for assistance with organization and editing.

Many stories and case examples are included throughout the book, most of them offered without recognition. However, we do want to acknowledge a few counselors and therapists who graciously provided examples of their relational engagement with clients: Andrea Gustin, Jamie Littleton, Hannah Acquaye, Debbie Joffe Ellis, Leah Brew, Jeff Zeig, Hilda Davis, Marlene Klaborg Larsen, and Michelle Perepiczka.

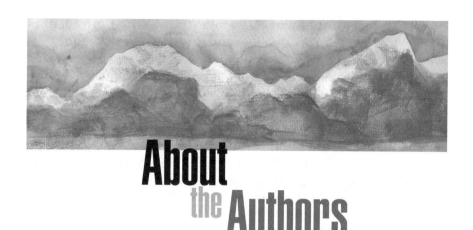

About the Authors

Jeffrey A. Kottler, PhD, is one of the foremost authorities on relationships in counseling and on advocacy efforts. He is the author of more than 80 books in the field that have been translated into more than two dozen languages. Jeffrey's books are used in universities around the world and are considered classics among practicing teachers, counselors, psychologists, health professionals, and social justice advocates. Some of his most highly regarded works include *On Being a Therapist, Changing People's Lives While Transforming Your Own: Paths to Social Justice and Global Human Rights, Creative Breakthroughs in Therapy: Tales of Transformation and Astonishment, Change: What Leads to Personal Transformation, On Being a Master Therapist: Practicing What You Preach,* and *Stories We've Heard, Stories We've Told: Life-Changing Narratives in Therapy and Everyday Life.*

Jeffrey has worked as an educator and counselor in preschool, middle school, mental health center, crisis center, university, community college, corporation, and private practice settings. He has served as a Fulbright Scholar and Senior Lecturer in Peru, Thailand, and Iceland, as well as worked as a visiting professor in New Zealand, Australia, Hong Kong, Singapore, and Nepal. Jeffrey is professor emeritus of Counseling at California State University, Fullerton.

Richard S. Balkin, PhD, is a professor and doctoral program coordinator at the University of Louisville. He is the editor of the *Journal of Counseling & Development*, the flagship journal for the American Counseling Association, and is past president of the Association for Assessment and Research in Counseling. His primary research interests include counseling outcomes, research methods, counseling adolescents, and cultural differences in counseling. He is a past recipient of the ACA Best Practices Research Award and the ACES Counseling Vision and Innovation Award.

Rick has published more than 60 peer-reviewed articles and book chapters, with the majority being quantitative in nature. He is the author of *The Theory and Practice of Assessment in Counseling* (Pearson) and has authored book chapters on research methods, as well as several articles related to research methods.

Part 1

Some Operating Assumptions About Relationships in Counseling

Chapter 1

What Do We Know, or *Think* We Know, About How Counseling Works?

Let's acknowledge at the outset that there are decades of empirical research, not to mention practitioner anecdotes, to support the power, influence, and efficacy of counseling. This is true across a number of theoretical orientations, clinician styles, contexts, clinical specialties, diagnostic issues, and client problems. However, in spite of the confidence we might feel in the power of our profession to improve the quality of people's lives, as well as to address their most challenging difficulties, we are by no means all in agreement as to *why* it works.

In this initial overview of what we know, or at least what we believe may be the case, we review some of the consensual assumptions and common precepts about what most consistently produces the most satisfying outcomes—for both clients *and* their counselors.

First, a Little History

Much of the interest in the counseling relationship began with Sigmund Freud's (1933/1916–1917) early work, which was followed by many of his colleagues and disciples, investigating the mechanisms of the so-called alliance that takes place in all therapeutic work. Luborsky (1976) distinguished between two different phases in this process; the first includes the supportive and caring "holding environment," and the second involves the client's own commitment and investment in the process. Bordin (1979) considerably expanded these ideas from a psychodynamic perspective to one that was far more encompassing and integrative. This model, which has now become known as the "working alliance," consists of three distinct but related features: (1) agreement on goals between counselor and client, (2) collaboration on the structure and content of the sessions together, and (3) respectful and intimate bonds that develop in the relationship. It is this third dimension of relational connection that Carl Rogers (1957) researched throughout his career, emphasizing the warmth, affection, trust, authenticity, and congruence that he found so critical in his work. Complementing Bordin's work were other theorists (e.g., de Shazer, 1985; Haley, 1963; Satir, 1983) who advanced more relational strategies, spawning specializations in marriage, couples, and family counseling. Essential to these theorists was the notion that what is occurring between two people is more important than what is occurring within each person (Bateson, 1972).

All of this is part of the foundational heritage of counseling as a profession. In one sense, it is what helped distinguish counseling from other allied mental health specialties such as social work, psychology, and psychiatry; that is, we have always been (and, we hope, always be) relationally oriented in our approach. Rogers (1980), perhaps more than any other thinker, defined the anthem of the counseling profession when describing the nature of empathy as both the ability and the willingness to understand others' thoughts and feelings from their own unique point of view. He believed this could only legitimately take place when the counselor was able to enter into the private perceptual world of clients, thus enabling the counselor to sense meanings about which clients may not be fully aware.

Empathy has its origins as part of the biological and social basis for human existence. This ability likely evolved as a way for members of a community to literally feel one another's pain and provide assistance as needed. Cozolino (2006) described empathy as more like a hypothesis than an actual sensation: "Shuttling back and forth between my head and what I imagine to be in yours, I generate hypotheses about your inner state based on my own thoughts and inner experiences" (p. 231). He posited that it is our shared neural circuitry that allows us to create models of others' internal states and make assumptions based on this resonance. Using the metaphor of cellular physiology, Cozolino suggested that just as neurons have synapses between them, so too are there *social synapses* in the spaces between client and counselor, or any other individuals. We communicate across those spaces in such a way that they alter brain chemistry in the same way that cellular structures and compositions are changed as a result of interneuron interactions. So-called mirror neurons, in particular, allow us to feel what others feel—as if it is our own experience. This remarkable ability, as we discuss later, is one reason stories have such a profound effect on people's lives, regardless of their form. When we are watching a film, television show, opera, play; listening to song lyrics; or reading a novel, we enter into the fictional world and fully imagine ourselves living in this alternative universe that provides vicarious experiences without danger or actual threat (Gottschall, 2012; Kottler, 2014).

The Counseling Relationship and the Era of Accountability: Two Opposing Forces?

For any of us who has been in the field for a while, we may remember a time before the strict oversight of managed care and the sometimes rigid parameters of prescribed "manualized" treatments designed to provide greater accountability. This was an era when counselors and therapists were actually allowed to determine for themselves, and their cases, exactly how often sessions should be conducted, how long they should last, and what should be the focus of treatment. Although there were some abuses of this system, it was a time of greater professional freedom in which counselors and therapists determined what was in the best interests of their clients.

In recent years, two terms related to greater accountability in counseling frequently have been used: *empirically supported treatments* (ESTs) and *evidence-based practice* (EBP). ESTs refer to specific techniques and strategies that reduce symptoms based on empirically controlled studies. EBP, on the other hand, refers to *any* evidence that affects client outcomes (Laska, Gurman, & Wampold, 2014). The issue of *evidence*, therefore, is the primary concern because there is ample support to conclude that the role of the relationship in client outcome is indeed quite substantial. In addition, "evidence" can take many different forms beyond quantitatively measured dependent variables, such as the anecdotal evidence that emerges from personal and professional experience.

Many of us might agree that that there have been times when the obsession with empirically supported interventions for specific presenting complaints has been taken a bit too far. Wampold (2001) has been particularly critical of the role ESTs have garnered in counseling practice and estimated that techniques account for less than 1% of actual client outcomes. Nevertheless, all of us today are expected to provide some evidence that what we are doing is helpful to others. To understand what we know and what we think we know, it might be helpful to explain how we got to this point.

Hansen, Speciale, and Lemberger (2014) provided a historical retrospective on the debate between ESTs and the role of the relationship in counseling. ESTs have roots in the biological premise of behavior espoused by Freud and behaviorism as exemplified by B. F. Skinner and others. As you are probably well aware, our profession has been fighting for respectability as a scientifically supported discipline that is grounded in research. Although humanistic ideologies, exemplified in the work of Carl Rogers, Abraham Maslow, Victor Frankl, and others, provided a counterpoint to the influences of behaviorism and psychoanalysis, the medical model also exerted a lot of pressure on nonmedical practitioners to utilize their *Diagnostic and Statistical Manual of Mental Disorders* ([DSM] American Psychiatric Association, 1952), which emphasizes ESTs for specific diagnostic entities and configurations of symptoms.

The *DSM*, originally published in 1952, was developed by psychiatrists in collaboration with the pharmaceutical industry. Although the latest incarnation of this "bible" invites input from other helping professionals—notably, psychologists—it is still heavily shaped by the medical profession, which treats conditions such as depression, anxiety, and other emotional disorders essentially as diseases ([DSM, 5th ed.; *DSM-5*] American Psychiatric Association, 2013). There has also been a noted preference for any therapeutic approach, such as cognitive–behavior therapy (CBT), that can be "manualized" and empirically tested. Needless to say, relational factors, which are often both indistinct and difficult to measure, have been relegated to categories of "nonspecific" or "common" factors.

Components of Successful Counseling Relationships

Debates and arguments, if not an actual war, have been waged among therapeutic practitioners regarding which approach or model is best. This has been going on for decades, with some arguing that the best way to help people is by focusing on their internal beliefs, or their innermost feelings, or their dreams, or their past unresolved conflicts, or their behavior, or the social constructions of the larger culture, and so on. At one time, these debates may have been useful, but we are pleased to report that more recent efforts have focused on what all (or most) successful counseling efforts have in common. In other words, instead of trying to figure out which single theoretical model is best for all clients, in every context and situation, regardless of their complaints, social environment, family configuration, and cultural background, attention has now turned toward those features that seem relatively universal across the spectrum of variables. The key question now is, "What are the common factors in counseling approaches that seem to be most important and useful?" Once these significant variables have been identified, the corollary question explores just how relatively important each of these factors might be. In the language of researchers, this is described as the "percentage of variance."

Identification of Common Factors

Many years ago, Jerome Frank (1971) published a seminal book about the nature of persuasion and influence within helping encounters. He viewed the various therapeutic approaches as "cults" in the sense that each had a rigid ideology that seemed impervious to compromise. Rather than necessarily accepting that what their proponents insisted was operative as a therapeutic ingredient in each conceptual framework, Frank settled on what he considered to be universal features of healing, such as the client's expectations, the counseling relationship, and the importance of faith in the process. Since that time, a number of other researchers (e.g., Duncan, 2014; Lambert, 1986, 2013; Norcross, 2011; Wampold, 2001) have investigated these common factors. In one early review (Grencavage & Norcross, 1990), five recurring themes were identified that are still considered important today: (1) what the client brings to sessions in terms of motivation, beliefs, personal characteristics, and expectations; (2) the counselor's personal characteristics; (3) the ways sessions are specifically structured to meet clients' needs and interests; (4) the change processes that are emphasized and accessed; and, finally, (5) the quality and kind of relationship that is established and maintained. In subsequent studies and reviews, this last feature—the relationship—has been found to be just as important as any technique that may be used.

Of course, it isn't *any* kind of relationship that is considered helpful to clients but rather the sort that has some particular qualities. Although certain clients may need or prefer more or less structure, as well as a number of other facets, it consistently has been found that the best helping relationships have a high degree of perceived and experienced empathy—clients feel understood, respected, and cared for by their counselors. Clients feel that there is a true partnership in terms of collaboration on their goals. In addition, the best relationships provide opportunities for ongoing sharing of input and feedback so that constant adjustments can be made as the process, stage, and needs inevitably evolve.

We will save you the trouble of wading through the overwhelming evidence, supported by countless research studies, that clearly demonstrates the importance of the counseling relationship by summarizing the key principles that we describe and apply throughout this book:

1. In all of its many manifestations, the relationship is central to all that we do in counseling.
2. Although we may be fascinated and drawn to study theories, models, and different approaches to counseling, it turns out that the particular choice we make is much less important than the kind of relationships we negotiate with clients.
3. Most counselors identify as integrative or pragmatic or eclectic, especially as they gain experience. What holds together all the different ideas they have incorporated is the way they are uniquely blended within the context of a helping relationship.
4. It would be far more useful to spend less time and energy learning new techniques and mastering new models and, instead, to become far more proficient and skilled at developing solid relationships with clients, regardless of their issues and background.
5. Issues of power, marginalization, privilege, and cultural background are not just facets of the relationship that should be considered but remain central components of any helping effort.
6. Successful relationships in counseling—or, for that matter, in any helping encounter—can take place in a variety of settings and contexts but still retain many similar features, which are personalized and adapted for each client.
7. Positive outcomes are most often associated with high levels of empathy, rapport, and relational engagement.

As we have stated, the relationship is a key component of any helping effort, perhaps even *the* most significant feature, but it is also not nearly enough. In asking the crucial question, "What leads to lasting change, both within counseling and in daily life?", a number of other factors have been identified that play an important role (Bohart & Tallman, 1999; Gianakis & Carey, 2008; Higginson & Mansell, 2008; Kottler, 1991, 2014; Lambert, 2013; Norcross, 2011; Paul & Charura, 2014b). We summarize the most active ingredients within constructive helping relationships in the following section.

What Makes a Difference in Promoting Change in Counseling?

- Positive expectations and hope
- Lifestyle changes
- Disclosure and processing of content
- Permission to explore new areas
- Feeling understood and heard
- Emotional arousal
- Facing fears
- Validating and normalizing feelings
- Collaborative goal setting
- Constructive risk-taking
- Reduction of stress
- Honesty and directness
- Rehearsal of new skills
- Task facilitation
- New insights and understandings
- Sensitive confrontation
- Challenge of dysfunctional beliefs
- Suggestions for resolving problems
- Modeling new behavior
- Creation of meaning
- Public commitment of intentions
- Social support
- Reframed narrative
- New options and alternatives
- Secondary gains eliminated
- Responsibility for consequences
- New resources accessed
- New solutions generated
- Understanding past behavior
- Planning for the future
- Interpretations of behavior
- Tolerance for ambiguity/complexity
- Inviting and responding to feedback
- Flexible adjustments over time
- Integrity and mutual respect
- Follow-up and accountability

Even with all of these additional variables that usually operate in complex and interactive ways, we may still conclude that relationships are the principal forum by which healing, growth, and change take place in counseling. These are not static entities; helping relationships are multidimensional and occur on different levels and within culturally specific contexts. Regardless of their setting, they are designed to maximize power and influence within a collaborative partnership, although each successive stage in the relationship requires a different kind and level of engagement. There may be differences of opinion between the client and the counselor as to the origin, source, and meaning of the presenting problems, but eventually a consensus is reached that further enhances the relational connection. As we mentioned earlier, the best of these relationships are characterized by agreement on goals and methods, open communication, mutual respect, and caring.

Common Factors and Outcome Variance

Before discussing further conceptualization of common factors theory, it may be beneficial to identify what is meant by *outcome variance*, which is a statistical term that reflects a percentage of impact, influence, or effect, usually expressed in relation to a normal distribution. This is often the way researchers choose to discuss what contributes to particular outcomes. For example, Michael Lambert (1986, 2013) followed Frank's original ideas to identify the four common factors that were believed to contribute the most to successful counseling cases. It was found that 40% of the outcome was determined by factors related to the client, 30% by the relationship, 15% by the client's hopeful or pessimistic expectations, and the last little bit (15%) the result of the counselor's preferred theory and techniques. Pretty interesting, isn't it? Although we may hungrily attend workshops and classes, read books, scour the Internet, and watch videos searching for the latest hot interventions, our efforts might be much better focused on strengthening our relationships with clients and harnessing their own resources.

Although these estimates are widely cited, not everyone agrees that they are set in stone. In fact, although the numbers conveniently add up to 100%, they were not derived from statistical analyses but represent best guesses from reviewing previous studies. Nevertheless, this does act as a reminder that the "Holy Grail" will not be found in any magical technique that has so far eluded us but rather in the less glamorous job of making our relationships with others more engaging and productive.

We wish we had learned this lesson long ago because each of us has spent many years as workshop junkies, not to mention lifetime students and scholars, searching for the next best thing that would render everything else obsolete. Perhaps like you, we have watched the masters in the field work their magic in demonstrations and then tried (often unsuccessfully) to imitate them. It took a long time to discover that what they did was unique to them and not easily replicated.

Subsequently, many others have attempted to sort out these variance percentages as precisely as possible. Duncan (2014), for example, honed in on clients' contributions to outcomes in counseling, including their initial motivation to seek help, available support system, particular complaints and problems, life experiences, resilience and hardiness, and what they want and expect from the sessions. However, many other factors are random, mysterious, or difficult to measure in the first place. In addition, none of this addresses the other important features such as the counselor's unique personality, approach, and signature style. It is, therefore, our view that many of these treatment effects ultimately can be connected to some relational components, either directly or indirectly. This is very good news because there are so many things that we cannot control, or even change much, such as what the client originally brings to counseling.

We may all agree that the relationship is key, perhaps *the* ultimate force and factor that determines the result of helping. However, that still doesn't explain the many paradoxes within counseling relationships that we may not immediately recognize because we live within them so much of the time (Kottler, Sexton, & Whiston, 1994). For instance, counseling is said to be based on reasonably equal, collaborative negotiations, yet it is pretty clear that most of the real power is lodged in the counselor's authority and position no matter what we claim otherwise. Likewise, counseling is conceptualized as being intimate and highly personal, even though it is also professional and distant at times with very clear boundaries. It is conceived as a rather spontaneous encounter but is often highly prescribed and ritualized. It is supposed to be real and genuine but is actually at times somewhat manipulative and filled with all kinds of distortions and projections. It is designed to foster independence but does so, in a way, via dependence in counseling. It is also advertised as safe and secure but can be somewhat dangerous, given that its structure is designed to produce changes. Finally, counseling is based on universal principles that have been supported by research and practice, yet it is adapted differently based on the cultural and individual context of the client and the counselor and their negotiated relationship.

Why Don't You Believe Us?

Despite all of the evidence reported, especially numerous studies indicating that client outcomes are predicated on the quality of the client–counselor relationship, it often seems problematic for practitioners and students to actually believe this and take it to heart. Most of us were originally trained to believe in the power of theories and techniques, taking classes mandated by accreditation standards. We offer specific classes that focus on particular approaches, skills, and interventions, and certainly these are important, but the subtext is that *this* is where all the action resides. This focus continues despite all the evidence and research that affirms that specific theories and techniques account for a very small part in client outcomes.

From early in a counselor's training, faculty and supervisors may instill the belief in the magic pill—that there is a technique or an intervention that will transform the client with a few sessions of active listening or disputing irrational beliefs. Such a belief is further strengthened by managed care and external funding agencies that emphasize these supposed ESTs.

Embracing regimented, manualized treatments that emphasize situation-specific techniques implies that almost anyone could do counseling with minimal training, if they just follow the template. The reality is that such practices can undermine the effort and hard work it takes to establish a deep and meaningful relationship with clients that is designed to empower the work that we do together. Such a relationship requires deep, deep listening, hovering attention, and intense concentration to capitalize on whatever is happening in the ever-changing moment. Counselors are required to take time to truly understand a person and to demonstrate that understanding through a genuine, accepting, and caring interaction.

Unfortunately, providing evidence of the client–counselor relationship through traditional research techniques such as clinical trials is difficult. The establishment and growth of a relationship is a unique process between two (or more) people that is not easily reduced to successive, incremental, invariant steps. Nevertheless, each of us is saddled with the responsibility of answering the ultimate question, "How do you know that what you are doing is actually working?", and each of us is required to provide reasonable evidence to support that claim.

Chapter 2

What Counselors Believe Matters Most— and Why Their Clients Disagree

If theory or techniques are not the major determining factors for successful counseling outcomes, then the key question for us to wrestle with is, "What else is important?"

Think of a case, *any* case, in which you tried to help someone and are confident there was a successful and satisfying result. Let's also stipulate that both you and the other person agree that things worked out just fine (this is not always true). Now, what do you believe had the most significant impact?

This is an important question, especially if you hope to duplicate the result with others in the future. It is absolutely critical that you have a handle on what you do that is most influential and that most consistently produces desired outcomes for the people you help.

One common practice for determining how well things are going is to take the most obvious course of action: Ask the client! That isn't necessarily the definitive answer considering that clients often don't know what happened or why, and even if they did, that doesn't mean they will tell you the truth. But it's certainly a good starting point.

Trying to Figure Out What Happened and Why

"Now that our sessions are coming to a close," the counselor says, "I'm wondering what you have found to be the most helpful in our work together?"

"Um, you mean what I liked the best?" The client appeared confused by the question, even though it seemed like the most logical place to begin the review process before the relationship ended.

"Well, it could be something you liked, but I'm more interested in what you thought made the most difference to you."

The counselor already has her own ideas firmly in mind of what she is fairly certain led to their breakthrough. It was just a few sessions ago that the relationship really seemed to deepen to a new level right after they talked through an ongoing conflict between them. The client had insisted that he wasn't really all that interested in learning to be more assertive at work and with his partner; he just wanted to avoid letting others get underneath his skin so often and so intensely. The counselor kept urging him to consider his ability to reduce his social anxiety as well as pushing him to take some risks and truly express himself more honestly. They had been practicing that in the last few sessions, and the change in the client had been dramatic. The counselor was so pleased and proud of all they had accomplished, and she was looking forward to hearing confirmation from the client that he felt the same way.

"I guess. . . ." The client hesitated for several long minutes while he was thinking, finally settling on a thought that was becoming clearer to him. "I guess it would have to be that time you smiled at me when I told you that story about what happened at work. You just shook your head and gave me this huge grin. Then you reached over and touched my arm. Remember that?"

Actually, the answer was no. The counselor had no idea what the client was referring to and had no recollection whatsoever of this particular interaction. Furthermore, she wondered why in the heck he was mentioning that clearly insignificant moment compared to all the other awesome things they had done together.

We wish we could say that this difference of opinion between client and counselor is rather unusual when each is asked to supply reasons for particular outcomes at the conclusion of the relationship. In fact, this disconnect is rather common between what counselors believe was most effective—usually their favored techniques and interventions—and what clients more consistently mention as aspects of the relationship in which they felt heard and understood.

So much of our field is driven by studies that interview, assess, measure, and observe what counselors think, believe, or do during their sessions. After all, counselors are the trained experts, so we are the ones best qualified to determine how, and to what extent, the counseling was helpful or not. Although there have been some

investigations into clients' perceptions and experiences (e.g., Binder, Holgersen, & Nielsen, 2009; DeFife, Hilsenroth, & Gold, 2008; Fitts, 1965; Hodgetts & Wright, 2007; Howe, 1993; Lambert & Shimokawa, 2011; Manthei, 2005; McMillan & McLeod, 2006; Reese, Toland, & Slone, 2010), the results of these studies have often been surprising, and sometimes disturbing. We are not suggesting that client reports are any more reliable, thorough, and accurate than those of their counselors who have a vested interest in writing case notes in the most optimistic way possible, but we are saying that there is, indeed, a difference of opinion between what practitioners often believe (or say they believe) is most important versus what their clients report was most helpful. This is the rather complex, confusing, and so interesting territory we want to explore in greater depth.

It's My Theoretical Orientation!

The power of relationship is difficult to fully appreciate, in part because there has been so much emphasis on one's chosen theory and approach, as if that is the key that will unlock the secrets of a person's troubles. Beginners are encouraged (sometimes required) to sort through the overwhelming choices available and to select a model that is most attractive or, in many cases, one that is favored by their instructor or supervisor. This may be a useful exercise for those getting started in the profession, but we believe other important corner pieces of the puzzle are lost as a result.

There is little doubt that the theorists who originally formulated and propagated various conceptual models of practices were highly passionate, influential, and charismatic. Each of them recruited a herd of devoted followers who were loyal to the cause and viewed opposing ideas as potentially threatening. Even today there is a "rock star" mentality among the field's most prominent figures who developed particular approaches, with their devotees paying homage to these apostles. The result has sometimes been a cultlike following of particular luminaries or models, as if they hold the essence of truth.

The selection of a theory is widely recognized as a core area of counselor preparation, a virtual requirement to graduate and pass licensing standards. We heartily agree that such an endeavor can indeed be useful in providing an initial framework for making sense of clinical issues, as well as their treatment. It is interesting, however, that research simply does not support that any particular theory is all that much better than most others. Remember that some estimates (Duncan, 2014; Wampold, 2001) were that the choice of theory accounts for less than 1% of the outcome variance, a virtually insignificant factor. Even the most optimistic figure of 15% (Lambert, 2013) is still not nearly as important as relational processes.

OK, So It's Not My Theory . . .

If there is not one single approach or theory that is optimal in every situation, with every client—one that guides us through periods of confusion—what are we to do when we are stuck or clueless? First of all, the experience of being (or feeling) stuck is itself driven by other myths and misconceptions.

Myth 1: The Client Is Stuck

When counseling isn't working, the first thing that many counselors do is blame the client for being resistant, uncooperative, or otherwise "difficult." Apparently, the client's personality configuration, lack of motivation, fears, self-sabotaging behavior, and perhaps even a toxic or nonexistent support system, are the reason for the poor results. The literature is filled with more terms than can possibly be imagined to describe such clients as hateful, personality disordered, reluctant, noncompliant, unmotivated, and so on, all of which imply that somehow the client's job is to meet our own expectations. In fact, in one sense, there are no really difficult clients—only difficult counselors who are unable or unwilling to alter their approach or adjust their style to better respond to where clients are and what they need in the moment.

The common perception, often presented to supervisors or noted in case files, is that the client isn't doing enough to get things going. We are big proponents of the idea that, ultimately, clients are responsible for their own growth and progress; however, we see problems in blaming clients when things aren't proceeding according to our expectations and plans. Our preferred theory is time tested and infallible, so it must be the client who is not cooperating with the program.

Myth 2: I Am Stuck

Of course, counselors aren't the only ones who blame external factors when things go wrong: Clients do this for a living! More often than not, they fully expect that we have some magic wand or instant elixir that will immediately cure them of any problem. In addition, clients are often inclined to attribute their difficulties to factors outside of their control, whether bad luck, poor genes, or others who just don't understand them. Likewise, when counseling isn't working as quickly as they expected and hoped, we are the ones who shoulder the blame. In spite of how we may reassure ourselves otherwise, it is hard not to take this personally and wonder if we are somehow doing something wrong or misguided. It is fairly obvious that the kinds of complex difficulties that clients bring to sessions rarely have simple solutions or respond immediately to any single intervention. Instead, efforts are more productively directed toward helping clients unravel within the relationship what it means to be—or feel—stuck.

We Are Stuck

Shifting the context from *you* or *I* to *we* represents an essential paradigm shift, one that recognizes mutuality and collaboration in the counseling partnership. This may seem rather obvious, but it is still incredibly difficult to sit back and watch clients suffering, recognizing that they can only move forward when they are ready. Of course, our job is to help them to become more willing and open to this process, as well as to find meaning and purpose in the value of the struggle. "If there is a meaning in life at all," Victor Frankl (1984, p. 88) observed, "then there must be a meaning in suffering." Like many other existentialists (and Buddhists), he considered pain and anguish to be not only inevitable parts of life but also valuable teachers.

By adopting the posture of *we are stuck* and searching for answers within the framework of the counseling relationship, the perception of "stuckness" changes. Rather than a client being stuck due to a particular issue, or the counselor feeling pressured to rescue the client, the impasse is conceptualized as an integral part of the journey. Further, it is the bond of mutuality and collaboration within the relationship that conveys to both (or all) the participants that "we are in this together." This helps contribute to hope and optimism for the future, one of the factors mentioned earlier that has a significant impact on successful outcomes. Part of our job is to help people who feel discouraged and dispirited find or create some faith in the counseling relationship so they ultimately can unravel what feels out of sorts. That is the basis of many of the favored brief counseling techniques—such as the "miracle question," "skeleton key," or "unique outcomes"—that ask clients to imagine a future in which they no longer have their problems.

So What Is Theory For If It Is Less Important Than We Think?

Conceptual frameworks and theoretical models are essential for the practitioner of any discipline. They help explain complex phenomena. They provide structure for systematic decision making. They develop hypotheses that can be empirically verified. They also alleviate our own discomfort with ambiguity and uncertainty.

The main point that we are emphasizing is that *which* theory is selected is less important (to a degree) than the idea that each of us find one that best reflects our values, beliefs, interests, and style—as well as those of our clients. We could even raise the point that none of us actually chooses a theory but rather that it chooses us!

Each of the models includes some attention to the relationship even if it is configured quite differently according to the preferred counselor role as an expert, parental or authority figure, transference object, coach, collaborative partner, instructor, or adviser. We would hope that these are not necessarily stable and invariant positions, considering that each client needs and requires something unique and different, depending on his or her cultural background, personal experiences, presenting problems, expectations, and preferences.

Although particular techniques are often associated with the theories that spawned them, it is no longer the case that anything we do is necessarily wedded to one conceptual model. The "empty chair" may have originated in Gestalt therapy, but it can be used in a variety of ways to identify and name irrational beliefs that are part of CBT. Likewise some of the signature interventions of "externalizing symptoms" (narrative), "meaning making" (existential), "reflecting feelings" (person centered), "goal setting" (behavioral), "lifestyle assessment" (Adlerian), "gender role analysis" (feminist), "exploring cultural worldview" (relational-cultural), "identifying attachment styles" (emotionally focused), and "exploring family structure" (systemic) are universally applied by practitioners of all persuasions and adapted to many different kinds of therapeutic relationships.

"It's My Wisdom and Experience!"

Counselors and therapists are the closest thing to gurus and sages in contemporary Western cultures. We are considered the experts and authorities on all things personal and interpersonal, expected to explain the intricacies of any problem and provide guidance to resolve almost any difficulty. We know stuff. We can do things that others can't touch. We can even read minds, or so it often seems.

There is also a common and logical assumption that veteran counselors are far more skilled and successful than those with less experience. They would have been able to devote more time to developing increased knowledge, mastering skills with greater fluency, integrating more options from a variety of sources, and gaining invaluable practice in finding out what works best in which situations. It is, therefore, a bit disconcerting (at least to veterans) to discover that this may not necessarily be the case. Advanced degrees, continuing education credits, even decades of practice don't necessarily lead to mastery of our craft and more satisfied clients (Balkin & Juhnke, 2014; Chandler, Balkin, & Perepiczka, 2011). Although it makes perfect sense that those with greater wisdom and experience would be better equipped to deal with an assortment of diverse clients and problems, thus far there isn't a lot of research support for this belief.

We don't wish to make any overarching statement that experience and wisdom are not critical components of a truly excellent clinician; however, we do want to provide some caution regarding some things that we may assume are true that are not yet supported by overwhelming evidence. We also hope this may be encouraging to beginners because their passion, enthusiasm, and excitement go a long way toward compensating for what they may not yet know or understand. Advanced practitioners in every profession often rely on shortcuts, take some things for granted, and may lose the perspective of treating every client as a singular, unique individual regardless of the familiar configuration of symptoms or cultural background.

"It's My Ability to Diagnose!"

Perhaps more than any of the claims counselors can make in terms of their own talents and beliefs, this one is perhaps the most entertaining. Why? Despite intense training, claims of a standardized system of diagnosis (e.g., the *DSM-5*), reputed experts in the field, and extensive research on symptoms and treatments of disorders, there is no evidence that consistency and accuracy in diagnosis has been achieved—ever! In a review by Vanheule et al. (2014) that covered selected clinical field trials for the past 4 decades, the accuracy and consistency of diagnostic assessments has not significantly improved. We will say that again: In spite of the widespread use of diagnostic systems that have been updated and revised every few years, practitioners are still not very accurate and reliable in their assessments (Aboraya, 2007). If you wonder, then, why the helping professions (especially psychiatry and psychology) are still so enamored with the current diagnostic system, it is because they have simply changed the standards of what is considered good enough.

How Do We Determine Accuracy and Consistency?

The key to understanding the accuracy and consistency of diagnosis is to understand "interrater reliability," which, you may remember, is the consistency or relationship among those who are making judgments about some common observation. It is a statistical value that describes the amount of agreement about some phenomenon, which can be quite useful. The problem, however, is that experts have not consistently agreed that particular diagnostic entities such as "schizoaffective disorder" actually exist or, if they do, that we can recognize what they are. To add to the challenges, it is sometimes the case that there are other coexisting or multiple conditions that "pollute" the purity of a single diagnosis, not to mention the ways that culture, race, gender, and socioeconomic class affect behavior and observations.

The *DSM* system was devised to make diagnosis a scientific enterprise, which is an admirable goal. Unfortunately, the ways in which we observe, analyze, and conceptualize client experiences are not easily reducible to a configuration of observable symptoms, especially when the process is intrinsically subjective and embedded in a relationship that contains almost an infinite amount of potential data that are not easily recognized, much less visibly observed or sensed.

Relationship Factors Affecting Client Conceptualization

The diagnostic and assessment process in counseling relies on a particular conceptual paradigm—and there are far more of them than just the standard *DSM-5* informed by the medical model. Whereas the *DSM-5* (American Psychiatric Association, 2013) subscribes to the idea of discrete categories of psychopathology, each of which is organized according to etiology, symptom clusters, and prognoses; counseling as a distinct profession has also embraced other models that practitioners often find far more functional and relational. A developmental model, originally part of our heritage as a discipline, assesses client experiences in the context of their appropriate life stage. A phenomenological model avoids labels altogether and instead uses rich, thick descriptions of clients' inner experiences. Also, of course, a systemic model diagnoses almost any client issue or problem in the context of relational factors within the family; so, even though many counselors rely on using the *DSM-5* for reimbursement, balancing the role of diagnosis in relationship to other models that inform us as counselors is an important skill set that separates counselors from other helping professionals.

For example, too often client conceptualization may be perceived as a matter of specific skill sets related to documentation, diagnosis, and treatment planning. Instead, we might use a more broad, flexible approach that addresses three primary questions that might concern us (Hill, 2014):

1. What are the client's identified problems, issues, and concerns?
2. Why is the client seeking help right *now*?
3. What does the client believe, think, and feel about this problem?

Even within this more basic structure, you may notice that what is missing once again is specific attention to relational factors that reveal valuable information about the client's functioning, either within sessions or in the larger world. Someone can tell us he or she is depressed, and it is certainly important to figure out what kind of depression might be operating. Is this a depressive reaction to something that happened recently, or is this potentially a biologically based endogenous depression with a long family history? Is the depression brief and intermittent or chronic and long-standing? Is it mild or absolutely debilitating? All of these questions are critical, but so is additional information related to how the experience of depression affects this person's relationships, daily functioning, and behavior within sessions.

There is also a danger for beginners to accept that diagnoses are static entities rather than dynamic processes that are situational, contextual, and continually evolve. Nobody, for instance, is depressed all the time, in every situation, and with everyone with whom he or she is in contact. Depression, anxiety, anger, loneliness, and other emotional reactions are triggered as much by environmental, contextual, and interpersonal factors as they might be by internal processes, so it is important to consider any diagnostic conceptualization as tentative, fluid, and strongly affected by interpersonal and contextual factors.

The previous statements apply as much to our own behavior as to that of our clients, because we are talking about what is clearly a relational phenomenon. Clients behave or present themselves in certain ways as a result of how the counselor behaves or responds. Imagine, for instance, that a client begins with the statement, "I'm depressed."

Consider all the different ways a counselor might respond to that:

- "You're depressed, huh?"
- "What's that like for you?"
- "That must be so difficult for you."
- "How long have you been depressed?"
- "When you say you are depressed, what exactly does that mean?"
- "How do you know you are depressed?"
- "Interesting."

We could go on, but you get the point. The counselor's response to the client's statements, in turn, leads the conversation in particular directions that result in possibly different kinds of diagnostic decisions.

Likewise, when both clients and counselors are asked to provide their own assessments of what happened in any given session, and what was most helpful, they often provide very different answers. Counselors are inclined to attribute positive results to their own accurate diagnoses, insightful interpretations, poetically formed metaphors, clever reframes of the problem, perfectly timed confrontations, well-executed role play, or other brilliant interventions, yet the interesting, if not amusing, irony is that clients rarely mention these things! They might notice or remember them. If pressed, they might agree that they were helpful in some way. However, most consistently, what clients report was most useful to them appears to have little connection to what their counselors believe was important (Bohart & Tallman, 1999; Duncan & Miller, 2000; Hodgetts & Wright, 2007; Knox, 2013; Lambert & Shimokowa, 2011; Manthei, 2005).

If counselors are rather attached to their techniques and strategies, clients who leave satisfied most often mention something about the relationship that supported and validated them. They felt heard and understood. They felt a strong personal connection to their counselor that led them to feel a safe and secure attachment. They felt encouraged and motivated to take risks and experiment with new behaviors. Also, clients frequently mention that they gained some new perspective (perhaps thanks to the interventions the counselors so adore) but only if it was embedded in a solid alliance. When there was some problem in the relationship, or counseling itself, the clients were still satisfied if the issues were directly addressed (Safran, Muran, & Eubanks-Carter, 2011). Unfortunately, in many cases, counselors may be unaware of the difficulties in the relationship or at least be unwilling to acknowledge them in such a way that the problems could be worked through.

Although we are talking about counseling relationships, these principles apply just as well to any helping encounter. When patients are asked what is important to them in a medical professional, they admit that expertise, competence, and experience are important, but it's also important to them to feel heard and understood, a phenomenon that is quite rare considering that the average patient has only about 18 seconds to talk about what's wrong before he or she is interrupted, and only 1 in 50 will ever get a chance to finish the story (Levine, 2004).

One client who consistently had trouble expressing himself in other relationships felt an immediate breakthrough with his counselor because, for the first time, he felt like there was someone who was actually hearing what he had been trying to say for a long time: "I was so utterly surprised to find out that someone was really and truly understanding what I was trying to say" (Fitts, 1965, p. 27).

On the most basic level, many clients come to counseling with a history of being (or feeling) mistreated, neglected, or otherwise unsatisfied in many key relationships from the past. The kindness and caring that we demonstrate models a very different kind of relational connection, one that is honest, direct, and authentic but also quite supportive and caring. Defenses are reduced in such a way that clients feel safe enough to experiment with alternative ways to function in their lives.

One of the most reassuring messages that we offer to beginning counselors, which often surprises them, is that it really isn't necessary to understand our clients, only to help them feel understood. This is a tremendous relief considering the reality that we sometimes don't even understand ourselves, much less anyone else. The brutal truth of the matter is that we cannot possibly understand the essence of a client's experience merely by spending a few hours in conversation. It is a myth in the profession that understanding is even possible given the complexity, uncertainty, and mystery surrounding any human life. The good news, however, is that once we enter a state of empathic connection with a client, sometimes even a kind of transcendence, we significantly increase the likelihood that he or she will at least feel understood. That is usually enough.

Just about the lamest response that anyone can offer to someone who is hurting is to say "I understand," as if that declaration is enough to persuade someone. We are required to demonstrate, if not prove, that we are on the same wavelength. We do that not simply by announcing this is the case but by showing, through our behavior, our reflections and summaries, our compassion and caring, that we are there with that person—every step of the way.

Counseling Side Effects

We talk a lot in our field about levels of competence, as if it is enough to be acceptably professional rather masterful and extraordinarily effective. *Multicultural competence* is the standard term thrown around all the time, as if it is sufficient to just develop a minimum level of proficiency in being sensitive and responsive to others. Once again, when clients are asked what matters most to them, besides fixing their problems, they most frequently say that they want to feel valued by their counselors, that they really matter as people, not just as professional cases (Cooper, 2005). They want to experience what has been described as "relational depth," the sort of intimate engagement that feels both comforting and inspiring (Cooper, 2005, 2013; Knox, 2013; McMillan & McLeod, 2006).

One of the "side effects" of almost any counseling experience is that clients are able to learn what it is like to be in a relationship with someone who not only listens carefully but responds with respect, authenticity, and caring. This often creates a new standard for all other relationships in the future. It also sets the tone for far more constructive negotiations related to differences of opinion or desired objectives.

One of the things that best predicts a satisfying and productive counseling relationship is that there is a clear consensus among all the parties regarding the goals that will be accomplished, as well as a commitment to follow through with these intentions (Tryon & Winograd, 2011). This holds true regardless of the specific counseling approach or theoretical model used, a subject we take up in the next chapter.

Chapter 3

Models of
Counseling Relationships

Every system and conceptual approach to counseling has formulated its own ideal construction of the kind of relationship that is best suited to accomplish the desired goals. Whether these objectives are to address symptomatic relief or underlying intrapsychic issues, cognitive processes or unexpressed feelings, present functioning or unresolved issues of the past, individual concerns or systemic dysfunction, different kinds of relationship configurations are possible, even optimal. Depending on personal characteristics and theoretical ideology, not to mention dynamics with each individual client, counselors may function in the relationship in a variety of ways, whether as an authority; parental; or benevolent figure. Each role would be designed to maximize the impact of the preferred interventions.

With dozens of theoretical frameworks in current practice, there is considerable disagreement about the ideal kind of relationship to maximize change, each with a different name, such as a working alliance, real relationship, collaborative partnership, corrective emotional experience, problem-solving adviser, and so on. In spite of these and many other differences, there is universal agreement on some desired features of the helping relationship.

A Smorgasbord of Relational Configurations

The particular approach to counseling selected by a counselor is not based solely on intellectual compatibility or even a supervisor's influence or institutional policies. Each of us discovers (or creates) a way of being with our clients that best capitalizes on our own strengths and preferences. Some practitioners love to delve deeply into the interpersonal dynamics that emerge during sessions, using authenticity, immediacy, and present moment disclosures to highlight these issues. Others take on a far more objective, even somewhat detached, clinical position and so negotiate relationships that are more formalized and structured. In each case, counselors operate within their own comfort level in terms of the ways they engage with their clients.

A person-centered approach, which has as its goals increasing self-acceptance and congruence, would emphasize a more genuine and authentic encounter. A behavioral approach might focus more on the relationship as leverage to reinforce constructive behavior and reward completion of therapeutic tasks. Psychodynamic counseling is more about promoting and working through transference reactions and unresolved issues of the past. Each theoretical orientation not only provides a framework for the ultimate goals of counseling but also suggests a relational structure for the best way to accomplish those objectives.

Of course, it is even more important that the particular kind of relational engagement that is negotiated is one that best fits the needs of any given client. You may prefer working on a deep, intimate level with clients, but in some cases it is far more advisable to keep strict boundaries and a certain emotional disengagement. Another counselor may like to help clients understand more clearly the impact of their internal thinking on their emotional reactions but then work with someone who is so emotionally restricted that a very different kind of relationship might be better designed to help facilitate increased expressiveness. That is one reason it is optimal for counselors to be flexible and adaptable enough to design and co-create different kinds of relationships depending on what may be required. We present some of the options as if they are offered in pure form, and Table 3.1 summarizes the processes involved in each of several common configurations.

Rather than stressing the differences between these various counseling approaches, we prefer to highlight the commonalities among them. We might all agree, for instance, that different aspects of the relationship would be emphasized at different points, depending on the client, the issues, and particularly the stage in the process. The key point here is that relationships continually evolve over time.

TABLE 3.1
Conceptual Models of Counseling Relationships

Theory	Primary Relational Processes	Counselor Roles

Psychoanalytic
Frued
	Identification
	Transference
	Unconscious desires and
	  wishes
		Position of neutrality and
		  hovering attention
		Interpret transference reactions
		Process countertransference
		  reactions

Humanistic/existential
Adlerian
	Empathy, respect, and caring in
	  intimate encounter
	Immediacy of feelings and
	  personal reactions
	Mutual understanding
		Authenticity, genuineness,
		  and congruence
		Focus on the here and now
		Operate as a facilitator and
		  catalyst by reflecting feelings

Cognitive behavior	Structured, collaborative
	  partnership
	Spirited and respectful conver-
	  sations about self-talk and its
	  impact
		Modeling of sound, logical
		  thinking
		Challenging irrational
		  thinking
		Teaching alternative ways of
		  interpreting experiences

Object relations	Creating and maintaining a
	  holding environment
	Focus on attachment issues
		Operating as parental figure
		Providing safe place to
		  work through unresolved
		  conflicts

Reality therapy	Involvement
	Collaborative relationship
	Trusting environment
	Avoid arguing, blaming,
	  criticizing the client
		Engaging in gentle, firm
		  confrontation
		Focus on how needs are met
		Encouraging choice to meet
		  needs

Narrative/constructivist/
  solution focused
	Collaborative, cooperative
	  relationship
	Clients are viewed as experts
	  in their own lives
		Counselors stress clients as
		  the experts
		Clients can best offer what
		  will be effective or
		  ineffective
		Counselor frames
		  opportunities for change

Relational-cultural theory	Mutuality
	Equal, empowering relationship
		Counselor is sensitive to
		  inherent power
		Transparent about values to
		  encourage client
		  empowerment
		Inclusion of client in
		  assessment and treatment

Stages of Relationship

So far, we have been discussing the ways that the relationship is usually structured according to a variety of approaches, but this oversimplifies the reality that the relationship changes over time, depending on the stage of treatment, the counselor's mood, the subject at hand, and what appears to be working best at any moment. You may begin sessions by initiating a fairly structured relational pattern but find that the client is both frustrated and unresponsive until trust is established. Once you loosen things up a bit, the client appears more engaged, but to the point that boundaries become too permeable. This calls for another adjustment, one that is carefully and incrementally negotiated.

Regardless of the specific conceptual model, there have been attempts to develop stage theories to explain the usual evolution of almost all counseling relationships (Prochaska & DiClemente, 1982, 1984, 1986). This transtheoretical model was designed to cut across different theoretical orientations and highlight the universal processes that often operate in almost all counseling relationships (Prochaska & Norcross, 2013).

It makes sense, for instance, that the first stage of counseling begins before we ever meet our clients. They imagine what we will be like. They have conversations with us inside their heads. They rehearse what they want to say and how they intend to present themselves. They consider the most important stories about themselves that they will share. They anticipate how we might react and respond to certain parts of their life narrative. This *contemplation stage* of the relationship sets the stage for what will initially follow, because the client is clarifying intended goals and solidifying expectations.

During the intake and first few sessions (if the counseling lasts that long), the *preparation stage* establishes relational norms, the behavioral "rules" for who does what and when. Very quickly, we notice that routines are established. The client tends to sit in the same place, begin the same way, and engage in a series of rituals to maintain comfort and safety. Naturally, we do the same things according to our own customs and preferences but also to develop as much trust as possible. In addition, new insights and understandings are discussed with the hope that they will lead to some commitment to take constructive action.

Regardless of the particular model, most counseling approaches include an *action stage* in which the relationship takes on a different form that is focused on problem solving and accountability. Frustration, disappointments, and setbacks are inevitable, and the relationship often alternates between being supportive and encouraging and being direct and challenging when things don't proceed according to plan.

Finally, the *maintenance stage* takes place toward the end of the relationship when a working alliance is long established and comfortable. Routines have settled in, and the relationship often becomes more egalitarian as the process moves toward closure and preventing relapses.

The point of this review is to emphasize the ways that counseling strategies and relationships should be matched not only to the client's presenting problems, personality, cultural background, and expressed needs but also to the appropriate stage of the process. This recognizes that, quite simply, people respond differently according to their readiness levels and to what is likely to be most helpful during any moment in time (Miller & Rollnick, 2012; Moyers, 2014).

Taking into consideration a client's expressed and implied preferences significantly increases the likelihood of a successful outcome (Swift, Callahan, & Vollmer, 2011). These preferences can be categorized according to the counselor's characteristics (style, personality, gender, age, race, language, sexual orientation), the counseling approach (direct, supportive, family, behavioral, problem solving, insight oriented), and the kind of relationship (supportive, confrontive, informal, authoritarian, business-like).

Relationship Shapes and Sizes

Every theoretical framework of counseling offers a distinctly (or slightly) different conception of how the process should proceed. There is an underlying philosophy, several theoretical assumptions, statement of desired goals, and usually a collection of favored techniques and interventions. Bring to mind a theory, any theory, and there is some immediate free-associated signature skill. Carl Rogers: reflect feelings. Albert Ellis: dispute irrational beliefs. Virginia Satir: sculpting. Fritz Perls: empty chair. Michael White: externalize symptoms. You could name a particular approach to counseling and also get a sense of the preferred relationship structure that is best suited to accomplishing the stated goals.

Consider the classic film, *Three Approaches to Psychotherapy*, originally released over 50 years ago. Three prominent theorists of the era—Carl Rogers, Fritz Perls, and Albert Ellis—each conducted a brief session with the same client, Gloria, to demonstrate their theories in action. Although the film turned out to be a fraud in the sense that Gloria was pressured and coerced to lie and say that Perls helped her the most, when, in fact, she was traumatized by that particular session (Rosenthal, 2011), it still clearly showed the distinctly unique ways that relationships were created by each of them. In analyzing the emotional climate that each of these famous counselors created, it was found that Rogers exuded mostly feelings of joy and deep interest, Ellis revealed anger, and Perls revealed contempt (Magai & Haviland-Jones, 2002). That, by the way, is what *appeared* to be evident rather than what was actually intended.

If the intention is to help clients explore deep, unresolved, existential issues related to loneliness and feelings of alienation, a relationship might be developed that is quite different from that of a counselor who seeks to increase a client's skills of assertiveness to counteract bullying. Even among practitioners who (say they) utilize one identified model with all of their clients, all the time, counselors will still likely adapt and shape the particular relationship according to what they think best fits that client, issue, and situation. Then again, what counselors report they do in sessions isn't necessarily an accurate representation of what may have actually occurred.

Within emotionally focused counseling, for example, practitioners have stated goals of creating the most optimal relationship to explore and facilitate modes of emotional processing, internalized affect regulation, and soothing the affect-attuned bond (Greenberg, 2014). The counselor would, therefore, attempt to enter into the client's internal frame of reference, follow that experience, and then try to guide and deepen it as much as possible to a place of increased self-acceptance. The goal would be to help the client better regulate his or her emotional reactions, an outcome that is believed to be far more likely if there has been a collaborative negotiation over shared tasks (Greenberg & Johnson, 2010). The warm, caring, trusting bond is important, perhaps even critical in this approach, but only when it is complemented with considerable attention to mutually agreed-upon structures and procedures.

In the earliest stage, the relationship is all about validation of the client's experience, particularly of struggles and suffering and its impact on various debilitating aspects of the client's life. Just as in its person-centered origins, hovering attention, presence, genuineness, caring, and empathic resonance all lead toward supporting the client's abilities and resources to regain emotional composure. Of course, this is important in every other approach as well.

To the emotionally focused counselor, "relational presence" has special meaning and remains the focus of much therapeutic activity. This means being completely open, receptive, and sensitive to every experiential moment, getting a sense of what the client is feeling, surrendering to the process as it is unfolding, and letting go of all one's personal concerns to feel empty and yet clear.

Once this exceptional, transcendent state of being infuses both participants, the counselor's role switches to more of a coaching relationship. While supporting and validating the client's current emotional reactions, the ultimate goal is to help the client develop alternative ways of responding to interpersonal and internal struggles. Although this is couched in the language of emotionally focused counseling, some features are familiar to many other approaches.

Another example is motivational interviewing, a direct descendent from person-centered counseling that focuses attention on empathic resonance and relatively nondirective listening (Miller & Rollnick, 2012). Although it was originally developed to work with substance abuse and other addictions, it has since been applied to a variety of problems because of its direct focus on the client's *decision* to change (Moyers, 2014).

Motivational interviewing relationships also emphasize collaboration and empathy attunement but concentrate on the first tasks of seeking consensus on a narrow focus that alters the way the client speaks about intentions and goals. The initial nondirective nature of the relationship then becomes far more targeted and focuses on language that expresses commitment to change. Although this approach is known for some specific techniques, it is still the relationship that is at the center of all the work. The relationship qualities inform the counselor about how far to push, when to back off, and how to mend things when the pace may have gone too quickly or too far. This is an important feature considering that the counselor often takes a stand of direct advocacy, hoping to encourage "change talk" that leads to constructive action.

In spite of their differences, there are some commonalities among all the various approaches in terms of what they agree are important features of any helping relationship. First and foremost, if the relationship is safe and trusting, then there is openness to mutual feedback. This often involves the counselor providing feedback to the client according to the particular theoretical premises. A reality counselor (choice theory) might focus on ways the client is avoiding responsibility for decisions and behavior, whereas a cognitive behavior counselor would hone in on irrational thinking. A person-centered counselor might provide feedback in the form of immediacy, how the client comes across in the relationship. A Gestalt counselor, by contrast, might use feedback to emphasize inauthenticity. Feedback cycles in the other direction as well in a safe and secure relationship, with clients freely able to communicate what they like, what they don't like, and what is most and least helpful.

Meaning making is another relatively common aspect of most counseling relationships, even though, once again, it may take different forms. Psychodynamic counselors create relationships that are specifically designed to search for the underlying unconscious reasons for present problems, as well as transference reactions. Constructivist counselors utilize the relationship to explore personal narratives. Existential counselors look at what gives meaning to daily life. Cognitive counselors help clients to better understand how their suffering results from internalized self-talk. Different kinds of insights are generated in the various relationship structures, whether the goal is to help people get more in touch with thinking, feelings, behavior, cultural influences, unconscious motivations, defenses, resistance, internalized scripts, or interactive patterns.

Empathy as a Unifying Dimension of All Approaches to Counseling

All the various models and approaches to counseling are united in their support of the most essential component of any helping relationship—empathy. Regardless of whether the basic goal is to promote deeper self-awareness; alterations in self-identity or internalized narratives; or changes in thinking, feeling, or behavior, it is through empathic connections that mutual understanding and support take place. In fact, empathy is considered the second greatest human achievement after mental consciousness (Ickes, 1997). According to Heinz Kohut (1977), empathy is as basic a human endowment as the senses of vision, hearing, touch, smell, and taste: It is the way we *feel* others.

Although early psychoanalysts did mention the importance of empathy in any therapeutic relationship, Carl Rogers (1957) brought this feature to the forefront as one of his "core conditions." For Rogers, it was not only about feeling empathically toward clients but also about being willing and able to accurately convey this deep understanding in such a way that others feel truly heard and supported. Along with the other core conditions of warmth, genuineness, congruence, respect, acceptance, and immediacy, the counselor's empathy was regarded as the highest therapeutic virtue. It is a component of every configuration, whether we call it the working alliance, real relationship, corrective emotional experience, or transference.

Counselors tend to be divided into two camps in the types of empathy they value (and practice). *Cognitive empathy* refers to the more analytic style of making sense of others' experiences by entering their frame of reference, whereas *affective empathy* is far more intuitive and focused on feelings. The most accomplished masters of empathy use *both* kinds to serve several functions (Howe,

2013). First and foremost, empathy provides a sense of safety and support in the relationship, a reassurance that the unknown territory explored is accompanied by a confident and understanding guide. Second, empathy helps clients to elaborate and dig deeper into their own thoughts, feelings, and desires. Third, such work within the relationship helps clients deal with emotions that often feel confusing or out of control.

In a counseling group, one participant had been discussing her feelings of inadequacy as a mother, feeling very much like a failure. For a moment, her face clouded over as she talked about falling short in so many areas, all of which seemed to the leader to be significant distortion and exaggeration. At that point, another member started to ask her a question, but the leader held up his hand to freeze the moment.

"Kelsie," the leader said to her in a whispery voice, "Right now, what's happening inside you? What are you feeling? It seems like something hit you hard just now, some feeling that you can barely hold back."

Kelsie looked at the leader, nodding her head in acknowledgment and seeming to feel grateful for the interruption. "Yeah, ah," she started and then hesitated.

"Go on," the leader prompted.

"Well, it's just that when Flynt asked that question a minute ago . . ." As she said this, she pointed accusingly across the group toward the member who asked the distracting question. "At first I felt relief," she continued. "I thought I was off the hook, that ya'll would back off and I could bury this stuff again. But then when you noticed that I was. . . . Well, when you forced me back into my feelings about all this, I figured it was finally time to deal with this stuff that I've been avoiding for a long time."

"It really helps to feel the support of everyone here and to know that we are with you," said the leader.

"Exactly!" Kelsie responded, then continued on with her story.

As we well know, empathy is considerably different from sympathy in that the latter is more about the concern or feeling for someone else rather than actually experiencing the same feelings while entering that person's world. "I know how you feel," a sympathetic listener might say, "I have had similar problems during a difficult time in my life." Such responses mean well, but they rarely convey the deep understanding that accompanies empathic resonance: "I can sense that you feel really lost right now, as if you are out in the wilderness all by yourself without any idea of which direction to head next."

Empathic responses such as this explain why teaching active listening skills is such an integral part of counselor preparation programs. It has become the tradition that learning to decode and reflect content and feelings are among the first skills taught to beginners. Unfortunately, relying too much on these mirroring skills can be perceived by clients as inauthentic, superficial, and annoying unless they are accompanied by more natural responses that are sometimes rather nonlinear and even paradoxical (Mozdzierz, Peluso, & Lisiecki, 2014).

Too much empathy is not a good thing either. Empathy is what leads us to experience what other people are thinking and feeling, and it makes it possible to have simulated experiences within various forms of storytelling. The attraction of video and online gaming, reality shows on television, celebrity gossip, novels, and movies is that our empathic abilities make it feel like *we* are the ones having these vicarious experiences. However, the epidemic of immersion in virtual realities, whether in the form of multiplayer gaming or online porn, provides testimony of the addictive nature of this alternative universe.

Empathy also can become counterproductive when we can't turn it off or control the responses. There are times when boundaries collapse and we feel too much of the client's suffering. The group counselor mentioned previously was working in another group recently when he noticed that one of the members started crying when she talked about her mother dying recently. "I was so tuned into her experience," he explained, "so connected to her, that before I realized it I was also crying with her, for her, and for myself as I remembered my own mother dying when I was young."

Empathy is clearly one of our greatest gifts, the main channel by which we connect with others. It also can become a burden when it feels intrusive, triggers a collapse in boundaries, or leads to a loss of control. In the previous example, the empathic resonance may have led to the counselor's strong personal reaction, but in this case at least, it seemed to increase his standing and credibility within the group because of the genuine and caring personal response.

Empathy has traditionally been understood to mean the counselor's ability and willingness to understand accurately the client's experience *without* losing awareness of the boundaries that exist in the relationship. Staemmler (2012), however, saw this conception as somewhat limited because of three considerations. First, the state of connection is seen as one-sided; that is, empathy flows only in one direction from the counselor to the passive client even though there is often *mutual* compassion and caring. Empathy in counseling isn't just about the ways the client feels heard and understood but also the corresponding parallel feelings the client has toward the counselor.

Second, the client is often objectified as a target of empathic listening rather than as an active participant in the process. Staemmler points out that this is a rather "cold" form of empathy, an intellectual rather than an affective reaction to what is being experienced. A much deeper form of empathy involves not just *seeing* the client's world but *feeling* it in a way that is acknowledged as similar. A number of humanistic theorists, such as Carl Rogers, Eugene Gendlin, James Bugental, Alvin Mahrer, and Irvin Yalom, talked about empathy as an "embodied" experience, a subjectively felt sense of another person that is, in its own way, a transcendent state of being.

The third limitation of empathy as it was originally conceived is that it is part of an individualistic rather than a collectivist worldview. The idea was that empathy was the means by which one individual, designated as the helper, would reach across a chasm toward another person who felt isolated; yet cultures with a collectivist worldview, interconnected networks, interdependent social systems, and internalized and integrated perceptions of self and others, reconfigure the experience of empathy as far more than an anecdote to individual isolation. Among clients from African, Asian, Latino, and indigenous backgrounds, empathy may not represent just an individualistic experience but also one that is embedded in a particular social and cultural context.

Expressing Empathy

In deep empathic connections, the kind that are reciprocal, even magical, participants enter into an altered state of consciousness that is not unlike a hypnotic trance. It truly feels as if two beings are synchronized, can read each other's minds, anticipate what each will say next, and feel each other's hearts beating.

While working with trauma victims after the series of devastating earthquakes in Nepal in 2015, I (Jeffrey) was approached by a 96-year-old man who told me through a translator that he had a number of aches and pains in his back, knees, and shoulders. I asked him if he had been sleeping outside on the ground because it wasn't safe for any of us to spend prolonged time inside buildings that could collapse at any moment, especially with aftershocks continuing every few hours. He shrugged and smiled. Then the translator left us alone.

The man didn't speak a word of English, and my command of Nepali was rather basic, so we spent a few minutes just staring at one another. Then he reached out and took my hands, staring into my eyes, his face now completely serious. He said some things to me in a soft voice. Unsure how else to respond, I squeezed his hands a little harder, feeling this incredible surge of love for this man I had just met. This guy was almost a century old in a place where the life expectancy was half that age. He had survived a hundred earthquakes, not to mention all the trials and tribulations of living in such a remote part of the Himalayas with no access to any medical care.

I sat with him and wondered how I could help him, how I could ease his discomfort and reassure him that the trauma of the earthquakes would eventually diminish. I couldn't speak his language, so I just sat with him and held his hands, smiling, staring into his eyes. We sat that way for more than 10 minutes—I know that because my wrist was turned in such a way that I couldn't help but see the face of my watch and the sweep second hand circling around and around.

Finally, the man released my hands, steepled his own beneath his chin in the customary gesture of "Namaste," a sign of gratitude and respect, and then shuffled out of the room with a wave over his shoulder. Now *that* was a profound experience—for both of us. I spent several idle moments during the day wondering if he had been as moved as I had been from our empathic connection. The uncertainty was later clarified when he returned in the afternoon for another meeting, dismissing my translator, and again reaching out for my hands. Just to hold them. Just to gaze into my eyes.

This was a kind of transcendent empathy, also referred to as paranormal empathy, meditative empathy, or an intersubjective state of consciousness, to which Staemmler referred. It is a state of heightened awareness of self, of other, and of the connections between oneself and someone else. These are admittedly rare experiences compared to the usual ways we go about our counseling business.

Each of the therapeutic models presents different ways of accessing and expressing empathic resonance. This can include empathic reflections of feeling that represent the gold standard of early skills classes, or it can involve nonverbal behavior, compassionate attitudes, communicative attunement, accurate interpretations of experience, or the development of rapport or successful collaboration with any other approach.

By way of summary, four different types of empathic responses are usually most helpful (Elliot, Bohart, Watson, & Greenberg, 2011). *Empathic understanding responses* communicate clearly, and reasonably accurately, the client's experience, or at least the facets that were shared in session. This is what we most commonly learned during early training as reflections of content and feeling: "I hear how difficult it is for you to talk about these issues. You are wondering how safe it really is to explore what you are feeling given that others like me have responded so punitively in the past."

Empathic affirmations validate rather than interpret or reflect the client's experience: "It takes a tremendous amount of courage and resolve on your part to continue to push through your ambivalence when you wonder whether the effort is really worth what you will gain. But regardless of the result, you should feel proud of the risks you are willing to take."

Empathic evocations help to probe, invite, facilitate, and draw out deeper explorations of innermost thoughts and feelings: "As difficult as it is for you to talk about your reactions to what happened with your parents, I notice that you seem to feel more relieved getting some of this out and in the open."

Finally, *empathic explorations* dig much deeper to excavate some of the hidden, buried, disguised, disowned aspects of the client's experience: "I notice that although you quickly moved on from talking about the feelings of hurt that have been festering for some time, you seemed to circle back to those issues again and again as if a part of you really wants to heal those wounds and yet you are afraid of the increased pain that may result."

Given the incredible variety and diversity of counseling approaches in the field, many of which appear to minimize relational and empathic features in favor of specific techniques, counselors have developed and refined their own unique ways of including empathy as a key component of the process. More recently, several of the most popular approaches have incorporated cutting-edge research from neurophysiology to support particular kinds of relational connections.

The Brain Thrives on Interpersonal Attachments

Every decade brings to the forefront a few novel, innovative ideas that seem to take the profession by storm. In the early years at the turn of the 20th century, it was all about the power of the unconscious, followed later by reinforcement theory, cognitive processes, attachment theory, or multicultural considerations. Most recently, we can't seem to get enough of brain-based explanations for interpersonal relationships that help to unify features of many of the models previously described. The precision, or at least the medical language, appears to offer considerable structure to explain how and why relationships can be so healing. The nature of relational attachments are now frequently being described as "integrative neurophysiological changes," "activated embodied mechanisms," "engrained patterns of emotion dysregulation," "neural net configurations," or an "oscillating cycle of internal versus external focus of connection" (Siegel, 2012). What all this means is that in spite of the metaphorical language we might use to describe and explain the power of relationships, some components clearly are driven by the brain's need for connection to thrive and grow at a purely neuronal level.

We have known for some time that people who suffer early interpersonal deprivation or isolation, or those who experience trauma, show signs that their brain's natural neuroplasticity has been impaired, resulting in disturbed physiological functioning. The brain's systems become recalibrated in such a way that stress hormones such as cortisol constantly flood the body, perceptual filters lose their accuracy, and memories become unreliable, inaccessible, or even remain impervious to long-term storage (van der Kolk, 2014).

It would appear that close, intimate, supportive relationships, whether in the context of counseling or any other helping encounter, immunize people against the potential for more extreme trauma and help those who do have problems to recover much more quickly. Even in rather extreme circumstances, it seems that the threat of physical danger can be moderated through interpersonal support. In one dramatic example of this that occurred during the bombing of London in World War II, some of the supposed "fortunate" children were sent into the countryside so they could remain safe from the Blitz. However, it was discovered by Anna Freud (of all people!) that these children experienced *more* stress and did far worse than those children who remained with their friends and family—even though they were subjected to constant violence and destruction (A. Freud & Burlingham, 1943).

This is just one reason why group counseling and other support groups have been found to be so intrinsically helpful, regardless of their particular structure and application. Human beings just do much better when they are surrounded by others who sincerely care about them. No matter how severely someone has been damaged or traumatized, or simply discouraged, sometimes it only takes one solid, trusting attachment with another to promote recovery and healing, and that is one reason most approaches to counseling seem to work reasonably well, even though they *appear* to offer very different structures (Laska et al., 2014).

So many of the clients we see have been (or felt) rejected, marginalized, or otherwise injured by interpersonal wounds that compromise their ability (or willingness) to trust others. They hunger for intimacy and closeness that is counterbalanced by an intense fear that rejection will be inevitable, yet it is precisely this human contact and attunement that leads to better physiological and emotional regulation and the resolution of the ongoing problems.

It is curious, but certainly understandable, that we have such strict prohibitions on touch within our profession because of fears that boundaries might be violated, especially in light of the history of sexual exploitation that occurred in the past. It is also unfortunate considering how much physical touch, hugging, holding, or rocking is associated with reducing emotional arousal and providing comfort. Instead, we refer clients for drugs to soothe their physiological systems. "How did we become so phobic about appropriate touching," Bemak and Chung (2015, p. 88) wondered, "and why do we let litigation become a driving force in defining healthy, responsive healing practices?"

Well, we do know why we've become so cautious about touching clients, even when they desperately crave physical contact. We discuss the so-called slippery slope in Chapter 9 on relational boundaries, but suffice it to say for now that although touching clients in a comforting, appropriate way is indeed highly desirable at times, it carries the risk of being misconstrued if the counselor misses some important cues. The context for physical contact depends very much on the age difference, gender, sexual orientation, and culture of the participants, as well as on the particular kind of relationship that has been created.

Similar to self-disclosure as a therapeutic intervention, most practitioners believe that appropriate physical contact can lead to "pivotal moments" (Harrison, Jones, & Huws, 2012). Even the most technique-oriented counselor will find instances when a comforting touch on the arm, a congratulatory or reassuring hug, or a literal pat on the back is just what is needed. We swing back to this subject a bit later to look more deeply at other boundary "crossings" that have the potential to intensify both help and harm.

If neurophysiological mechanisms and brain-based interventions are now increasingly popular, then attachment theory, originally developed by Bowlby (1978) and others, has significantly shaped a number of therapeutic models, a few of which (emotionally focused, relational-cultural, and relational psychodynamic counseling) feature it quite prominently. In addition, attachment theory is now seen as one of those "common factors" that integrates all approaches, just as empathy is considered the glue that holds everything else we do together.

Of course, the counseling relationship is far too complex to explain with any single theoretical model, even if attachment theory offers one such structure. We may know that "secure attachments" lead to far better outcomes in counseling, regardless of the approach used, but we don't really understand the intricacies of how and why this occurs (Diener & Monroe, 2011). For instance, we may think it is important that *we* feel attached to our clients, but, in fact, the only thing that really appears to matter is that *they* feel attached to us (Ligiero & Gelso, 2002).

It's All About Hope

In the chapters that follow, we talk more specifically about the skills and strategies associated with relational enhancement, but we end this discussion with a focus on hope. Just as it is important for you to feel hopeful that your investment in reading this book will result in clearly observable positive outcomes that make it worth your time and energy, so too do our clients rely on hope as a primary impetus for change. Beyond all else that we do in counseling, the relationships established, regardless of the particular theoretical framework, are designed to encourage hope and optimism for the future despite the challenges clients face and the disappointments of the past (Larsen & Stege, 2012).

Hope is one of the common factors that is considered to be crucial to successful counseling (Duncan, Miller, Wampold, & Hubble, 2010; Lambert, 2013). Hope is framed in a variety of ways—as optimism, faith, strength-based resources, agency thinking, pathways thinking—but it is considered to be an essential part of any successful helping effort because of its multidimensional impact including affective, cognitive, interpersonal, behavioral, contextual, and temporal features (Larsen, Edey, & LeMay, 2007).

Hope is likely related to clients' sense of well-being (Yalçin & Malkoç, 2015). As mentioned previously, how connected counselors feel toward their clients isn't as important as how connected the clients feel toward the counselor. Likewise, counselors' optimism is less important than clients' own beliefs about what might be possible (Coppock, Owen, Zagarskas, & Schmidt, 2010). When clients feel they are safe and secure in a relationship, they are more likely to entertain optimism for the future.

Part 2
Relational Strategies and Interventions

Chapter 4

Skills and Strategies
for Promoting Therapeutic
Relationships

The relationship-oriented work that we do in counseling begins with a certain set of beliefs and attitudes about the process. One of the first of these is related to the assumption that there is something about the relationship itself that is intrinsically healing for many people. Most of us would agree that this is usually not enough to promote major changes, but it sure is the catalyst for most of what follows.

There may be considerable debate in the field about which counseling approach is superior to the rest, or at least best suited for particular problems and situations depending on the empirical support available, but one area of almost universal consensus involves the generic skills and therapeutic options that are most often useful. Our standardized accredited curricula mandate a particular skills course that helps us develop basic competence in active listening, verbal encouragers, reflection and paraphrasing, summarizing, immediacy, and other responses that are designed to efficiently and effectively form and maintain constructive relationships with clients. *basic*

At a more advanced level, we go beyond mere listening to "deep *advanced* listening," becoming more fully present during interactions, "holding" others' sadness, and providing even more expressive caring and compassion. We also learned empathic attunement, balanced within certain parameters that are designed to protect clients from exploitation and also protect ourselves from emotional "leakage." Depending on our theoretical preferences and therapeutic style,

45

we also learned how to adapt our relationship skills to help clients accomplish their goals, which we hope have been mutually and collaboratively identified.

How Counseling Reveals Relational Patterns

There is an assumption, often useful, that the ways clients behave in counseling may illustrate some of the issues that crop up in their daily lives. This represents a sample of behavior that often uncovers dysfunctional patterns. Someone who has intimacy and trust issues isn't going to immediately open up with a new counselor who is essentially a stranger. A client who backpedals every time he is challenged, appearing to change his mind, probably does that with others in his life. Someone who consistently appears argumentative and annoying most likely does that in other areas of her life. In other words, the relationship is not just a way to gain leverage for promoting changes and facilitating growth; it is also a valuable means by which to assess relational patterns.

It could reasonably be expected that whatever interpersonal style clients bring to counseling is a variation of what they do in the outside world. If they appear passive, withdrawn, and unusually deferential, or combative and challenging, this could very well be an operational pattern. The behavior that is demonstrated offers a glimpse into what clients often do to get themselves in trouble, or at least compromise their best functioning.

"I'm not sure I agree with you," the client says before you can even finish the thought. You are surprised because this seemed like a rather benign statement that was offered very tentatively. You had just noted that the client seemed uncomfortable once you departed from his planned agenda for the session, and you wondered aloud whether that was the case in his relationship with his children who frequently rebelled at what they called his controlling behavior.

"Actually," you try again, "I was just . . ."

"I don't care what you were trying to do. I'm offended by that accusation."

You step back, quite intrigued with the interaction that is taking place. It strikes you as clearly indicative of exactly the kinds of problems this guy has been complaining about at work and at home: how nobody "gets" him and he constantly feels attacked— just as he does now.

Before you even consider how you might best deal with this situation to defuse the tension, you utilize the relational interaction as a diagnostic aid to better understand not only this client's experience but also the reasons he might find himself in difficult situations. It has all unfolded right before your eyes.

Counselors use the counseling relationship in all kinds of ways as a diagnostic and assessment aid, most of which rely on what Combs, Avila, and Purkey (1971) referred to as "self as an instrument." We monitor our own reactions to what is happening in the relationship, observe patterns in evidence, and make connections to the presenting issues. We also ask ourselves a series of questions regarding what might be happening in the relationship, especially during times when we encounter problems or conflicts:

1. How is the misunderstanding between us the result of a cultural context that isn't being fully acknowledged? We discuss this a lot more in later chapters, but for now we point out that often we miss nuances in meaning because of unfamiliarity with how behavior is situated in the client's past interactions within his or her family and identified cultures (gender, ethnicity, socioeconomic background, etc.).
2. How is what is happening between us representative of parallel processes that occur in the client's life? Another interesting and related question involves considering how the pattern is familiar in our own lives. In other words, relational patterns in counseling reflect client past experiences, counselor past experiences, and the interaction between the two.
3. In what ways is the relational pattern that has become entrenched in counseling sessions somewhat limiting? Once we have a sense of what that might be, we have greater understanding of ways to alter those established templates.

We can also consider not just what the client is doing, or not doing—that is, creating blocks or barriers—but especially our own behavior and perhaps unwillingness to be more flexible. After all, therapeutic relationships involve real living human beings, each with his or her own issues and personal reactions to what is happening between them.

Working With Transference Reactions

The classic, historical conception of therapeutic relationships is as a transference phenomenon in which the client projects onto the clinician feelings and perceptions that originate in earlier life experiences, often from childhood. The client's feelings and perceptions from earlier life experiences can provide a window into unresolved issues that spontaneously arise during sessions, largely as a result of distorted, exaggerated, or imagined feelings that are directed toward the counselor. Sometimes these feelings are indeed real reactions of anger, resentment, affection, even love, that are "earned" through the interactions that do take place in the relationship. For example, clients who may feel they were deprived of support and love earlier in their lives may be more inclined to seek such validation during sessions. Those who have felt abused and mistreated by previous authority figures may project those feelings onto their counselor. As we become aware of these patterns, we are better positioned to alter their trajectory in more constructive ways.

Although there is considerable debate surrounding exactly how transference should be defined, and how it is manifested, counselors may respond in different ways to the inevitable conflicts and misunderstandings, as well as to the opportunities for learning, that develop as a result.

1. *Immediacy interactions.* Comparable to but not exactly the same as in humanistic/existential counseling, the more generic form simply brings attention to the immediacy of any moment in a session, bringing attention to something important that might be playing out in the client's nonverbal behavior, observable actions, or sensations within the body: "I noticed as you were talking about the way your colleagues at work treat you that you were looking curiously at me, as if something was triggered, some reminder. You started folding your arms and leaning back in the chair. Talk about what's happening for you right now."

2. *Explorations of thoughts and feelings.* Through the use of probes, prompts, reflections, and open-ended questions, the counselor encourages clients to look more deeply at how their reactions to something that was said or occurred in session might reflect some strong feelings about the way the sessions have been proceeding: "You hesitated for a moment when I asked you about some things that happened when you were growing up. I notice you do that a lot, as if you are rehearsing what to say and how to say it in a way that won't reveal too much all at once. I wonder what it's like for you to spend this time with me?"

[handwritten margin notes: "I noticed X, talk about what happened there..."]

[handwritten margin notes: "You hesitated when I mentioned X, I wonder if you are editing what you want to say..."]

3. *Imaginings and fantasies.* It is sometimes useful to ask clients to reveal some of their innermost beliefs and perceptions about the counselor: "You've mentioned in the past that you often feel rejected when you share something really personal about yourself, as if others usually don't understand what you mean. What about with me? What do you imagine that I might really think about you?"

4. *Linking patterns.* This intervention represents one of the ways we make connections between the client's behavior in a session and ways he or she might act with significant others. This is perhaps the most direct use of transference, drawing attention to interaction patterns throughout life that also play out during the counseling relationship: "I can't help but observe that every time I compliment you or say something to validate your experience you brush it off. You literally wave your hand at me as if it doesn't mean anything. You've described earlier that was how your father often responded to you after you told him anything you felt proud of. I wonder what connections you see between what happens between us and what you have felt previously growing up?"

For those who are not trained in psychoanalytic methods, there is still relatively universal recognition that the counseling relationship consists of both distorted, exaggerated, projected features (transference) and genuine, authentic, personal engagement (real relationship). There is little doubt that, at times, our clients see us not as we are but rather as they imagine us to be, or perhaps as someone else who resembles a figure from the past. Likewise, there are instances when our own biases, past history, associative memory, and distorted perceptions lead us to view particular clients in ways that are less than accurate. Ignoring these relational issues as they arise in sessions can short-circuit progress and lead to breaches that end counseling prematurely (Gelso & Bhatia, 2012).

Clearly, not all clients profit from transference interventions, nor is a focus on this area even necessary or appropriate. I (Rick) once worked with a 16-year-old client who had significant anger issues toward his father. During one session, in the middle of a conversation, the boy abruptly asked me, "Can I sit on your lap?"

I wasn't sure if he was being serious or was just trying to get a response out of me. All I could think to do was repeat what he has asked me, trying to buy some time. "You want to sit on my lap?"

"Oh," I didn't mean it like that," he backpedaled, reading my surprised reaction. "I was just, you know, thinking that, maybe, we could hang out some time, maybe see a movie together."

I completely missed what was really happening and took what he was saying literally, which felt a bit creepy. Instead of reflecting the intimate feelings he was experiencing related to me as an older male figure who provided him with the caring and support that he desperately wanted, I reacted self-protectively, quickly indicating that this would not be possible. As a result, he shut down, and it took considerable time to repair his uncertainty toward me.

With some clients, in some situations and contexts, transference issues can be significant areas for exploration. Carefully selected, targeted, and judicious transference interventions can be extremely useful and well received (Hoglend, 2014). Excessive use of these interpretations, however, can sometimes lead to unfavorable results.

On the simplest level, essentially what we are often wondering, if not asking clients aloud, is: "What is it like for you to be with me?" The second question we occasionally consider is just as important: "What is it like for me to be with you?" Both inquiries lead us to consider ways that our own personal reactions can become clues as well as blockages to further enhancing the relational bonds.

Sharing of Self in the Relationship

The use of self-disclosure in counseling is potentially among the most powerfully impactful interventions but also the most abused and self-indulgent. From the very inception of the profession, we were warned to avoid talking about ourselves and to remain relatively anonymous to facilitate transference reactions. Interestingly, however, Freud himself personally ignored this prohibition (in 43 cases) in his own work, frequently crossing all kinds of boundaries because of his investment in his patients' lives (Lynn & Vaillant, 1998).

Most contemporary counselors and therapists, psychodynamic practitioners among them, now acknowledge that self-disclosures are inevitable, with some schools of thought (humanistic, existential, relational-cultural, feminist) emphasizing a far more egalitarian relationship in which sharing of self is a favored strategy. Everyone does this to some extent, although its frequency is often underreported because there is a big difference between what people say they are doing—or not doing—and what actually occurs behind closed doors.

Those who avoid sharing of themselves at all costs because of fears of violating boundaries or perceived ethical violations risk hurting clients in other ways (Barnett, 2011; Zur, 2009). Imagine, for instance, that a client is told briefly and simply by his counselor that the next 3 weeks of sessions will need to be cancelled, with no further explanation. The client leaves wondering (or likely perseverating), "Is my counselor going on vacation?" "Is she going into the hospital for some kind of operation? I wonder if she has cancer?" "I don't think she really likes me that much, and that's why she is avoiding me on purpose." The point is that withholding information can sometimes be as provocative as revealing too much.

Self-disclosure is a difficult skill to use effectively. It must be introduced in such a way that it directly relates to the client's needs and does not seem distracting or inappropriate. Let's face it: Clients are often already insecure and used to being treated as less than equals. When a counselor takes the focus off the client and tells a personal story, it may once again communicate this inequality of power. Unfortunately, all of us are more than familiar with a few colleagues (or former instructors or supervisors) who talk *way* more than they should about themselves. They tell long-winded, heroic stories about how wonderful or amazing they are, and the audience is often left wondering, "So why is he telling us this?"

At best, such excessive self-disclosures waste time and risk boring clients or pushing them away; at worst, they represent florid narcissism and disrespect, as well as incredible insensitivity and cluelessness. Nevertheless, incisive, well-timed, selective, and targeted disclosures can be among the most important tools at our disposal, especially if the goal is to deepen the relationship.

All types of self-disclosure are not the same. Some are deliberate, planned, strategic interventions that have a specific defensible rationale as they are applied in a given situation and context; others are spontaneous or sometimes impulsive offerings. Self-disclosures can occur inadvertently as well when clients search for information online and via social media or deduce certain things based on personal objects in the room. Clients can also make assumptions about the counselor's life based on visible eating habits (green tea bags, espresso cup, Snickers bars, bottle of bourbon—just kidding!), physical attributes (size, weight, tattoos), clothing (T-shirt with slogan, hijab, yarmulke), or jewelry (wedding ring, Star of David, cross, expensive watch). Additional clues about the counselor are revealed accidentally if he or she is encountered outside the office.

Generally speaking, self-disclosures occur in several varieties that begin with simply revealing basic information about ourselves such as our degrees, licenses, specialties, and professional training.

This can sometimes cover basic personal information as well, such as when a client asks, "Are you married?" "Do you have children?" "Have you watched this show that I've been talking about?" Except in the most unusual circumstances, it would not seem appropriate to sidestep these questions with an evasive response such as, "You are wondering whether I'm married or not."

Disclosures can involve sharing similar concerns to those mentioned by the client, offering insights (or advice) based on past experiences, providing examples from one's own life, and immediate thoughts and feelings about the client, the relationship, or the way things are going so far:

> *Version 1:* "I'm so pleased with the progress we've made so far and all that you have accomplished in the last few weeks. I feel so proud of you!"
>
> *Version 2:* "I'm a bit disappointed that you elected not to follow through on what you said was so important last week. It's as if you aren't treating these sessions very seriously."

The clearest distinction between these two types of self-disclosure, which are functionally quite different, is between their immediate and nonimmediate focus (Audet, 2011).

Immediate disclosures take place in the moment, in the here and now, and reveal the counselor's direct and honest feelings about what is happening in the relationship: "When you back off like that, cross your arms, it feels like you are punishing me for pushing you too hard. I feel sad every time that happens because it seems like we have to start over again." *Nonimmediate disclosures* bring up things from the past: "When I was your age, I remember going through a similar series of challenges that I had to overcome." Although both kinds have their value in some circumstances, the evidence seems to point to immediate disclosures as potentially being more useful and appreciated than nonimmediate ones because of the ways they deepen the relationship (Farber, 2006; Knox & Hill, 2003).

For our purposes, we are most interested in distinguishing between times when self-disclosure is most helpful, when it is relatively benign, and when it is clearly inappropriate. For example, although self-disclosure may be spontaneous and unplanned, unsolicited self-disclosure is less likely to be accepted by the client and may decrease the client's perception of the competence of the counselor (Cashwell, Shcherbakova, & Cashwell, 2003). In the most advantageous circumstances, self-disclosures are used to accomplish several goals, to strengthen the relationship, or to achieve specific outcomes by doing one or more of the following things:

1. Facilitating increased intimacy and closing psychological distance: "I remember a time when I dealt with something similar to what you are describing, and I also felt pretty helpless."
2. Normalizing behavior: "I also struggle at times with getting everything done, because I could be better organized."
3. Modeling greater humanness and fallibility: "I think you are right in pointing out that I pushed you too hard, and I apologize for that. I think I just became impatient, perhaps because I want so badly for you to pull yourself out of this tailspin."
4. Highlighting ways of dealing with shared experiences: "When I had once been let go from a job without any warning, I chose to see this as a new opportunity to reinvent myself; but also like you, it took me awhile to recover my disappointment and discouragement and motivate myself to move on to the next stage of my life."
5. Demonstrating ways of thinking or responding differently: "What I tell myself in similar situations is that even though I can't control what other people do or say, I do have the power to change how I respond to them."
6. Sharing immediacy of feelings in the moment: "Right now, I feel so much closer to you as a result of your revealing so much of yourself."
7. Emphasizing or teaching an important life lesson: "I was never a very good student in my early years. It wasn't until I realized that I could redefine myself, that I could be a completely different person if I so chose, that I was able to reach so far beyond what I ever thought was possible for me."
8. Demonstrating a parallel process: "I'd like to tell you a story about something that happened to me recently, and then I'd be interested to hear from you how you see this as being directly related to your situation."

Ultimately, the purpose and goal of any self-disclosure is to create a more trusting and constructive relationship to accomplish counseling goals. There seems little doubt from the evidence that this, in fact, can often result if the disclosures are appropriately timed, relatively brief, and relate directly to the client's needs. They are a lot less likely to be viewed as helpful by clients when the relationship is not strong or when they involve sharing personal problems that are still going on in the counselor's life (Bloomgarden & Mennuti, 2009; Maroda, 2012). The main challenge is to strike the right balance between being too withholding or too forthcoming about personal feelings, especially because the attention is taken away from the client temporarily. That is one reason why it is important to use this challenging skill carefully, cautiously, judiciously, sparingly, and briefly.

Once again, we emphasize that whether or not self-disclosure is experienced by clients as helpful, or essentially a waste of time, depends very much on the quality of the relationship as it is experienced by the client (Hanson, 2005). Identifying the client's preferences related to counselor self-disclosure may also be critical. When the client could benefit from counselor self-disclosure and the counselor refuses, the counselor is likely to be viewed as less competent and relational; however, unsolicited self-disclosure by the counselor can result in the same negative outcome (Cashwell et al., 2003). When in doubt, the ultimate conclusion is that less is more.

It is to be expected that various counseling models utilize self-disclosure in different ways. Emotionally focused and attachment-oriented counselors use personal sharing as a means of providing a corrective emotional experience, perhaps creating the kind of respect and intimacy that had rarely been experienced previously with someone in a position of authority: "I find that I respect you more than ever for challenging things I've said that don't fit with your experience." Cognitive behavior counselors might limit personal sharing to examples that model rational self-talk: "I tell myself that it isn't a catastrophe that it's raining again outside but that it is only a little disappointing." Feminist counselors might talk about some of their core values and beliefs, especially those related to oppression and privilege: "I don't think it's okay that you are treated that way because you are gay. You seem somewhat blasé about that incident, but I notice that I am furious at your supervisor for his insensitivity and disrespect." Humanistic counselors would, of course, be much more fluent and open, conveying aspects of transparency, genuineness, and personal authenticity: "I feel so close to you right now, like we have finally touched each other in a deep, deep way."

Although we have treated self-disclosure as a discrete and specific skill, or a manifestation of a particular approach, it also can be viewed more globally as part of an integrative process that can simultaneously accomplish several goals by enhancing the relationship and facilitating client motivation and commitment to the process (Ziv-Beiman, 2013). By way of summary, the results from research on the subject are mixed; nevertheless, we can reach a few reasonable conclusions. The first is that most (but not all) clients appreciate counselor self-disclosures and find that it makes the relationship feel more safe, secure, and reciprocal; they feel less like an object and more like a valued person. Second, self-disclosures are more likely to be helpful to clients when they are:

- Related to what is being discussed in the moment;
- Infrequently introduced;
- Intimate but not *too* intimate;
- Relatively brief with only relevant details; and
- Smoothly integrated into the conversation so the client isn't left wondering how this relates to him or her.

Finally, self-disclosures are among the most powerful, potentially transformative, and also risky things we do. They have the potential to strengthen relational connections like nothing else, but they also can lead to reducing the counselor's credibility and, at times, even sabotaging the relationship because of what is experienced as a boundary violation.

Deepening Relationships

We may have been taught how to create and maintain relationships with clients but not necessarily how to deepen them. The process is a gradual, moment-by-moment experience often characterized by a series of incremental steps (Knox, 2013). It begins with an initial slowing down of the pace because the client is feeling increased vulnerability after opening up about something particularly difficult. The counselor responds, not by pushing but, in one sense, by backing off to create more space for the client to proceed slowly and carefully around this sensitive material. In this vulnerable place, the client sees clearly that the counselor also recognizes and acknowledges this state of exposure. The counselor concentrates primarily on holding and supporting the client during this stage, offering reassurance that the relationship is safe and that the client is not alone in this journey. Each successive step the counselor takes is informed and guided by the client's responses, matching carefully what seems to be most appropriate in the moment—always in the moment.

If the relationship is going to deepen, that will happen at the client's behest, inviting the counselor to join him or her at another level of intimacy and trust. If the counselor successfully communicates understanding and acceptance, this often leads to feelings of relief and well-being, followed by greater self-acceptance. When clients feel affirmed and validated, they report feeling more alive and energized by the possibilities for the future rather than discouraged. It is at this point that the counselor steps back a bit to allow for deeper reflection about the meanings of what transpired and how it might relate to other aspects of functioning.

So, how do you know when you have achieved deep engagement with a client? It certainly can't be assessed alone by what clients say happened. They tell us things we want to hear. They engage in deceptive strategies for the purposes of image management: They want us to like them above all else. They lie because it's interesting, it's fun, and sometimes even empowering to fool someone in a position of great authority. They exaggerate their symptoms at times, and at other times they disguise or hide what is really going on.

Obviously, if clients distort the truth and exaggerate or minimize their symptoms, counselors may provide inaccurate assessments of outcomes. It isn't that unusual for a counselor to believe that a relationship is going fabulously well when the client is actually quite dissatisfied with the results. After all, counselors have a vested interest in emphasizing that counseling is perhaps going much better than might be reasonable to assume. We are eternal optimists and usually look at the bright side of things whenever possible.

With these cautions in mind, assessments can still be reliably undertaken to provide some indication of a client's feelings and reactions to the relationship, an enterprise that many find absolutely crucial to successful outcomes (Duncan, 2010; Duncan & Miller, 2000; Duncan et al., 2010; Hatcher & Gillaspy, 2006; Miller & Hubble, 2011). The Working Alliance Inventory (Horvath & Greenberg, 1989) is one such measure specifically developed and aligned with Bordin's (1979) theory of working alliance. A benefit of this measure is that the counselor can evaluate the depth of the relationship based on clients' reactions to something they found helpful in sessions (Knox, 2013). When such conditions are met, clients are inclined to agree strongly with statements such as, "I felt like my counselor understood me," "My counselor and I seemed to know what each of us was thinking," "It felt like something magical happened," "My counselor truly cares about me," and "I felt a close personal connection with my counselor." Cooper (2005) has divided these reactions into different domains of experience (see Table 4.1).

TABLE 4.1
Domains of Relational Engagement

Domain	Features
Self-experiences	Sense of aliveness, heightened awareness, clarity, congruence, slowing down, peacefulness, self-acceptance, revitalization
Experiences of others	Authenticity, genuineness, transparency
Experiences of relationship	Intimacy, closeness, trust, blurring of boundaries, collaboration, feelings of deep affection
Experiences of the moment	Unique and rare, surprising, spiritual or mystical connection, flow state of complete immersion

Considering what this relational depth feels like, the key question for us is, "How do we increase the likelihood that our counseling alliances achieve this end?" There is little mystery here because we have been hearing for decades about the core conditions that emphasize safety, warmth, genuineness, and nurturance. Still, not much can be accomplished in this realm without the full cooperation and participation of the client, who must feel committed to this intimate encounter. In some cases, this intimacy is neither necessary nor even desirable.

When such depth is useful to further counseling goals, one overriding skill—or, more accurately, quality—has been found to make the greatest difference, and that is the counselor's *presence in the moment* (Geller & Porges, 2014). This refers to our ability, and willingness, to completely immerse ourselves in the poignancy of whatever is being experienced in any given moment, to be truly and completely there. This sounds good, but it is really, really difficult to do on any kind of continuous basis. We get distracted. We lapse into fantasy. We are triggered by something the client says and go off into our own stuff. We feel bored or disengaged at times and don't keep focus. You can do you own personal study on the subject, but how much of the time would you estimate you are absolutely paying attention, with baited breath, to everything a client is saying and doing? What percentage of the time are you fully present in sessions? We've heard estimates ranging from 20% to 75%, depending on the client—and the counselor's mood and state of mind.

Not surprisingly, Carl Rogers (1980) stated that the times he was at his best occurred when the connections between him and his client became almost ethereal:

I find that when I am closest to my inner, intuitive self, when I am somehow in touch with the unknown in me, when perhaps I am in a slightly altered state of consciousness, then whatever I do seems to be full of healing. . . . Our relationship transcends itself and becomes a part of something larger. (p. 129)

Relationships are enhanced not only when we are closely in touch with the client's inner states but also when we are intensely aware of our own feelings, thoughts, and bodily sensations. This comprises our "filtered internal dialogue," which forms the basis for some of our most incisive process observations (Teyber & Teyber, 2014). Imagine, for example, that a counselor decides to say out loud what she is actually thinking during a significant moment: "I'm feeling confused and lost now as you continue to tell this story that I've heard you talk about before. It seems as if you'd rather stick with something that is safe and predictable than risk getting into new territory you have been avoiding. I have noticed that every time I try to broach the subject of your impending divorce you quickly change the subject."

One reason being fully present is so rare is because it requires so much commitment, focus, energy, and preparation. Sometimes, that is not enough because whether the counselor feels present or not doesn't count unless the client experiences this sensation too (Geller & Greenberg, 2012). Let's take a look at what can be accomplished using this challenging skill:

- Assess client reactions to seminal moments
- Clarify and focus on specific content
- Bring out hidden, implicit issues that are having an impact
- Emphasize collaboration in relationship
- Link together several relevant points
- Confront resistance and reluctance
- Heal ruptures in the relationship
- Take the relationship to the next level of engagement
- Model and demonstrate more authentic ways of being
- Teach greater awareness of interpersonal behavior
- Discover meaning, payoffs, secondary gains, and consequences of interpersonal patterns

What we are describing resonates with Rogers's earlier remarks. Engaged relationships operate at optimal levels when the participants enter into a kind of altered state of consciousness characterized by increased awareness of self and other(s), intense focus, enhanced sensitivity, emotional arousal, and a feeling of being grounded. The quality of the therapeutic relationship is improved by as much as one third when counselors receive mindfulness training and become more aware of internal and interpersonal processes (Razzaque, Okoro, & Wood, 2015).

Although mindfulness has a lot of different meanings and applications, for the purposes of our discussion it includes several components that are most often associated with stronger relationships (Hayes, Strosahl, & Wilson, 2012; Shapiro, 2009). The first is an internal awareness of one's own inner feelings, thoughts, and body sensations without distractions. This is followed by an exquisite awareness of clients' reactions and internal states, as well as focused, hovering, yet open attention to whatever is happening in the moment. Finally, there are feelings of compassion, not only for others but also for oneself.

This state of intense and total engagement takes on many of the features of a hypnotic trance in which we totally lose ourselves in the interaction. Time slips away. We almost lose our sense of self as we enter into deep engagement with the client.

When Techniques Get in the Way

We are quite aware that many counselors, especially those in the beginning stages of their careers, are hungry for relatively foolproof techniques and strategies, preferably something new and innovative on the scene that renders everything we've ever known obsolete and magically leads to an almost instant cure. Oh, and these techniques would be simple, easy to learn, and immediately applicable to almost anyone and any issue.

We have reason to be wary of "succumbing to the allure of novel procedures and fancy theories, particularly those that promise quick and dramatic cures," advised Efran and Fauber (2015, p. 31) in their criticism of this infatuation. They cite systematic desensitization and implosive therapy as the kinds of popular techniques that once took the profession by storm but turned out to be a bunch of quackery, unsupported by evidence and offering the same relief as any other rituals. They repeat once again what we and so many other researchers have been saying for the last few decades: It isn't really about the techniques but the relationship within which they are embedded. That is one reason so many counseling approaches have now put the relationship in the center of their treatment even as they continue to utilize their signature techniques.

Sure, a plethora of strategies have been systematically studied and supported by empirical evidence. Many of the studies used regimented treatment protocols that provide a highly structured series of interventions. However, regardless of the extent to which researchers delineate a treatment strategy, the therapeutic relationship remains a confounding variable. Further, potential participants in the studies who lack the ability to implement the treatment will likely not be included. In other words, such interventions are usually implemented by competent practitioners who are already enthusiastic and highly skilled in applying the protocol. These ideal circumstances do not resonate with those of us who are first learning the method and cannot immediately replicate the successful results reported in the studies.

By focusing too much on techniques, skills, and strategies, sometimes we lose the ability to sense and feel what is actually happening in the moment. It is when we are in that "relational zone" that we are often better able to capitalize on our natural ability to access preconscious thoughts, feelings, reactions, and intuition that often lead us to unexpected and rich moments of meaning.

Of course, it is better to have more therapeutic options rather than fewer unless one becomes confused and flooded with too many choices. Those who remain committed to one theoretical orientation may sometimes be (or feel) restricted in the kinds of relationships they are "permitted" to construct and maintain. Traditional applications of psychoanalytic, behavioral, strategic, humanistic, or any other variety of counseling prescribe fairly specific configurations and qualities of the relationship that reduce degrees of freedom in other areas.

Perhaps one of the exceptions that is often prevalent in any approach to counseling is the "technique" of making process observations about what appears to be happening in the relationship at any moment in time. These comments tend to deepen levels of engagement and "bring immediacy and intensity" to the stage (Teyber & Teyber, 2014, p. 334). They are not "truths" but rather expressed awareness that is offered tentatively, sensitively, and is subject to further scrutiny. Then again, we believe that the best relational skills and techniques aren't really specific interventions as much as they are infused into the very spirit of the interaction when we ask the question, "What is going on between us, and what does this mean?"

Enduring changes occur when clients are helped to experience "corrective emotional experiences" or "novel interaction experiences," the kind that break old dysfunctional patterns and lead to far more self-enhancing ways of relating to others. This is what forever alters clients' internalized beliefs about themselves and what might be possible. This is what assists them to increase their range of interpersonal options in all their future relationships.

Although we heartily agree that particular techniques and strategies are consistently helpful in establishing and maintaining the kinds of relationships that lead to successful outcomes, we insist that everything starts with the attitudes we bring to the encounter. It so happens that a positive, optimistic attitude goes a long way toward promoting therapeutic gains, not just encouraging hope in the client but also encouraging the counselor to adopt positive beliefs about what is possible. It would appear that neutrality is overrated as a counselor trait, because one of the best "techniques" in our repertoire is our own confidence that the healing powers of the relationship will help clients to better manage their emotional states (Peluso, Liebovitch, Gottman, Norman, & Su, 2012).

Efran and Fauber (2015) lamented that beginners in the field, in particular, are always trying to figure out how to *act* like counselors instead of just *be* themselves. We make things so much more complicated than perhaps they need to be, especially when we think that relational connections are all about techniques and strategies. We are obsessed with the newest, latest, great thing: "In the search for simple explanations for their clients' suffering, they [counselors] tend to find an attachment injury behind every relationship issue, a traumatic event to account for any symptom, and brain research to support every clinical maneuver" (p. 31). They hope to "declutter the therapeutic canvas" by suggesting that we try to clear our minds, as much as possible, of all the assumptions that might get in our own way. Once we have done so, they insist we are in a far better position to immerse ourselves in a client's story, undistracted by the constant search for the next best intervention.

Chapter 5

Customized Relationships: Differences Within and Between Individuals, Families, Groups, and Cultures

Like so many adolescents involuntarily referred for counseling, Jeremy was less than enthusiastic about the idea of attending sessions. One could even say he was determined to do his best to make life as miserable as possible for his counselor so that they could share some mutual suffering. To add to the burden, the counselor was already conducting 20 individual sessions each week, in addition to quite a number of family and group sessions, far more than he could fit into each of his 60-hour work weeks.

"I had to prioritize who in my caseload needed individual time the most," the counselor explained, almost apologetically. "At one point I just had to ask all the kids in one of my groups who needed—or wanted—to meet with me on any given day. At least that way I talked with those who were most motivated."

Because Jeremy never asked for a session on his own, the counselor only talked with him occasionally, and there didn't seem to be much progress. That's why the counselor was so surprised when he was pulled aside by Jeremy's father who told him, "You are the first person to ever reach my son."

"I am?"

In fact, the counselor didn't think he was reaching Jeremy at all.

"Yeah," the father immediately agreed. "He says you work really hard. And you are one of the few shrinks—that's what he calls you—that ever seemed to care about him."

One reason the counselor was so surprised by this feedback was because there was so much emphasis in his agency on using their standard treatment protocols. The power of the relationship was hardly ever even mentioned, and if it was discussed, it was only in the context of a relatively extraneous variable that must be monitored. In addition, the particular sort of relationship this counselor had negotiated with Jeremy hardly fit the usual standard we consider when things go well—it was not especially intimate and engaging, but apparently it was rather meaningful to the client. In fact, the only thing that the counselor could think of that must have been significant to Jeremy is that he noticed how hard the counselor worked to help *others* in the group, even though he was mostly a bystander.

Exceptions Are the Rules

The case just described is surely rather unusual, but then our main point for this chapter is that *every* client we see should be part of an absolutely unique and specialized relationship designed to best meet his or her individual needs. This not only means the kind of relationship that is co-constructed—intimate or business-like, informal and spontaneous or demarcated and prescribed—but also the level of engagement that is optimal to maximize influence.

This is not a static arrangement but is ever shifting in light of the client's reactions and feelings, needs and interests. There is a continuous mirroring effect in which the counselor makes momentary adaptations, staying closely attuned to the client's internal states. In fact, it is more like a *mutual* calibration in which each participant in the relationship makes moment-to-moment adjustments to inner states of arousal, dampening, intensity, and self-soothing. It is thus a process of interactive, mutual influence to regulate and manage both internal states and interactive patterns. Nolan (2012), for example, described how, with some of his more stable clients, he can sail to "dark and unknown islands" with smooth and direct navigation, whereas with his traumatized clients, the conditions are considerably rougher, with unexpected "high seas" that can become quite dramatic.

Most of us would agree that when it comes to relationships, one size clearly does not fit all of our clients. First of all, each person enters the room with a set of expectations about what he or she thinks will occur. Some clients have rather grandiose and unrealistic goals, such as that we will listen to their story and agree that they are not really the problem; it is everyone else who is at fault. Other clients will do the exact opposite and blame themselves unmercifully for everything that has ever gone wrong in their lives. Each of these scenarios suggests a different kind of relationship to best forge an alliance.

Individual personalities respond best to different kinds of relationships. Some clients are gregarious, others shy. Some are highly narcissistic, arrogant, and self-involved, and others are self-deprecating. Some are demanding and feel entitled to special treatment, and some find it hard to express their needs in any form. Some respect established boundaries, and others take delight at testing the boundaries at every opportunity. We feel an instant connection with some people and not much of one at all with others, no matter how much time we spend together. Some present themselves rather formally, and others are loose and spontaneous. Each of these personal characteristics interacts with our own qualities and preferences, leading us to accommodate clients in different ways.

We have talked about individual features so far, but larger cultural forces are also at work that dictate specialized relationships. We would have a different kind of connection with someone who shares many of our own values, beliefs, and customs than with someone who presents norms that are unfamiliar to us. If someone "belongs" to a corporate culture, she might very well expect (and demand) a relationship in line with that as opposed to the expectations of someone who works in a factory, farm, charity, or university. One's religious tradition, native language, family upbringing, ethnicity, gender, and age cohort also influence what could become an optimal relationship.

The client's motivation and readiness level guide particular relational strategies. Prochaska and DiClemente's (1986) seminal work on stages of change and clients' readiness to deal with their addictions was instrumental in developing motivational interviewing and its manualized version, motivational enhancement therapy (Miller & Rollnick, 2012). With someone who is highly engaged, committed, motivated, and impatient to get moving, we can do certain things we would never attempt with someone who is visibly reluctant, ambivalent about change, and perhaps angry at being forced to seek help. It is also relevant to know something about what has worked best in the past.

We have also emphasized that the particular stage of counseling matters. What we do in the beginning is different from what we do in the middle or at the end. The same client may sometimes want and need a relationship that is more supportive, but at other times require a far more direct and confrontive level of engagement. This varies in the evolution of stages but also oscillates session to session, even moment to moment.

Finally, there is the presenting problem and how that may strongly influence what type of relationship would be best for that issue, context, and situation. Imagine five different clients who are scheduled in a day. The first one is an adolescent boy who doesn't talk much at all, just pouts a lot because he resents that he has to attend sessions just because he talks back to his teachers. Client number two suffers from stage three cancer and is learning to live with the uncertainty of a fragile life. The third client hates his job as an accountant and wants guidance about other career options he might consider. The fourth case is a guy who just found out his wife is having an affair, and he has big-time trust issues. The last client is highly anxious, medication doesn't put a dent in her stress, and she is practically vibrating. No matter how you usually work, what theoretical approach you favor, we are certain that the relationships you establish with each of these clients would hardly resemble each other. After all, some people need to be held; others need to be kicked in the seat of the pants.

Relationships With Groups and Families

The challenges and difficulties we might face when developing relationships with individual clients are magnified many times when working with more than one person in the room. Couples who come in for help usually already have a fractured relationship and some breach of trust; at least one of the partners often feels suspicious or less than enthusiastic about seeking help for a relationship about which he or she may feel ambivalent or even may be prepared to abandon altogether. For those who work in group settings, the relational complexities are overwhelming. Various coalitions, alliances, and festering resentments are added to the initial challenges of creating the necessary trust and intimacy in the room. The transference reactions, projections, and strong feelings that might normally just be directed toward the counselor are now magnified by a factor of 10 or 100 with all the interconnections between and with each group member. Family counseling is often even more complicated because all of the participants are related to one another with a long history of complaints, ghosts, and secrets.

The original encounter group movement launched by Carl Rogers and company was essentially structured (or rather *un*structured) as a relational cure. The main idea, perhaps best explained by Abraham Maslow, was that a high-functioning group, with solid cohesion, has so much more potential to produce lasting changes than any individual modality, the equivalent of 1 + 1 = 11. The facilitator may have operated in a nondirective style, but it was designed to maximize relational engagement and work through feelings toward one another in the moment. The leader's job was to help members build their own therapeutic community, which would make it safe for them to share unexpressed feelings, work through their interpersonal difficulties, and, at times, reenact problems from the outside world.

Nowadays, group and family sessions are far more structured, just as counselors and other professionals are so much better trained to capitalize on other strategies beyond personal sharing among members. Nevertheless, navigating all the intricate, intimate, and intense interpersonal goings-on in groups sometimes feels like it is more than we can possibly manage.

Felipe is rambling on and on, and you feel completely disconnected from the proceedings and bored out of your mind. You wonder if it is just you and the uneasy relationship you sometimes experience with Felipe, but you scan the group and notice that several others have checked out as well. You start to say something to Felipe, helping him to get to the point, but then see two others out of the corner of your eye whispering and smirking. You abruptly stop for a moment and turn to them.

"I'm curious what you were saying to one another?" you ask, holding out your hand to request patience from the member who had been speaking.

"Oh, nothing," one of them says, and the other nods her head in agreement.

"Hmm. That's interesting. Because as Felipe was talking, I noticed that the two of you were sharing some remarks that seemed to be about him, or perhaps about me interrupting him."

Before you know it, others jump in, taking sides, supporting Felipe because they feel you were rude to cut him off in the middle of his story or jumping in to defend the other two for their behavior, which you found disruptive. You look around the group and are flooded by all the feelings you have for each member, as well as by the uncertainty you feel about what really might be going on behind the scenes. You know that many of the members remain in contact with one another outside of group, despite warnings that this can undermine the process. You think you have a handle on who is close to whom, as well as where possible sources of conflict might reside, but these are only hypotheses that have yet to be confirmed.

It turns out that group cohesion is almost *everything* in this therapeutic modality or, for that matter, any collection of people working together for a common goal, whether personal growth or corporate productivity. Specifically, this means that participants (a) observe clear boundaries of appropriate behavior that are consistently enforced, (b) feel a sense of safety and security, and (c) express a greater range of personal reactions that are more authentic and honest (Paul & Charura, 2014a). The relationships include both a type of "vertical" cohesion, referring to the relative closeness and empathy that a member feels toward (and from) the leader, and "horizontal" cohesion that describes any member's relationships with others in the group (Burlingame, McClendon, & Alonso, 2011). Both of these are important for productive work to take place.

A number of other curative factors have been described as well (Corey, Corey, & Corey, 2016; Gladding, 2015; Kottler & Englar-Carlson, 2015; Yalom, 1975), and we discuss them next. Many of these factors also connect to relational influences.

Vicarious learning. One of the most remarkable features of group work is related to all the mysterious and interesting ways that members learn all kinds of things simply by watching the action and personalizing what is occurring to their own lives. Often, they may do that very quietly, without saying a word. We have stopped trying to predict who grew and learned the most in any group (or class) because so much of the action takes place behind the scenes. Sometimes the person who is talking the most doesn't translate anything into constructive action, whereas members who may have appeared disengaged are quietly going about initiating major changes in their lives. Observational learning is a key feature of any group setting.

Reenactments and rehearsals. Because we live in a world of groups and clients frequently come to counseling in the first place because of interpersonal dissatisfactions and conflicts, group counseling is an ideal place to work through these issues. Whether in role plays, family reenactments that play out, or transference reactions to the leader or other members, there are numerous opportunities to examine, refine, and alter interpersonal patterns, both as they play out in sessions and in those conflict areas that originally brought them into counseling.

Providing feedback. Where else in the world can you really hear about how you come across to others and feel safe doing so without the usual defensiveness and perceived threats? Groups are ideal for clients to practice new behaviors, as well as engage in their usual patterns, and then find out how others perceive this. We try to do this during individual sessions, but it is not nearly as effective because of our authority position and what it might trigger. In group settings, clients can hear opinions and reactions from a variety of people and, if there is reasonable agreement, consolidate what was offered in such a way that patterns can forever be changed. "Do you know you raise you voice at the end of most sentences, turning them into questions instead of statements?" one member tells another. "It makes it hard to take what you say seriously. Maybe that's why you feel so ignored a lot of the time, even in here with us."

That might be interesting feedback indeed, especially if others chime in with similar input that makes it more difficult to ignore what was said. Even if the feedback is not particularly accurate, it still gives the individual an indication of impressions. This can open up another opportunity for the person giving feedback to learn what is most and least helpful. Once again, remember that all kinds of things are happening to others in the group who are watching this interaction and perhaps applying some part that speaks to them.

Deep intimacy. People, in general, and clients in particular, are often hungry for closer connections with others. Even those who have an assortment of friends and acquaintances still yearn for deeper intimacy given the usual kinds of superficial conversations that take place. Perhaps more than any other part of the experience, group members report that they enjoyed and felt fulfilled by the caring and support they felt toward and from others. In some ways, they say, they feel "ruined" because now they expect so much more from *all* of their other relationships.

Mutual support. "I've never told anyone this before, but when I was in school, I got busted for drugs even though it was expunged from my record." After disclosing this secret, another member confesses after nodding her head: "There's been something I've wanted to tell you as well, something that I've buried so long it is eating me up. I was abused in all kinds of ways when I was younger."

Whatever clients bring to the group, they are virtually guaranteed to feel some validation for their disclosures, no matter how shameful they might feel. The counselor's main job is to make absolutely certain that this occurs, that members are consistently offered the social support they need to feel understood and make desired changes. Given the kind of dysfunctional social groups that control and influence clients, especially those struggling with addictions, the counseling group provides a much healthier alternative.

Characteristic interpersonal patterns. We have mentioned previously that there is an assumption, or at least a hypothesis, that the ways people behave and respond in group offers clues to how they are likely to act in the outside world where they consistently encounter difficulties. If someone is shy and withdrawn, or angry and provocative, or manipulative and controlling, it is reasonable to conclude that this pattern may be the source of trouble elsewhere.

A group member tells another that she finds him a bit intimidating and, at times, disrespectful, an observation that most others validate by nodding their heads in agreement. When the guy answers challengingly by saying, "Oh yeah? How so?" the woman immediately backs down and says, "Never mind." A discussion follows that explores how this pattern plays out in each of their lives outside of the group, how the man sabotages himself by pushing others away at times, and how the woman rarely follows through on expressing herself in an honest and authentic way. How fabulous that both of them can practice alternative ways of being in the group now that their issues have been named.

Appreciation for individual and cultural differences. There has been some preference in the field to recruit homogeneous groups consisting of clients who have similar problems with assertiveness, grief and loss, parenting, depression, or other issues. However, we prefer to create the most diverse groups possible in terms of age, culture, background, and presenting issues, providing a more realistic and representative microcosm of the outside world.

Universality is a big theme in groups—we are not alone in our struggles and can relate to everyone else on some level—but there is also a greater respect for and appreciation of member differences. Every time one member attempts to offer advice to another, a common scenario, the leader gently steps in to block this ineffective response that often results in people feeling misunderstood. Each time someone in the group attempts to speak for others, the leader intervenes to make sure that each person takes ownership of his or her beliefs and opinions and feelings. Any time a member makes a comment, or even a joke, that might be interpreted as culturally insensitive, the leader forcefully explains that insensitive remarks related to age, gender, race, religion, culture, or sexual identity will not be tolerated. For no extra charge, every group member learns to be more tolerant, more flexible, and more responsive to people who are different from him or her.

Healthy norms and boundaries. The example just described is only one of many norms and rules established, negotiated, and consistently enforced to make sure the environment remains as safe and enriching as possible. There are rules related to time parameters, structure, and appropriate behavior, all designed to ensure that the work completed is as efficient and constructive as possible. This creates a certain comfort level and clear expectations about what is considered both unacceptable and optimal behavior. We especially like one of the consequences of this policy: it teaches members to set clearer boundaries in all of their relationships outside of the group.

Role experimentation and risk-taking. Ideally, counseling groups provide a forum in which members can experiment and practice being different in a variety of ways, sometimes even reinventing themselves. The overarching question we might ask is, "If you could change who you are, change the way you typically behave in your world, what would you do differently?"

That is both a powerful and an overwhelming question, one that people rarely consider is even possible much less actually doable in the group. Yet the changes that often take place become contagious, and members become dizzy with the freedom of knowing that just because they have been acting in a particular way so far doesn't necessarily mean it has to continue.

"So, I know I don't talk much in here because I'm shy and I . . ."

"You mean you *used* to be shy," the leader interrupts.

"Excuse me?"

"I was just pointing out that just because until now you have been shy in *some* situations, and with *some* people, doesn't mean you will *always* be that way. Right now, right this moment, you could make a decision to be different. In fact, you already did that when you jumped in to confess this part of yourself."

"Touché!" another member agrees with a laugh.

Assertiveness and conflict resolution. Clients often come to counseling because they are having problems with someone else in their life: a boss, a partner or spouse, a coworker, a family member, or a friend. These conflicts might dominate their lives in ways that create tremendous stress and discomfort. What better place to work on these issues than in a setting in which there are all kinds of opportunities to confront someone or to assert oneself? In fact, some of the most productive—and uncomfortable—encounters that take place are those in which someone feels hurt and speaks up to confront that person. If this behavior can be generalized to other relationships in which problems exist, it can make a huge difference in interpersonal behavioral options in the future.

Modeling fully functioning behavior. Consider how you really learn to be a good counselor. Does it come from reading books like this? Do you learn the most from sitting in a classroom or workshop listening to someone lecture to you and run through a group of slides? Do you read the latest issue of your favorite journal and find yourself immeasurably changed forever in your style and effectiveness?

Although these sources are helpful, much of what we learn about good counseling and bad counseling results from watching others at work. We systematically filed away the things we like and those we don't like. We seek first to mimic, and then to internalize, the best of what we observe in others we admire, whether in our own counseling, in supervision, by watching videos, or in live demonstrations.

Public commitment and accountability. Last but not least, groups are ideal places for clients to declare goals they intend to reach. By sharing them out loud, they will be held responsible by others to follow through on their commitments. If these relationships are indeed cohesive and caring, then people do feel a much greater sense of obligation to do the things they know they need to do but that are still really frightening or difficult. It is one thing to tell a counselor that you will complete an assignment or initiate some therapeutic task, and it is quite another to share this with a whole group that is cheering for your success.

All of these relational factors operate in family and couples sessions as well, but sometimes with much more intense interpersonal dynamics because of entrenched patterns, intergenerational legacies, long-standing resentments, circular causality, and all the other systemic influences. Diagnostic and assessment procedures are focused much more on interpersonal communication patterns than they are on intrapsychic dynamics within the individual. Different kinds of coalitions and alliances are formed than those we might observe in a counseling group, but they nevertheless strongly influence behavior within and outside of sessions. Once again, the counselor must navigate complex allegiances and trust issues that take place vertically (each family member's relationship with the counselor) and horizontally (the dynamics within the family).

Salvador Minuchin (1974) emphasized that until such time as the counselor finds a way to "join" the family, to become a part of their system, it is difficult to influence them in a meaningful way. Thus, the first and foremost task is to build connections with each participant, but to do so in such a way that all feel included. This sounds good in theory, but so often we have observed counselors talking primarily to whoever holds the most power rather than balancing attention between and among everyone.

Differences Within and Between Cultures

The context in which the counseling relationship occurs varies from individual to individual and even from session to session. One moment, someone might be thinking, "I love my counselor!" and the next moment, the client may leave thinking, "I can't stand my counselor!" The pressure of listening, empathizing, confronting, encouraging, and validating, all within a single session, can be very confusing! Now, add components of cultural differences to the uniqueness of experiences, and you may find relating to the client becomes even more challenging. Within the framework of the multicultural counseling competencies developed for our profession, attention to diversity and privilege are paramount (Ratts, Singh, Nassar-McMillan, Butler, & McCullough, 2015).

When counselors validate the discrimination that clients have endured, they demonstrate openness to diversity and communicate understanding to the client. Consider how an overarching view of privilege and marginalization can affect the counseling relationship.

I (Rick) recall working with Jay, a 16-year-old African American male client, in which the nature of our relationship was challenged due to my perceived (mis)understanding of privilege and marginalization. I was meeting with Jay and his mother when she confronted her son for doing poorly in school. "You are so smart!" she scolded him. "You can make good grades. But you don't!" Then she broke down into a tearful plea for Jay to live up to his potential and to discontinue relationships with kids she perceived as having a negative influence on him.

Jay just sat there quietly, passively, barely showing any glimmer of having heard his mother. I could see that she was fuming mad, and it was becoming contagious as I felt really annoyed as well. Finally, I spoke up and encouraged Jay to respond, perhaps with impatience in my voice.

Jay just looked at me with scorn and shook his head. "You have no idea what it is like to be Black and good at school!"

Jay was, of course, absolutely correct. His life was way outside my own experience as a relatively privileged, affluent, older White male. "You're right," I immediately agreed with him. "Your mother and I don't know what that is like for you. But I was hoping you could tell us more about that."

Although parental involvement and emotional support are relevant predictors of school achievement, for African American males in particular, pressure associated with a peer group can be a much more influential predictor of success (Butler-Barnes, Estrada-Martinez, Colin, & Jones, 2015; Eaman & Altshuler, 2004; Stinson, 2011). Notable, however, is the importance that relationships play in school achievement. In fact, poor relationships with school counselors, teachers, and administrators were identified by minority adolescents as negatively affecting their performance (Vega, Moore, & Miranda, 2015). In examining Jay's experience with peers and school, his worldview played an important role in his perceptions related to school, peers, and family.

Unfortunately, counselors sometimes have an unrealistic perspective of what it means to be culturally competent, much less masterful in this area. Historically, competencies in multicultural counseling were focused exclusively on ethnic differences (Weinrach & Thomas, 2004). As a result, textbooks on multicultural counseling were less focused on other aspects of diversity, such as gender identity, sexual orientation, religious beliefs, biracial/multiracial identity, dominant language, even geographical and environmental locations. Moreover, the notion that within-group differences of a homogeneous group are broader than between-group differences is a predominant view in multicultural counseling (Reynolds, 2008). In other words, the unique characteristics of individuals who are identified within a particular group are often more prevalent than differences between different groups.

For example, consider what happens when a counselor conceptualizes or identifies a client as Asian. What does that really mean? Does the client reflect a heritage from Japan, China, Taiwan, North Korea, South Korea, Malaysia, India, Pakistan, the Philippines, Vietnam, or another country categorized as Asian? Can we honestly identify this categorization as homogeneous? Clearly, cultural differences among these groups are pervasive—hence the large within-group variance. However, despite the notion that individuals of Asian descent represent a homogenous group (and that notion could easily be debated), that does not mean that the processes involved for developing positive counseling outcomes are different. Put a different way, the common factors of counseling really are *common*. For example, Dewell and Owen (2015) evaluated clients' reports from Asian American and White clients to identify cultural differences in the helpfulness of counselors' actions during the counseling process. However, no differences between White and Asian American clients were found. More specifically, the extent to which clients endorsed helpful information and feedback from the counselor, emotional/interpersonal learning, and a strong client–counselor relationship were not notably different between Asian American and White clients. Dewell and Owen concluded that counselors' adaptation to cultural differences should occur after a counseling relationship has been established. In other words, counselors may wish to consider multicultural issues when selecting an intervention, but establishing a deep, meaningful, working counseling relationship is important regardless of culture.

So, if by focusing on perceived cultural differences, we end up engaging in stereotyping our clients—the very action we are attempting to avoid by adopting a multicultural counseling perspective—how do we promote an openness to diversity and encourage the kind of counseling relationships that are most compatible with diverse clients? The key is that cross-cultural counseling goes beyond the core conditions of empathy, genuineness, and unconditional positive regard and includes a focus on diversity and privilege.

A movement in the field during the past few decades has focused on characteristics of various ethnic, religious, racial, socioeconomic, gender, and other differences, as if these factors hold the key to unlocking the secrets of making contact with all who fit that category. Such general knowledge about the values, beliefs, history, and preferences of Native American, Latino(a), transgendered, Muslim, or Vietnamese American individuals is certainly valuable. However, we know that the differences within each group are often greater than those between groups, especially when we consider distinctions in socioeconomic status and geographical location. There is nothing more dangerous than a little knowledge that leads professionals to treat all members of a diagnostic entity, cultural group, or any other singular variable pretty much the same.

It is a myth that any of us belongs to a single culture, regardless of how meaningful one's religious beliefs, how strong one's ethnic or racial identity, or how attached one might feel to affiliation with any particular group. Melanie was born in Vietnam, although her actual ethnicity is somewhat uncertain. She had been discovered as an infant, abandoned in a garbage heap, and through remarkable good fortune, she ended up on the last plane leaving Saigon before the collapse. She looks Vietnamese, or at least Asian, but because her parental origins are unknown, Melanie has no idea. Once she arrived in the United States, she was adopted by a nice Italian family and raised within their family culture. Because of injuries she sustained as a baby, she has limited eyesight and other physical disabilities. She works as a counselor in a woman's shelter.

When Melanie's counselor asked her about her cultural background, Melanie didn't know where to begin to try to explain the confusion and complexity of her multiple identities. She has never been to Vietnam, never even eaten at a Vietnamese restaurant (that later changed), but still partially identified with aspects of her (presumed) homeland. She has been brought up in an ethnically conservative Italian home but has no physical resemblance or behavioral characteristics similar to those of her parents and siblings. Because of her eyesight problems, which have progressively grown worse, she is actively involved in the culture of the visually impaired. However, if she had to name the culture that most dominates her worldview, her political beliefs and values, and her priorities and interests, and even defines most of her close friendships, it would be the culture of counseling.

We mention this one example to illustrate the complexity of cultural identity, how it is rarely a single feature but rather includes many different parts of us. Any relationship we establish with a client consists of multidimensional links to more than a half dozen cultural groups, which include not only the usual suspects but also cultures related to the client's interests, hobbies, and other priorities. When Melanie was asked which of her many cultural identities was most influential in shaping her values, she said something similar to the following, which we have tried to re-create from memory.

> I have had a number of problems throughout my life. I was one of the few non-Whites in my school. I was teased constantly because I looked and acted so different. Plus I could never see that well, so that created a lot of difficulties for me. I could never play sports. I couldn't really even see much in school at all. I had few friends. And everywhere I went I didn't belong. I'm not really Vietnamese. I'm not really Italian. What am I?
>
> We moved to southern California when I was about 6, and I remember when my family first went to Disneyland. This was a

fantasy that I'd always heard about and dreamed about because it was the exact opposite of my early life. We had season passes, so we'd go there frequently and it became a second home. You might think this is funny, but once I got in college I got a job there, jumping even more into the culture. And it is a culture for sure. Trust me. It's a culture that I have since internalized even though I know that sounds weird.

It turns out that identifying with Disney culture is what Melanie attributes to finding her way out of so much confusion in her life. It is an unreal world but one that is so overly structured, planned, and controlled that it gave her a feeling of safety. Yes, it's sanitized and artificial and contrived, but it is also organized extremely well around providing enjoyable experiences.

Once Melanie explained this to her counselor, they developed their own "Mickey Mouse" language to talk about her struggles. Melanie and her counselor eventually settled on this as the common ground between them, as the unique and customized way that they could relate to one another in a language that literally struck home. This is our goal for any client, an outcome that is far more likely when we let go of our assumptions and standard operating procedures and instead meet clients on both hallowed and new territory.

Developing Customized Relationships

So far in this book, a cogent argument has been put forward about the importance of empirical evidence to support the counseling relationship. Hovarth, Del Re, Fluckiger, and Symonds's (2011) research is particularly compelling, because it includes an analysis of almost 200 studies that show a clear connection between the quality of the alliance and the eventual counseling outcomes once sessions ended. What is missing, however, is an understanding of what constitutes the best kind of relationship. It turns out that quantitative research hasn't been that useful in this regard.

Fortunately, there have been several qualitative studies, including one by Strong and Nielsen (2008), who evaluated the interactions between clients and their counselors. The identified themes appear to correspond with attempts to emphasize the client's strengths and resources and to develop a shared understanding of their mutual experiences.

Many of the favored counseling theories, such as Adlerian, person-centered, existential, Gestalt, and narrative, adopt a phenomenological perspective that emphasizes understanding issues from the client's point of view. This is in contrast with an alternative approach that might dismiss the client's concerns as unimportant or irrelevant. Certainly, there are times when the client's perspective appears counterproductive, and our job is to introduce alternatives that might be more helpful. For instance, someone might believe quite stubbornly and passionately that the reason for his troubles is bad luck. Although it might be the case that he's had some tough breaks in life, attributing his relative success in life to luck is probably not in his best interests. Our job is to acknowledge and honor his perspective but in such a way that we can carefully negotiate an alternative way of thinking about his own power to take greater charge of his life.

Historically, counseling and psychotherapy have been problem centered, especially when we consider our reliance on diagnosis and corresponding specific treatments. Someone comes in and reports she is depressed, and we immediately kick in differential diagnosis to determine what kind of depression would signal particular avenues of action, whether CBT, hospitalization, or referral for medication. It's interesting, however, that more strength-based approaches correlate better with more positive outcomes rather than those focusing on the problems themselves. The tough part, however, especially for beginners, is that it is much easier to conceptualize cases in terms of their diagnoses and problems, and, of course, third-party payers and agency policies "reward" such behavior. The reality is that clients can rarely be reduced to singular problems that have clear, simple solutions.

Perhaps the most complex finding of Strong and Nielsen's (2008) research is the development of shared understanding between client and counselor. There are many ways that this takes place, including empathic understanding, counselor self-disclosure (addressed later in this book), and communication of immediacy within the counseling relationship. Certainly, we have to be careful when self-disclosing to clients, or addressing the context of the counseling relationship in a session, but these types of relational strategies are important to demonstrate not only that we do understand clients but that we are truly with them in their struggles.

Chapter 6

Relational Strategies and Interventions for Trauma

Supportive and close relationships are part of all counseling efforts, as well as general satisfaction in life, but they are crucial when working with survivors of trauma, abuse, neglect, and personal tragedies. This is especially the case with natural disasters that strike people in such random and unpredictable ways, challenging the very sense of control people have over their lives. Personal relationships, both before and after a traumatic event, are key to successful recovery, adaptation, and potential growth (Calhoun & Tedeschi, 2013). Social support, in all its various forms, whether through family, friends, or a counseling relationship, provides a number of benefits. It is interesting to note that it doesn't seem to matter whether the person simply believes in the support or whether it is actually present (Cohen, 2004).

Within counseling relationships focused on recovery from trauma, clients' *perception* of support and validation is absolutely critical, among other factors. These factors may include helping clients share their stories in ways they haven't felt comfortable doing previously or helping them reconceptualize their stories in more self-enhancing ways. Clients are encouraged to develop new ways of looking at themselves, at the world, and at the primacy of all their relationships. They are able to learn new coping methods that assist with emotional regulation and self-expression. Just as important, the counseling relationship provides a model for ways clients can seek support from others, which is critical during times of struggle.

In such relationships, the counselor is often far more personally affected, and involved, in the client's story. "Listening and being touched by a trauma narrative," observed Werdel and Wicks (2012), "may serve as much-needed validation that a survivor's experience (their trauma and healing) matters not merely in the life of the survivor, but in a broader, shared narrative" (pp. 140–141). In other words, we become partners in this healing process, a unique relationship that has far-reaching effects on both participants.

Relationship Empowered Treatments for Trauma

Many of the sanctioned methods and evidence-based treatments for trauma have been developed in the Western world and are ideally suited for those who share this cultural worldview. In places where traditional psychotherapy and counseling are relatively unknown, counselors face special challenges when using strategies that may emphasize values or features that are not necessarily applicable or even appropriate.

Working in a culturally competent or respectful way involves the counselor in focusing on four significant features: (1) choice over the ways the relationship is structured; (2) feelings of control over the proceedings, including the content and pace; (3) empathy that communicates empowerment within the relationship; and (4) respect for the client's capacity to regain some semblance of self-efficacy with support and caring (Goldsmith, Barlow, & Freyd, 2004). The relationship is all about empowerment but doing so in a way that acknowledges and respects the local cultural practices and values, especially in places where it is not normally appropriate to talk openly about fears and other feelings.

There is a disconnect between the intervention-based strategies, the evidence-informed practices, and the ESTs for trauma that we teach and use versus the relationally based work that is taking place in our offices. A whole laundry list of signature methods appears in the literature, each with its own acronym: DBT, TF-CBT, EMDR, and dozens of others (see Table 6.1). Each method focuses on a particular set of techniques while often ignoring the relational connections that truly empower our work with survivors of catastrophes (Murphy & Joseph, 2013). This is especially ironic, considering that 30 years of research has consistently demonstrated not only that the relationship is the most essential ingredient in counseling survivors of trauma, and almost any other client, but also that relationship accounts for twice as much of the outcome variance as does any specific, favored

TABLE 6.1
Specific Trauma Approaches

Approach	Definition
Trauma-focused cognitive behavior therapy	Combines cognitive behavior, family, and humanistic approaches to address emotional and behavioral problems with children/adolescents who have been exposed to traumatic events (Cohen, Deblinger, Mannarino, & Steer, 2004).
Eye movement desensitization and reprocessing	Technique in which the clinician tracks eye movement as a means to ameliorate trauma symptoms, especially those connected with PTSD (Davidson & Parker, 2001).
Direct therapy exposure	Behavior therapy technique that involves a safe, direct confrontation of stressors related to PTSD (Boudewyns & Hyer, 1990).
Mindfulness-based stress reduction	Mindfulness-based program incorporating such techniques as meditation and yoga to reduce stress and improve quality of life (Hayes, Villatte, Levin, & Hildebrandt, 2011).
Trauma adaptive recovery education and therapy	A strength-based approach emphasizing educational and skill development strategies to regulate emotions and reduce/manage stress (Ford & Russo, 2006).
Stress inoculation training	Cognitive behavior approach emphasizing stress management when exposed to stressful situations (Meichenbaum & Cameron, 1989).
Skills training in affective and interpersonal regulation	Uses skills training to teach management of emotions and interpersonal relationships (Cloitre, Koenen, Cohen, & Han, 2002).
Imagery rehearsal therapy	Cognitive behavior strategy that uses visual imagery to treat chronic nightmares (Krakow & Zadra, 2006).
Critical incident stress debriefing	A brief, crisis intervention process in a small, homogeneous group setting; participants have all been exposed to the same traumatic event. This single-session format is not a replacement for counseling (van Emmerik, Kamphuis, Hulsbosch, & Emmelkamp, 2002).

intervention method (Krupnick, 2013; Lambert, 2013; Norcross, 2011; Wampold, 2001).

Although the particular trauma methods highlighted in Table 6.1 have their fair number of fans, not to mention some research support, they often downplay, if not denigrate, the value of relational connections to empower their strategies. Whether clients' presenting issues include primary trauma or not, there is compelling evidence that clients are more satisfied with their counseling when (a) they feel heard and understood; (b) their story was acknowledged and believed; (c) they were helped to identify personal strengths and resources; (d) sessions promoted deeper understanding of how the events affected behavior; (e) counselors solicited meaningful feedback from clients and then adapted what they were doing to better meet expressed needs and interests; and (f) clients perceived their counselors as compassionate, caring, warm, and, most of all, hopeful about the future (Meichenbaum, 2013).

The category of trauma includes diverse and varied kinds of issues and problems. Those who are survivors of physical or emotional abuse, neglect, or incest as children will likely develop more complex and severe symptoms than those who experience some acute disaster (earthquake, flood, accident, violence) with no previous preexisting mental or physical condition. In the first case, we are dealing with a chronic, relatively intractable condition of many years, or decades, whereas the second scenario involves a sudden trauma, an unforeseen event beyond anyone's control.

Healing Through Presence and Touch

In 2015, when devastating earthquakes killed 10,000 people in Nepal, leaving hundreds of thousands of others homeless and without basic necessities, I (Jeffrey) led a medical team to the epicenter of the 7.3-magnitude quake. We were the first responders in the Everest region of the Himalayas, and it looked like a nuclear bomb had exploded, leaving piles of rubble where structures had previously stood.

Our team consisted of a special forces medic, two nurses, a medical assistant, a hospital administrator, a few translators, and me. I had been through Red Cross training for disaster relief and imagined that I was well prepared. In fact, I was so far out of my element that it felt like I was on another planet. There were no hospitals or clinics or even other medical personnel to refer any of our patients to for treatment. The only medical supplies at our disposal were those we managed to smuggle into the country—antibiotics, pain killers, suture kits, splints, surgical supplies—and it seemed that almost everyone had some kind of infection, festering wound, or symptoms of trauma.

During the next few weeks, we saw a succession of more than 800 patients streaming in from the mountainsides, presenting an array of symptoms. I was reduced to conducting 15-minute trauma sessions as the lines outside my tent grew longer. One man brought his brother, who was obviously schizophrenic, to see me. The brother was clearly a danger to himself and others. He would throw rocks at people walking by, would not eat, and usually talked to himself most of the time, rarely responding to anyone else. He would not look at me the whole time we were together nor respond to any question. He just rocked back and forth and giggled.

A mother brought in her adult son who was severely depressed. As best as I could gather, he had been depressed for 5 years, but since the earthquakes he had become inconsolable. All he did was walk back and forth, nonresponsive to anyone or anything. Another man sought my counsel about a head injury and vertigo. He wanted my reassurance that he would regain cognitive functioning. An older woman presented memory problems, backaches, and headaches that all seemed age appropriate but were more severe after the earthquake and sleeping outside on the ground for a week. I listened to a woman who was hearing voices, of either ghosts or God. Given that choice, I told her it must be God speaking to her because she was special. I asked her what God said to her, but she either didn't know or wouldn't say. I saw a 5-year-old girl, then a 6-year-old boy, one after the other, both presenting the same symptoms of frequent urination and bed wetting.

One after another, after another, they lined up outside, hoping for a cure, for answers, for reassurance. I held their hands, looked into their eyes, and admitted to them that I was terrified as well with the aftershocks continuing every few hours. I explained about the effects of trauma on the body, but much was lost in translation. I reassured them that they were not alone, that we all felt the same way.

A little 3-year-old girl was brought to see me, the same age as one of my granddaughters. Her father had just died from a head injury; the mother was now a widow and would be required to spend 1 year in mourning, so it was supposed to be my job to tell her she was now an orphan. I looked at this smiling little girl, playing with a stuffed animal I offered to her, and it just broke my heart. I could feel myself losing control, tears running down my cheeks, and so excused myself for a moment and walked out of the room to regain my composure.

I thought to myself how fate had put me in this place, at this moment in time. My chest hurt. I felt so flooded with emotion from all the accumulated stress, all the stories I had heard, all the people I had seen. I felt so helpless at times, so inadequate to provide the help and support everyone needed, and now I was given this gift: I could save this child, literally save her life and give her a future, by agreeing to provide her with a scholarship so she could have an education and a future.

That single act is the one and perhaps only time I'm pretty sure that I made a difference. All my other supposed trauma counseling was almost completely relational: I had nothing to offer these people but my literal presence to share their fear and suffering. Many of my sessions consisted almost entirely of literally holding people in my arms.

It is apparent that much of Jeffrey's counseling focused on relational connections with clients. There was little time to spend with each family or person and few available resources. Providing accurate information about the nature of trauma and its aftermath was helpful, just as it was desirable to allow people to share their stories, but much of the reassurance and support from the sessions seemed to come from expressions of caring and physical touch.

Like any counseling issue, trauma is contextual and embedded in a person's cultural and family background, prior experiences, and unique responses to the events that transpired. As previously mentioned, not all types of trauma are the same. Survivors of earthquakes or other disasters are dealing with acute conditions, whereas those who were subjected to abuse, incest, assault, or neglect experience a different sense of disempowerment, helplessness, and disconnection from others. The counselor's role often concentrates on far more than symptomatic recovery; it also includes restorative work on intimacy issues.

What's Different About Relationships With Traumatized Clients?

Some unique and complex issues frequently crop up with clients who have experienced severe trauma, as a result of either prior life events or more recent catastrophes. The relationship must be constructed in a way that provides maximum safety for especially fragile and vulnerable people yet also provides the sort of therapeutic features that will produce the best outcomes.

A number of sources have made recommendations for practitioners that are based on current research and consensual standards (Johnson & Lubin, 2015; Levers, 2012; Murphy & Joseph, 2013; van der Kolk, 2014). Ten of these recommendations follow.

1. It is important to appreciate the great complexity of these cases and to demonstrate a degree of patience and caution, given the increased fragility and vulnerability of traumatized clients. In other words, sometimes it is important to build the relationship slowly and carefully, respectful of the person's pace.
2. The counselor must be able to tolerate more intense emotional arousal and expressiveness, especially related to anger and anxiety. This is a problem especially for counselors who like to be emotionally engaged because they are more likely to have strong reactions to clients' stories and presentation, reactions that may range from disgust, anger, or frustration to sadness and despair (Courtois & Ford, 2013).

3. As much as possible, downplay the authority role to minimize the acting out that could occur as a result of abuse survivors' having been betrayed by those in positions of power and authority. Become aware of the "traumatic transference" issues that could arise, whether you are psychodynamically inclined or not.
4. Deal explicitly with the inequities of power in the counseling relationship. Counselors are in a strong position of authority and may trigger emotions that are re-creations of past injustices. This is especially the case with instances of oppression, racism, prejudice, or bullying, in which the counselor may resemble past antagonists.
5. Explore and monitor attachment, avoidance, and defensive responses to closeness (which may have been devastating in the past). Understand that trust is one of the main issues to work through in the relationship. Watch out for clients' rescuer fantasies and idealization of the counselor.
6. Create a "holding environment" that is warm and supportive, even loving, but with sufficient boundaries to prevent overindulgence and excessive testing of limits. Model a healthy, nonexploitive relationship, even with the power differential, to demonstrate that it is possible to feel trust without betrayal.
7. As much as possible, involve family members in the recovery. People who have suffered trauma feel disconnected not only from themselves but also from others who were once close to them. Individual counseling can reinforce the feeling of being "other," being different, being an outsider, being a victim, being alone in the struggle. Counselors sometimes avoid such family work because it is so challenging and potentially emotionally volatile and unpredictable (Barnett, 2014).
8. Because of the high prevalence of borderline personality disorder and other personality disturbances associated with childhood trauma, it is important to deal with impulse control, acting out, and emotional regulation (van der Kolk, 2014).
9. Take a "principled" relational stance. As stated by the posttraumatic growth researcher Stephen Joseph (2011), recognize that between one third and one half of those who experience trauma will be able to find or create significant benefits and growth as a result of this experience. The relationship thus becomes a forum for talking not only about suffering and pain but also about what was learned and what has changed for the better.

10. Monitor your own personal reactions to the trauma stories, becoming vigilant to secondary trauma or compassion fatigue.

Recognize that boundary and ethical issues in relationships become far more complex and challenging in trauma work because the usual safeguards, structures, confidentiality, even physical environment, often become more fluid and flexible (Baum, 2010; Mailloux, 2014). Usual work spaces may be compromised, along with the counselor's own familiar detachment and objectivity. In addition, countertransference and the counselor's personal reactions may become much more of an issue; in the case of shared trauma, the risk of client and counselor retraumatizing each other is increased (Phelps, Lloyd, Creamer, & Forbes, 2009).

The Relationship Is a Start, but Is Not Nearly Enough

The focus of this book is on relational issues when counseling clients, whether traumatized or not, and a solid alliance provides the foundation for all that follows, although it may not be sufficient to solidify lasting changes. Carl Rogers was correct in proposing that relationship factors are a necessary condition for counseling, but he was not quite accurate in claiming that they are sufficient conditions. As mentioned earlier, the relationship (or the counselor) is not the most influential factor in producing positive outcomes in counseling. Positive outcomes are largely determined by factors related to the client's characteristics, including levels of motivation and commitment, personality qualities, and presenting issues (Norcross & Lambert, 2011).

With respect to trauma, there is far more going on than psychological numbing or emotional disturbances that might respond to relational support. Increasingly, there is evidence that trauma reactions involve an assortment of neurophysiological changes (van der Kolk, 2014). These changes occur at almost every level of the brain, hormones, and nervous system. For example:

- Recalibration of the brain's alarm system (hypervigilance)
- Adrenal glands release stress hormones (cortisol, adrenaline) that flood the system
- Sensory overload when thalamus filter system shuts down
- Perceptual distortions colored by alterations in brain chemistry
- Inhibition of Broca's area of the brain devoted to speech
- Executive functioning and decision making impaired

- Intrusive memories
- Difficulties with emotional regulation
- Sympathetic nervous system stimulates anger and anxiety
- Parasympathetic nervous system leads to emotional numbness
- Elevated heart rate, blood pressure, respiratory functions, and muscular tension during "fight or flight" overreactions
- Autoimmune system compromised

This helps explain why clients sometimes just can't put their jumbled thoughts and overwhelming feelings into words—no matter how trusting and open the relationship and how patient and encouraging the counselor might be. When there are intrusive emotions, sensory overstimulation, arousal of the autonomic systems, and a series of extreme physical reactions in the body, it is far more difficult to even talk about what is bothersome. Fisher (2014) described one example of this. Instead of following a more traditional path of connecting a client's current traumatic struggles to past events in her life, or challenging and regulating her extreme emotional responses, Fisher focused on goals that were specifically targeted to soothing and regulating the nervous system.

Given the breadth and depth of the ways trauma affects the body, brain, and mind, it is clear that relationship variables can only provide a foundation for the many interventions that follow. These interventions include strategies to reduce hyperarousal (deep breathing, meditation, mindfulness, self-regulation, medications) and to facilitate integration of disturbing memories, as well as to encourage deeper and more intimate connections with others for support, both within the counseling relationship and in the outside world.

Once a trusting alliance has been established along the lines we have discussed previously, many other therapeutic tasks, including the following, may be included in counseling:

1. Building social support within the client's world
2. Reframing a victim mentality to that of a survivor or, better yet, a heroine or hero
3. Conducting a risk assessment of self-harm
4. Including exposure-related desensitization activities when needed
5. Exploring and working with family issues that may directly or indirectly be related to the presenting problems
6. Introducing useful coping skills to deal with recurrent disturbing memories

7. Inviting storytelling and work on narrative deconstruction
8. Facilitating cognitive processing of dysfunctional and irrational thinking
9. Addressing issues of guilt and remorse, as well as forgiveness of self (and possibly) of others
10. Challenging excessive ruminations about past events over which there is no control
11. Working on emotional regulation of extreme emotional reactions including anger, frustration, and acting out
12. Discussing spiritual and other meaning-making conversations that promote deeper understanding when appropriate and indicated

The idea of deeper spiritual and meaning-making conversations can be framed in a number of ways, depending on the cultural and religious traditions of clients and their personal interests and values. Much of what we do in any counseling encounter is to help clients dig deeper into the meaning of their experiences and to understand their own behavior. The relationship can act as leverage to balance extensive attention to the client and to what the client is experiencing to include growth opportunities that are often associated with any potentially life-altering event or experience (Park & Ai, 2006).

Growth and Learning After Trauma: For the Client and the Counselor

The field of positive psychology has been around for half a century, beginning with Abraham Maslow's early work on self-actualization and Carl Rogers's studies of fully functioning behavior. However, the idea of "posttraumatic growth" after a debilitating event or experience was first popularized by Tedeschi and Calhoun (1995) when describing the ways that self-perceptions, interpersonal behavior, and alternations in life priorities, spiritual beliefs, and values all become transformed after surviving some adversity.

When we speak about how counselors are affected by their work, it is usually couched in negative terms of countertransference, secondary trauma, loss of control, projective distortion, and other kinds of "collateral damage" from getting too close to others' suffering. However, tremendous gifts are offered by our clients as well, from their resilience and their courage to their willingness and openness in sharing their stories with us. We learn so much from watching and listening to them and from joining them during their journey toward some kind of enlightenment, if not peace.

Werdell and Wicks (2012) highlighted some of the important lessons that can be learned, not only by clients who suffered trauma but also by the counselors who accompany them along this journey. These benefits are commonly reported by those who experience posttraumatic growth after life challenges that tested them and forced a reevaluation of life priorities.

1. Life is fragile and ultimately uncontrollable, in spite of all efforts to manage every conceivable possibility.
2. Sometimes *why* things happen is much less important than *how* certain actions can lead to different outcomes.
3. Close calls with death or disaster, whether directly or vicariously, lead to reassessment of values and priorities, as well as a search for greater simplicity.
4. We may not be able to prevent bad things from happening to us, but we can choose how we deal with them—and allow such events to instruct and influence us for the better. It is often true that what doesn't destroy us makes us stronger and more resilient.
5. True integration of a traumatic event—for client or counselor— occurs during moments of deep reflection, sharing one's story, and periods of solitude and mindfulness that help us explore and find meaning in suffering.
6. To immunize oneself against future life challenges and traumatic events, build greater social support and relational connections to others. People don't react in the same way to identical events; their reactions depend on their internal resources, coping skills, and preexisting condition.
7. Forgiveness and compassion, for oneself and others, helps us tremendously in letting go of guilt, remorse, regret, and ruminations.
8. Spiritual rejuvenation is often a consequence of surviving trauma and can become an important asset for meaning making.
9. Reexamine and reprioritize the value and role of all relationships, before, during, and after the traumatic events.

How and why people respond and recover so differently from traumatic experiences is both interesting and endlessly complex. Some people become permanently debilitated; others stabilize afterward and seem to flourish in unanticipated ways. Clients (and counselors) who are most likely to grow as a result of life challenges and trauma acknowledge their fears and difficulties in a way that focuses on new possibilities for the future rather than dwelling on the nightmares and failings of the past. The paradox of posttraumatic growth is that it isn't about denial and positively framing experiences but involves an intense and thorough exploration of life in a very different context (Neimeyer, 2001). It is a very special relationship indeed that makes such a difficult process possible, one that helps clients develop a different kind of "narrative cohesion" to their survival story, one in which they triumph even as they lick their wounds. Essentially, our job in such a relationship is to help clients rewrite the stories of their lives or at least the part they experience as tragic or debilitating (Neimeyer, 2012).

We also must acknowledge that what clients report about their *perceived* growth does not necessarily accurately reflect the reality of what may, or may not, have changed. Clients sometimes share all kinds of distortions, exaggerations, or outright lies. They tell us things to win our approval. They attempt to manipulate us. Some clients live in a world where they can't seem to tell the difference between what really happened and what they prefer to remember. Nevertheless, given that the relationship is built on mutual trust, we must take what clients say based on reasonable faith; to do otherwise would involve continually questioning, if not interrogating, clients about the veracity of their reports. Second, if people do, in fact, believe an illusion of growth, even if it is not totally supported with evidence, maybe that's enough for the present time.

Counseling relationships with trauma survivors place tremendous strain and additional burdens on the practitioner, often leading to various degrees of stress, emotional arousal, compassion fatigue, and vicarious or secondary trauma as a result of the nightmare stories shared in sessions. Some of the early warning signs for this symptomatology include a devaluing of work, emotional exhaustion and flooding, and decreased empathy as a self-protective defense. It is imperative that such relational wounds be addressed and healed through other forms of mentoring, supervision, or counseling, or at the very least through social support from family, friends, and colleagues. We have discussed how posttraumatic growth frequently accompanies the experiences of trauma survivors and also can benefit their counselors—if we have a way to process feelings and explore more deeply the meaning and positive outcomes that may have occurred. It is imperative that we be willing and able to reach out for relational self-care resources to sustain us during times when we might feel most personally and professionally challenged and confused. This enables us to model for our clients exactly the kind of resilience that we hope to facilitate in their lives.

Chapter 7

Exchanging Stories to Solidify and Fortify Counseling Relationships

I (Jeffrey) sat in awe of how this story unfolded during an informal, unscripted conversation that took place in the lobby of our hotel when we working in Nepal before, during, and after the earthquakes of 2015. One of the girls we support was despondent because her father had forbidden her to continue her education, informing her that it was time for an arranged marriage. This young woman was absolutely brilliant and had planned to go to medical school, and now her dreams were dashed. I was sitting with two of my counseling students when she asked us what to do. Through her tears, she confessed that as much as she wanted to be a doctor, she just couldn't disobey her father in her culture.

We tried several interventions. We consoled her. We offered support. A few of the students offered their own advice and suggestions, but each attempt only seemed to make things worse. The breakthrough occurred when Karla, an immigrant from Mexico originally, shared her own story of hardships that required her to disobey her father in a culture where that was not permitted to do so. The fact that she was now a graduate student, that her family and her father were now so proud of what she had accomplished, got through to the Nepali teenager in a way that nothing else could touch. When she hugged us afterward, it was with considerable relief that she had now found a path she could follow.

What is truly remarkable about this story is that it is not the least unusual: you have a dozen or more stories of your own. It is commonplace that people's choices become clearer and that the trajectory of their lives can be indelibly altered just by hearing someone else's story.

The Power of Stories

Consider this question: What do counselors actually *do* in their work? What specific skills, interventions, and behaviors would someone witness in a typical session? To state it another way, imagine that an anthropologist from a foreign culture (perhaps Venus or Jupiter) were to watch us in action, taking notes to report on what this counseling stuff involves in case they wanted to import it for their own people: What would she (or it) see?

If you were to make a list of the sorts of skills and techniques that you might use in a typical relationship with a client, what might you include? This isn't a complicated question. These "bread and butter" types of interactions hail all the way back to your first counseling skills class, which included, perhaps in order of frequency, nonverbal acknowledgments ("Uh huh," "I see," "Hmm," "Oh yeah?"), restatements of content, reflections of feelings, and interpretations, explanations, and summaries of what has been said. Less often, but sometimes more powerful, confrontations, reframing, challenging beliefs and assumptions, and prescribing therapeutic tasks might be included. You might add others that come to mind, but this is the standard stuff that usually dominates our actual behavior—with one notable exception, which is rarely part of any training program or offered for continuing education, yet it is one of the most common things that we do. In fact, we could (and will) make a case that so much of what we do within counseling relationships is listen to client stories and then tell stories of our own. In essence, we are professional storytellers (Kottler, 2014). More than that, all our relationships are created and bonded through storytelling—the feature, more than most others, that makes us uniquely human (Gottschall, 2012).

From the earliest African cave paintings and Egyptian hieroglyphics to the contemporary vehicles of plays, novels, operas, song lyrics, television shows, films, puppet shows, blogs, posts, even texts, graffiti, and tweets, we spend most of our lives sharing stories with others. We do this through conversations, confessions, gossip, and written communications. Unfortunately, many of the stories we tell ourselves—and others—are not very empowering, especially when people paint themselves as victims of circumstances or antagonists in a world beyond their control.

Powers of Influence and Persuasion

Jerome Frank (1971) noted long ago that our primary job is to convince people to do things that they really would rather not do. They come to us with a not-so-hidden agenda and prefer that our work be quick and painless. Most of all, they want us to agree with them that they are not really the problem—it is everyone else who doesn't appreciate or understand them. Even among those who do acknowledge that they have considerable work to do on themselves, they still may feel reluctant to take the necessary risks and expend the required energy and commitment to alter lifelong self-defeating behaviors.

We attempt to influence our clients to experiment with new options, make hard decisions, and confront aspects of themselves they have long been ignoring. We urge clients to take charge of their lives. We debate with them about alternative courses of action that may be in their best interests. We use everything in our power to try to make a difference.

How we accomplish these tasks may appear to be directly related to the core skills previously mentioned—things like reflecting, challenging, and presenting rational arguments for why new choices might be better than existing ones. However, as we know from the political world, it is *very* difficult to get anyone to question his or her entrenched belief systems. After all, when was the last time you changed someone's mind about his or her favored political candidate or religious tradition?

In one sense, we are faith healers. Data and information and rational arguments certainly have their uses, but often they are not nearly as effective within a helping relationship as offering a story. Sometimes the indirect and more emotionally evocative option of storytelling is the best way to solidify a relationship as well as to more subtly and effectively influence clients in enduring ways.

Consider your own most influential teachers and supervisors: What is it that you remember about an especially effective class or workshop? What has stuck with you over the years when you recall a particular mentor? More often than not, it is the stories that were shared, especially those that resonated with you in a very personal way, that seemed to penetrate your soul.

In our field we tend to privilege and honor data over stories in an assortment of ways, emphasizing ESTs, EBP, standardized assessments, reliable measures, meta-analyses, and medicalized treatment practices. This has certainly lent greater scientific rigor and consistency to our profession and helped us gain respectability in the larger world. It is also a bit daunting (and bewildering) that certain books offered to people who are suffering from psychological problems achieve results comparable to those of counseling (Hirai & Clum, 2006; Jack & Ronan, 2008). Of course, all stories are not the same, and the most influential books must be of high quality and directly relevant to the person's issues and interests.

It's interesting, for example, that fictional stories are more influential than nonfiction books like this one (Appel, 2008; Appel & Richter, 2007; Burns, 2008; Levitt, Rattanasampan, Chaidaroon, Stanley, & Robinson, 2009; Paul, 2012; Zipes, 2006). Think about why that might be the case, especially given that self-help books are specifically designed to resolve personal difficulties. Of course, if they really worked all that well, then there wouldn't be so many thousands more of them published each year.

Fictional stories, in particular, are so powerfully influential precisely because they are made up: The reader or listener suspends disbelief and critical thinking to enter into the story and join with the characters in an intimate and relational way. That is the reason people become so attached to the characters in television shows, movies, novels, and reality shows. They really do feel like close, intimate friends whose welfare is deeply important to us—even though they aren't real. Mirror neurons make this possible. The human brain has evolved in such a way that we can accumulate vicarious experiences through stories without risking our own safety (Hess, 2012; Iacoboni, 2008; Rizzolatti, & Craighero, 2004). You have to admit that being hardwired for vicarious learning is a fabulous way to explore the world, experience all kinds of adventures, and indulge in a variety of amazing activities that would never have been possible any other way. Evolution has made it possible for us to learn all kinds of things about ourselves, about others, and about the way things work without actual physical risk, and it is certainly true that we can learn and experience so much more by fully entering into a story as if it really is our own experience.

The implications of this are profound. One way to intensify and strengthen our relationships with clients, as well as to better influence them, may be through sharing stories, whether they are fictional, metaphorical, or personal anecdotes. Fictional stories may open up a number of alternative options, introduce new ways of looking at problems, and provide alternative possibilities that clients may not have considered.

Deep work often can be completed through sharing or consuming fictional stories, precisely because they do spark a high level of emotional arousal and vicarious identification. Because they rely on imagination, they train greater cognitive flexibility and promote empathy and sensitivity to others' experiences. They teach people to search for and interpret hidden motives and the innermost thoughts within characters' minds. They also serve to help immunize us against fears and anxieties by preparing defenses against perceived or imagined threats.

Functions of Storytelling in Counseling

All human relationships are bonded through shared stories. A new client comes in, and the first thing you ask is, "So, what's your story?" The client already knows the expected rules, so he tells you the story about his current situation. His parents and teachers are on his back and he's in trouble. He hates school with a passion.

Curious about the vehemence with which he talks about his experiences, you prompt him to tell another story to excavate some possible reasons for his negative attitudes. You find out that he has a reading disability that has been mostly denied and ignored by his parents. He blames them for all his misery, plus his teachers suck.

You nod your head in understanding. You also recognize that it's going to be pretty hard to work with this version of his core problems in which he is a victim of circumstances beyond his control. So you introduce an alternative narrative in which he is cast in a heroic role as someone who has been misunderstood and unappreciated but has persisted in soldiering onward, even without much support.

It was a good try, but he doesn't buy it. You try a different approach later in the session, telling him a story from your own life when you also had problems in school, not because of any disability but because of feelings of isolation because you were so different from others. This wasn't quite true, but it *felt* that way to you at the time. You stop to see if he makes the connection. He either doesn't see it or would prefer not to acknowledge the insight. Instead, he folds his arms and yawns, staring out the window.

Feeling somewhat stymied and confused about what to do next, you decide to just make up a story on the spot, pretending to ignore him and mostly just seeming to entertain yourself. You speak in soft whisper, barely audible, so much so that you notice the boy leaning forward to catch the drift of what you are saying.

It happens to be a fairytale of sorts, a story about a prince who will someday inherit a kingdom, but only if he obeys his parents' wishes at all times. As much as he might enjoy the position and power, the prince decides that he'd rather have his freedom and so disobeys his parents, ignores his tutors, and generally makes himself a pain in the butt. It doesn't matter where the story goes next, because the counselor is now certain he has the boy's interest. That is a start.

Counselors use stories in many different ways in their relationships. We might reveal personal information about ourselves as the counselor did in mentioning to his client that he had had similar problems. We might also use personal examples to model behavior we are teaching, such as saying, "Yes, I once had similar issues to yours, but rather than pretending they would go away, I chose to confront them. Would you like to know what happened?"

Self-disclosures tend to bridge distance in the relationship by emphasizing commonalities in experience. They also humanize us in ways that make us more accessible. This is especially true when we use stories from our lives as teaching points as well as to plant hope for the future: "I do know what you are going through. When I was your age, I also struggled with some problems. They may have been a little different from what you are experiencing, but I found that the challenges taught me some valuable lessons I still use today."

As we mentioned previously, self-disclosures are also among the most abused and poorly executed counselor skills, especially when practitioners are self-indulgent or excessive in their personal stories. In their best form, self-disclosures tend to be relatively brief and sparsely used, be directly relevant to the discussion at hand, and focus on the client immediately afterward. When used appropriately, such stories can become utterly transformative for the relationship.

Stories as Coded Packages

In all their forms and adaptations, whether as self-disclosure, metaphors, teaching tales, or even recommendations of films or books to read, stories present "coded" information in an efficient package. That is essentially the power of metaphors: They represent issues discussed instead of confronting them directly. They contain symbolic features, often disguised or even deliberately obtuse, so as to appeal to unconscious processes (Burns, 2001; Lankton & Lankton, 1989). In their best and most influential form, these stories are pragmatic, flexible, and collaborative creations, shaped by context and the client's own language and symbolic representations. They may sneak up on clients through their "packaged" potential insights, but they also encourage greater imagination and abstract thinking.

Just as illustrated in the previous example, stories capture attention and interest in ways nothing else can touch. Our brains have evolved in such a way that they process almost all experiences as stories, whether we are talking about the random fragments of dreams or the 10-second fantasies that dominate waking life. Even statistics are simply efficient stories about a phenomenon.

Stories seem to automatically create a hypnotic induction that places us in an altered state of consciousness. We willingly agree to enter a different world because stories don't "work" unless we do so. As soon as you utter the words "Once upon a time . . . ," listeners go into a trance.

Storytelling can do so much more, including:

1. Provide a different form of "direct experience" through vicarious identification.
2. Evoke strong emotional reactions that inspire, motivate, or ignite passion.
3. Resonate with cultural and historical traditions within the community, tribe, and social, political, and environmental context.
4. Bypass resistance and defensiveness through subtle introduction of concepts and ideas.
5. Appeal to multiple dimensions of complexity and cognitive processing.
6. Facilitate recognition of patterns across life experiences.
7. Provide a digestible and palatable meaningful "diagnosis" (alternative story) that is destigmatizing.
8. Introduce overarching, organizing scaffolds to understand phenomena and life experiences.
9. Present a canvas upon which clients can create their own work of art to capture their experiences.
10. Introduce alternative realities (fantasies) that facilitate creative thinking.
11. Teach significant adaptation and problem-solving skills through vicarious experiences.
12. Present alternative pathways and options for viewing problems and their solutions.
13. Access unconscious processes through metaphors.
14. Externalize problems such as in narrative counseling.

15. Provide opportunities for rehearsal of new behavior through surrogates.
16. Reframe and reconstruct trauma victim stories into courageous tales of survival and achievement.
17. Promote restitution, renewal, and redemption when stories are recast in one's own life narrative.
18. Have staying power that haunts clients in ways that direct advice or information can't touch.
19. Assist in the existential search for the meaning of life path.
20. Create "secret" passwords that act as reminders and reinforcements of prior insights.
21. Provide adjuncts (bibliotherapy) to sessions that support lessons learned or challenge dysfunctional beliefs.
22. Lead to critical evaluation of parallel issues that might otherwise feel threatening.
23. Promote wisdom, tolerance, and flexibility in thinking about self, others, and the world.
24. Become contagious narrative "viruses" that reproduce and are transmitted to others.
25. Encapsulate the mystery of change, including features and processes that we will never fully understand.

If we distill all of these points into a central theme, the main point is that stories work best when they are contextualized in the client's world. We negotiate with clients within the relationship to create multiple versions of their stories. We challenge them to consider the ways the stories they tell themselves are not only the result of internalized beliefs but also are the result of culturally influenced discourses from media and societal norms, many of which lead to oppression and colonization, especially with regard to feeling oppressed and marginalized.

Recommending Stories Outside of Sessions

We all recognize that most of the important work in counseling takes place outside of sessions when clients are applying what they learn. All counselors devise ways to assign homework, prescribe films or books, or otherwise move conversations into action. Typically, counselors might recommend self-help or nonfiction books that focus on relevant and parallel issues, perhaps the standard ones on trauma or depression or anxiety. We could be a lot more inventive and likely be more effective if we expanded our perspective to include real or imagined stories about identified issues. This could include autobiographies about mental illness (Jamison's [1995] *An Unquiet Mind* or Greenberg's [1964] *I Never Promised You a Rose Garden*), fictional novels about abuse (Walker's [1982] *The Color Purple*), family dysfunction (Conroy's [1986] *The Prince of Tides*), alcoholism (Frey's [2003] *A Million Little Pieces*), racial identity (Dorris's [1987] *Yellow Raft in Blue Water*), depression (Plath's [1963] *The Bell Jar*), bullying (Palacio's [2012] *Wonder*), or autism (Haddon's [2003] *The Curious Incident of the Dog in the Nighttime*).

Film or television-based stories can be just as compelling. Counselors might recommend *Silver Linings Playbook* or *Running with Scissors* to delve into mental health issues. Every month, another film is released that deals with some sort of emotional or family problem that might resonate with our clients. A number of resources offer counselors hundreds of choices for how they might intensify the work in sessions through the use of films matched to particular presenting issues, whether depression, panic disorder, abuse, sexual assault, or family conflicts, among others (Solomon, 2001; Ulus, 2003; Wooder, 2008).

Recommending stories is a time-honored part of counselor training, especially for instructors and supervisors who recognize the potential power for diving deeper into issues that can further enhance relationships both with the mentor and also within the group or cohort. We find it fascinating to watch relationships evolve and develop in classrooms and supervision groups as a direct result of participants having opportunities to share their own stories with one another, often sparked by a story they were reading. One example of this occurred in a group counseling practicum in which the students were assigned to read Yalom's (2005) *Schopenhauer's Cure*, a novel about a group in action. Typical of Yalom's fictional writings, the story is both compelling and complex, stirring up all kinds of issues for beginning (and advanced) counselors who lead groups, including but not limited to deep discussions of death, anxiety, boundary issues, and intimacy. It is also rather rare that we are offered stories like this that reflect (reasonably) accurately what we really do in our jobs.

When students are required to read this novel before class even begins, we have found that it has a huge effect on their behavior in terms of their willingness to be more self-disclosing, authentic, and open about some of their own struggles. They see options for how they might interact with others that they had not previously considered. They identify strongly with particular characters in the novel. Many reported that it felt like they were actually members of the group themselves, lending support to the earlier discussion of mirror neurons and how they make us feel as if we live *inside* stories.

Most of us have favorite stories we like to recommend, regardless of the medium. Some of these choices may be based on our experiences in the past in terms of books or films or shows we have recommended that had the most positive outcomes, but others are related to our own lived experience. Think, for a few moments, about the stories that had the most potent influence and impact on your life, perhaps even revealing the reason you wanted to be a counselor in the first place.

Relationships With Stories

Yes, people do have relationships with particular stories, sometimes quite strong ones at that. It really isn't surprising, considering how much time people spend each day immersed in stories that dominate their lives—an average of 3 hours each day watching television, an hour listening to music lyrics, plus all the time spent watching movies, reading books, sending and reading texts, emails, and tweets, dreaming, daydreaming (2,000 per day, lasting an average of 14 seconds each), plus all the time in conversation with others (4 hours) listening and telling stories. Even interactions between parents and their children are primarily structured around telling stories that are essentially induction scripts for how to behave and follow moral codes, an average of one every 7 minutes (Kottler, 2014). *The Cat in the Hat* by Dr. Seuss, for example, is really about learning not to trust strangers and to clean up after you make a mess.

Among some indigenous peoples, stories are just as real as any other experience. Some Native American tribes believe that when you think you are dreaming, you are awake, and when you think you are awake, you are really dreaming (think about that). For tens of thousands of years, stories were the only way that critical information about the best hunting grounds or seminal events within the tribe could be passed on from one generation to the next.

One of our favorite stories about the intimate relationships that evolve related to stories occurred when an anthropologist was visiting and studying a remote village in Africa. She had been there when a television was first introduced to the tribe, so she was hardly surprised when all the villagers abandoned the traditional storyteller to flock to this new device that presented pictures and sounds to accompany stories from all over the world; yet she was utterly perplexed when, after a few days, everyone returned to the campfire and abandoned this "story box." When she asked the villagers why they would prefer this far more basic option, they told her that it was true that the television knew many stories, but the storyteller in the village knew *them*. It was the relationship with the storyteller that mattered as much as the story itself.

Stories hold our cultural legacies. Just as our clients remain connected to us for the rest of their lives through the stories we offered them, as well as those they shared with us, so too all human lives are composed of those stories that touched and shaped us the most. They provide a common cultural heritage, whether told around a campfire, read to children before they go to sleep, or presented as the cultural artifacts of a community. Stories like *Red Riding Hood* and *The Wizard of Oz* do not just entertain but also instruct us in moral lessons that bind us together. They provide children with opportunities to literally confront their most terrifying fears in the form of wicked witches and other monsters.

Most of the stories told, either within the context of counseling or in the larger culture, are tales of transformation. As Joseph Campbell (1988) noted long ago and literature scholars have observed (Booker, 2004), a few basic plots provide the templates for almost all the stories ever told. These structures are familiar to us all, and they deal in the same kinds of story lines: fighting monsters (*Frankenstein, Star Wars*), rags to riches (*Cinderella, Ugly Duckling*), quests (*Finding Nemo, Don Quixote*), voyages and return (*12 Years a Slave, The Wizard of Oz, Hunger Games*), or rebirths (*Christmas Story, Dances With Wolves*).

These stories usually involve some sort of physical, psychological, or spiritual journey that leads to a crisis or trauma. The challenges that are faced require the protagonist(s) to confront difficulties by relying on new resources, and sometimes assistance from a mentor, guide, muse, the supernatural, or a higher power. Whether the story is *Harry Potter, King Arthur, Star Wars, Shrek, The Wizard of Oz*, or *Cinderella*, some kind of transition or transformation results in a reconceptualization of self or one's vision of the world. The goal is almost always connected to becoming the narrator of one's own life (Josselson, 2003), and the action almost always takes place within the context of a crucial relationship with a guide, thus providing a parallel process for the listener or viewer to personalize and internalize.

If our only job was to recite stories, or listen to those told by others, our profession wouldn't require so much training and preparation. The reality, however, is that we do so much more than that because our job is to help clients retell stories that feature them in roles as survivors, or even heroines, rather than mere victims. Each theoretical orientation has its own name for this process. Brief or strategic counselors might call this "reframing," narrative counselors call it "re-authoring," cognitive counselors call it "challenging beliefs," and so on. In all of these permutations, we collaborate with clients to take the story they initially present, in which they may have felt helpless and powerless, and help them construct a version of these events in which they think of themselves in a more empowered way.

The Desperate Need for Relational Storytelling

Eighteen seconds is the answer.

What's the question?

How long does the average patient have to tell his or her story to a doctor about what's wrong before the narrative is interrupted?

In the past 30 years, incredible advances in the technology of health care (robotic surgery, MRI scans, stem cell transplants) have taken place in the practice of medicine, yet nothing much has changed in terms of relational connections. Only 1 in 50 patients is allowed to finish his or her story to a doctor, and more than half of patients leave the office not understanding what was explained to them and why (Levine, 2004). No wonder doctors are often so frustrated with noncompliance when their patients don't follow their orders—their patients never got a chance to talk about their full concerns and didn't understand what was expected.

We suppose that result is very good news for the future of our profession, because, more than ever before, people are desperate to find someone to whom they can tell their stories without constant interruptions. Given the widespread use of mobile devices, we rarely have anyone's undivided attention today. People check their phones constantly throughout the day—during meetings, conversations, counseling sessions, even during sex. Regardless of what you are doing, the frequent bings and buzzes of mobile devices beckon. Even if the people you are with have the good sense to ignore the alert and stay with you (which rarely seems to happen), you can see the look of temporary distraction in their eyes as they split their attention between whatever heartfelt subject you are talking about and the life-changing message they imagine is waiting for them as soon as they can extricate themselves from your presence.

With everyone's constant distractions and multitasking, counseling sessions will likely continue to serve a primary function of providing relational space to honor stories with full and complete attention. Perhaps the biggest and most frequent mistake that a counselor or any storyteller can make is to fail to adapt and personalize the story for the particular audience, culture, context, and situation. People frequently memorize jokes and recite them verbatim, just as counselors have a catalog of greatest hits that they may rely on without taking the time to refashion the narrative to fit the situation. Yashinsky (2004), for example, considers himself an accomplished storyteller who is used to beguiling audiences with his craft, but he recalled sharing one of his best anecdotes with a group of Inuit children in northern Canada and getting no response whatsoever—just blank looks. In one part in the narrative, the character falls into a mud puddle, which was always guaranteed to generate hearty laughter, but this time it elicited shrugs and boredom. Then he realized that these children lived in a snowy world and had never seen a mud puddle; it was unfamiliar to them. When he retold the tale with the character falling into a pile of snow, he got the expected reaction of delight.

This illustration highlights the critical importance of making sure that any stories we tell are clearly embedded and customized for each client relationship. If we truly want to become more accomplished in our craft, we might be well advised not only to invest in new theoretical, technological, and EBPs but also in our powers as relational storytellers. Whether speaking to an individual client, working as a family or group counselor, delivering a speech to a large audience, being interviewed in the media, or telling a story in a social setting, the real growth edge is related to becoming a powerful storyteller, the kind that leaves people in laughter *and* tears.

The best stories, of course, are those that move people emotionally, that touch their souls, that present such indelible images that they will never be forgotten. Deconstruct any great speech, any viral TED Talk, and they all have embedded within them a compelling story that resonates with the audience, that moves, informs, and inspires them. Great stories have vivid emotional coloring that elicit strong feelings of joy, fear, sadness, and even confusion. In fact, the best stories may not even initially make sense but require the listener or reader to do the real work of converting ambiguity and complexity into something personally meaningful. That's why great stories are collaborative partnerships between the listener or reader and the storyteller. Metaphor innovator and researcher Steve

Lankton (Lankton & Lankton, 1989) once remarked that the best stories should be elusive, ambiguous, mysterious, and only slightly relevant to the client's presenting issues. That way, the client must figure out the connections to his or her own experience. Whether you agree with that approach or not, it does emphasize the recognition that stories are not something just offered to someone else but rather involve collaborations and individualized interpretations.

Counselors can improve their storytelling proficiencies in several ways if this is a priority (Duarte, 2010; Gallo, 2014; Hsu, 2008; Ingemark, 2013; Kottler, 2014; Maguire, 1998; McKee, 2003; Reynolds, 2012; Simmons, 2006; Spaulding, 2011). First of all, give yourself permission to be far more dramatic, playful, and creative in the stories you invent and share. Include much more density of sensory details in storytelling to make the tales truly come alive. This is what helps to activate all the senses of the brain, not just visual processing but the senses of sound, touch, and smell as well. Finally, the whole purpose of telling a story in counseling is so that the client can connect with the narrative in such a way that it becomes his or her own experience. You want the client thinking, "So, how is that related to *me* and my situation?" Usually, this is accomplished by introducing one character or metaphorical feature that represents the client and the particular issues discussed.

In all their various forms and manifestations, stories are the glue that hold relationships together. They represent the most poignant, courageous, tragic, humorous, and seminal experiences of our lives. They are the indelible memories of our deepest connections to those who have influenced us the most.

Chapter 8

Innovative, Creative, and Practical Strategies for Enhancing Relational Effects

"I'd been having these reoccurring visions, almost waking night-mares, ever since my house had been broken into," a client reveals. "Just as I walked in the door, I could hear them run out the back. What would have happened if I'd been there when they showed up? I just can't get that out of my head."

The client had been referred for eye movement desensitization and reprocessing therapy (EMDR) for trauma and went as directed by her physician. "She was the nicest lady," the client reports about her therapist. "She had me do these things that seemed really weird with flashing lights or something. I didn't really understand it all, but I could tell she was totally into it. But basically I just really liked that the lady listened to me and all, so I kind of just went with her program. I guess it helped, but I don't really know exactly if it was those lights I was supposed to look at or whether it was just that I finally had someone who understood what happened."

Of course, the research on EMDR is a bit unclear as well, making it difficult to sort out which aspects of our work with clients are the most important ingredients. We have already discussed how the empirical research on interventions and techniques is less than convincing. It is problematic that, even in well-controlled studies, the researchers often don't take into account the different skill levels of the counselors, the different ways the techniques are applied, the depth and kind of relationship established, and so many other intervening variables that can't be isolated or even identified.

Nevertheless, even if techniques and strategies aren't necessarily important to the client, or the outcome, they sure matter a lot to us!

Throughout our narrative, we have focused on the premise that the relationship is the primary component that promotes healing within the context of counseling. We have made the case that strategies and theories play a less prominent role, especially when compared to the influence of the alliance once it is negotiated and customized to meet the particular needs, interests, issues, problems, personality, and cultural context of the client.

We described earlier how it has become the tradition within our field that strategies and techniques have been linked to particular approaches. Thus, the skill of interpretation is related to psychoanalytic theory; the empty chair, to Gestalt theory; the miracle question, to solution-focused theory; challenging beliefs are part of cognitive behavior theory; and so on. This has now evolved to the point that many new singular strategies are considered approaches on their own, whether art therapy (e.g., Schroder, 2004), equine-assisted therapy (e.g., Bachi, 2012), animal-assisted therapy (e.g., Chandler, 2006; Chandler, Portrie-Bethke, Barrio Minton, Fernando, & O'Callaghan, 2010; O'Callaghan & Chandler, 2011; Stewart, Chang, & Rice, 2013), music therapy (e.g., Duffey & Haberstroh, 2013; Hendricks & Bradley, 2005), floratherapy (e.g., Perryman & Keller, 2009), adventure therapy (e.g., Gass & Gillis, 2010; Gillis, Gass, & Russell, 2008; Gillis & Simpson, 1991), or play therapy (e.g., Landreth, 2012; Ray, 2011).

This is a chapter about creative therapeutic work, and we applaud these innovations even though they usually emphasize the technique over the relational considerations that actually empower them. After all, it's not likely that the relationship with a horse, a dog, a flower, or a toy is going to be all that useful without a solid alliance with the counselor who is using that particular strategy. More precisely, it isn't these objects or tools themselves that hold healing power but the *relationship* that clients develop with them that matters most.

Enhancing the Counseling Relationship

It is more than a little ironic how often we invest our time, money, and resources attending workshops, seminars, continuing education programs, and advanced training to learn the latest newfangled technique that is supposed to render everything else we know obsolete. We flock to programs on EMDR, DBT, EFT, MBCT, and all the other acronyms, hoping to get a handle on the next miracle cure. We jump on the hypnosis or creative arts bandwagon, as if adding art or music or inductions to our practice will make all the difference. We are not suggesting that learning new interventions isn't useful, although not necessary, but rather that devoting our time to this singular task flies in the face of what we do know and understand about what best empowers our work. With that in mind, we want to review what we do know and understand (so far) about what matters most.

Give It Time

Relationships take place not only in a context of personal engagement, cultural interactions, and environment, but also in moments of time. They represent a kind of evolution with successive stages of development in trust, intimacy, and task completion. In other words, relationships take a certain amount of time before they become as satisfying and productive as we—and clients—might like. How *much* time is required depends on all kinds of factors, such as the client's readiness and motivation, the nature of the presenting problems, external influences such as financial or insurance resources, and, of course, the counselor's own beliefs and approach. Some counselors believe, for instance, that a lot of work can be accomplished rather quickly in a few sessions, and others might insist it takes months to make "real" progress.

It is often the case that time really does heal most wounds. This is true whether people seek counseling or not—they do often get better on their own, even if it may take much longer. Counseling relationships usually improve as well over time and are viewed by most participants as helpful once things progress (Elad-Strenger & Littman-Ovadia, 2012). Unfortunately, with the pressures of managed care and institutional policies, we are often forced to move things along far more quickly than would be best indicated, focusing on measurable outcomes that result from specific interventions.

Spend the First Moments Wisely

Quiz: What is the *principal* goal of the first counseling session?
   a. Complete necessary paperwork and intake forms.
   b. Conduct an initial interview and mental status exam.
   c. Conduct a thorough diagnostic assessment.
   d. Develop a treatment plan with specific outcome measures.
   e. None of the above.

We don't quibble with the importance of these necessary tasks that we are certainly required to complete, but the single most important goal of a first counseling session is to get the client to return for another one. Except in those rare crisis situations in which a single session is all we've got to make a difference, we can't do much to help someone unless we have the structure and reasonable time to do so.

It is during the first few minutes, sometimes even the first *moments* of the initial session, that first impressions are formed and the client decides whether or not this experience is going to be helpful or a colossal waste of time. Just as in all other kinds of relationships, we are programmed by evolution to form immediate reactions as to whether someone, especially a stranger, is going to be useful, annoying, or perhaps a danger to us. With that in mind, you would imagine that we would spend that first meeting doing everything and anything in our power to make sure that clients feel welcomed, honored, and validated.

Compare that logical plan to what actually happens for most clients. They show up, often against their will in the first place, more than a little anxious and uncertain about what is to be expected. They are suffering in some way and have considerable doubts whether this counseling stuff is going to be all that helpful. In many cases, they are looking for any excuse to bail out, one that will be convincing enough to get others off their backs.

They show up and are usually greeted with innumerable forms to fill out. "Have you attended counseling previously? If so, when and where?" "What medications are you currently taking?" "How were you referred to this agency?" "How would you describe your sleep habits?" "Are you currently experiencing depression, anxiety, or loneliness?" "How often do your drink alcohol or use other drugs?" "Describe your family history of mental illness." We hit them with these incredibly personal questions before even meeting them.

Next we greet them in the waiting room, escort them into the office, and look over the forms, asking further questions about any blank spaces or confusing responses. Then we proceed with the formal intake interview. We've known this person for exactly 5 minutes, and we start asking them all these personal, intrusive questions: "When you say, here, that there has been a history of addictions in your family, how are you most inclined to medicate and soothe your own anxiety? How often do you smoke marijuana?" "It says here that you aren't currently in a romantic relationship. How often do you use porn to masturbate?"

Needless to say, it is a wonder that anyone returns after we greet them this way. The only saving grace is that the medical system has so depersonalized health care that clients are used to this sort of treatment. On some level, it seems ridiculous that we even ask people to disclose so many intimate, personal details of their lives when they don't even know us. It is not just that we are asking them where the pain hurts, like a physician might, but we are pushing them to reveal the most difficult, disturbing, shameful aspects of their lives.

The contemporary realities of counseling virtually require us to collect necessary background information, but we at least have some choice in what we explore and how we do it. For instance, clients are more likely to have satisfying and productive initial sessions when we spend more time discussing sociocultural background and personal history rather than asking about their problems and diagnostic symptoms (Nakash, Nagar, & Kanat-Maymon, 2015). Although, at some point, we will be expected to provide that information for the sake of supervisors, agency policies, and documentation for third-party payers, it may not be in the best interests of the client to do so until we have some kind of working alliance.

Your Perspective Matters, but Not As Much As You Think

We have mentioned previously that the key factor that predicts the best outcomes is not how the counselor views the relationship but rather what the client thinks and feels about it. This is a relatively recent revelation because researchers have usually found it a lot more convenient, not to mention easier to get ethics approval, to talk to counselors rather than clients. It is also consistent with the belief that we are the experts and know what is best, not to mention that we are supposedly more reliable and accurate informants. When you think about it, that is almost amusing in that it has often been assumed that we are the ones in the best position to judge what the *client* is getting out of the sessions. On the other hand, we've said before that clients aren't always able to describe what helped them the most, or at least aren't able to do so in a very comprehensive and precise way.

Clients aren't really that interested, or care very much, about our own research agendas, which is why so many studies have been centered on "captive audiences" such as college students. Naturally, this skews the data available. The end result is that counseling research is overwhelmingly focused on navel gazing—there is simply an overabundance of research in which we look at ourselves instead of our clients' actual experiences.

The good news is that the counselor's assessment of the working alliance can be predictive of counseling outcomes; it's just not the complete picture. When both the counselor and the client are asked to assess the quality of the relationship, maybe it's not too surprising that the client's opinion matters a lot more. So, although our perspective of the counseling relationship might be helpful, having an idea of the client's perspective is even more helpful. The challenging part, of course, is how to get that reliable, truthful input.

There are a lot of formal assessment tools, some that ask clients to fill out feedback forms at the end of every session. Although we can imagine that such information would be invaluable for making adjustments in what we are doing, and how we do it, it seems easier and simpler, not to mention more relational, to just ask clients what they liked, and what they didn't like, about the session. It also helps when we return the favor by providing them with feedback reporting on what we thought was most interesting or useful.

This is a chapter about creative ways to enhance the relationship, so it is worth mentioning that one of the signature ways Michael White and David Epston (1994), cofounders of narrative therapy, provided strategically framed feedback to clients was to send them letters after every session summarizing their take on what had happened. This developed as a way to make sure they were all on the same page, so to speak, but it also enabled the counselors to shape the interpretations most advantageously.

Empower—and Challenge—Clients

There is a common adage within our profession that clients are experts on their own experience, except in cases when we don't seem to trust their judgment. When we talk about "empowering" clients, it is more than just encouraging them to take the lead in sessions by asking, "What would you like to work on today?"

In the last few years, there has been a notable shift in thinking away from the traditional psychopathological model, which focuses almost exclusively on what is wrong, dysfunctional, and problematic in people's lives, and instead honing in on strengths and resources. Influences from positive psychology and brief therapy have encouraged us to be more balanced in the ways we help clients to examine what is going well in their lives as well as what is difficult for them. If you've ever worked with those who struggle with chronic pain or intractable illnesses, or who have just adopted a very pessimistic attitude toward life, then you know how challenging it is to get them to talk about exceptions to their difficulties, including times when they are feeling pretty good.

Counseling relationships tend to be further enhanced when counselors adopt a more strength-based rather than problem-focused approach, one that acknowledges symptoms but doesn't necessarily dwell on them (Oddli & Ronnestad, 2012). Instead, clients report that it was especially helpful to them when they are asked to examine what has worked best in the past and when they are frequently asked their own opinions about what to do, emphasizing their own inner wisdom.

We also empower clients by using language that encourages choices during and throughout counseling. This means that we check in with clients about what we understand and provide clients with the opportunity to agree, disagree, or add to our understanding. There is a rich history of using metaphors in counseling to communicate understanding and to confirm the accuracy of our perception. For example, rather than merely reflecting what a client says in a session, as if it were some indisputable truth ("It sounds like you are ready for a change"), we might instead invite the client to more actively confirm or elaborate on what he or she really means.

There are other times when we might use more tentative language to challenge clients, especially those struggling with self-esteem issues. For example, when working with survivors of abuse, we often encounter clients who verbalize feelings of self-blame and guilt over their own suffering. One potentially effective strategy to enhance the counseling relationship and empower clients is to challenge their entrenched views of themselves: "It seems that you are angry at yourself for staying in this situation with someone who repeatedly hurt you, but maybe some of this anger you feel toward yourself is misplaced."

Being Creative and Innovative

Earlier in the chapter, we identified the creative strategies counselors use to enhance relational effects, and we emphasized the practical processes that actually do affect the counseling relationship in a positive manner. What, then, is the role and purpose of being creative in counseling? Creative moments are more likely to be used when the problem-solving process appears to be obstructed—when the client and the counselor appear to be stuck (Kottler, 1992; Lawrence, Foster, & Tieso, 2015).

The counselor's use of creativity in counseling emanates from a moment, such as an intervention or interaction, that is both original and beneficial to the client (Gladding, 2008). Such novel and beneficial experiences are most likely when the relationship established feels safe and permissive for *both* participants. In other words, you are far more likely to experiment, take risks, try new strategies, or think outside the box when you trust the client enough to be forgiving if things do not inevitably work as well as planned in an initial effort.

We sometimes feel a moment of hesitation when that voice inside our head is saying, "Go for it!" We are considering doing or saying something that we've never tried before, something that seems a bit wild and crazy, but it just might get through to the client in a way that nothing else has. It is during that pause for reflection that we consider the risks versus potential rewards. If we feel relatively safe and trusting with a particular client, we will be more inclined to reach beyond what is comfortable and familiar and try interventions that might take things to a whole new level. Being creative doesn't necessarily mean being more effective or helpful, but it often does shake things up a bit, which may be what is most needed when sessions appear to have reached an impasse or the relationship has become dull and predictable (Duffey, Haberstroh, & Trepal, 2009).

Application of Established Techniques in Novel Ways

We offer a simple truth: There really are no special techniques or strategies to enhance counseling relationships. As we've said time and again, it's not about any particular approach but about the relationship going to a deeper level when we are fully present. That's a lot easier said then done, even for counselors. Consider how often we "leave" the room and lapse into fantasy, become distracted by our own thoughts, or become triggered by something the client says or does that sends us off into our own unresolved issues.

Immediacy and Presence

There may be no single trick or magical incantation that deepens relationships, but there is one key, if not a secret, and it involves talking about whatever is happening in the moment, for each of us, but especially for both of us together. We have emphasized being fully present several times, but it's worth mentioning once again in this context of creative strategies when previous efforts have proven less than useful.

"I'm wondering what is happening right now," the counselor says aloud, interrupting a story the client has already told a few times before.

"Excuse me?"

"This moment, right now, what do you think is going on between us?"

"Um, I'm not sure what you mean. I was just telling you about the way my kids barely speak to me, how they . . ."

"Yes, I'm aware of that. We've gone over that same ground many times. I can see how much that bothers you, how helpless you feel. We've talked at length about how you have to wait for them to come to you, how the more you push them, the more they back away. But the part I was wondering about is why you launched into that story just at the moment you seemed to feel some tenderness toward me. So I was just trying to imagine what that was like for you, what you were feeling at that moment when we seemed so connected. Or at least that's the way it felt to me."

"I don't know. . . . I mean, I'm not sure exactly."

"I can sense that this conversation is becoming uncomfortable for you, that your eyes flitted over to the door, as if you were looking to escape."

[Laughs] "Ah, well, maybe you're right! This is getting a bit weird."

"And by 'weird,' you mean what exactly?"

"You know, like, kind of, you know, strange."

"You mean it is uncomfortable and difficult for us to talk about our relationship like this?"

[Nods head thoughtfully.]

"You know, it's a little uncomfortable for me to," the counselor admits. "But just a few minutes ago, I felt so close to you. For the first time, it felt like we were really connecting with one another. And then, there was that uncomfortable pause for a moment, remember?"

[Client nods.]

"And then it was almost as if you wanted to run from those feelings, and so you went back into that familiar story you tell me every time you don't know what else to say."

"So," the client asks, "what exactly are you saying?"

"How about, you tell *me*?"

"Well, I'm not sure exactly, but I think you are saying that I kind of ruin things when someone tries to get close to me. That's what I've done with my kids. And I think you are saying that's what I do with you. Is that what this is about?"

Although this dialogue exemplifies many of the features of a deepened relationship, it is probably idealized by presenting so many different issues in such a brief amount of time. Nevertheless, the major themes are addressed here with a complete absence of "technique." Instead, the counselor is doing her best to use what some approaches call "immediacy," and others might refer to as "mindfulness" or "being fully present."

Advanced Empathy

Long ago, Carl Rogers talked about the concept of "advanced empathy," a way to take counseling relationships to a much deeper level and to facilitate mutually transformative experiences. This was alleged to go far beyond so-called basic empathy, which reflected initial thoughts and feelings. More recently, it has been suggested that a number of creative enhancements are related to this process, the first of which involves reflecting much deeper feelings.

One example of the creative use of empathy is described by Neukrug and his colleagues (Neukrug, Bayne, Dean-Nganga, & Pusateri, 2013) when they state that "you can't get there until you've been there," meaning that it is our own felt experience that transports us more completely into the client's world. The most creative part of counseling, they argue, is when we are able to more accurately and fully reflect the essence of the client's experience in such a way that it leads to new understandings. Although it has been found consistently that deeper levels of empathic connection result in better outcomes, they are also quick to acknowledge that they have no way of knowing just yet whether these more creative variations produce still greater benefits.

A client says, "I can't believe she just walked out on me," and perhaps standard operating procedure might be to respond with something like this: "I can tell you are pretty angry about that." However, once a working alliance has been established, we often have the freedom to test hypotheses that might take things to another level: "I sense that the anger you are feeling right now is also holding a lot of disappointment and loss, blaming yourself for not picking up on things much earlier."

Whereas this second response might be described as simply more "advanced" in the way it possibly captures the client's fuller experience, it also signals a willingness to do far more than actively listen to what has been said. Another example of creative adaptations of deep empathy occurs when counselors use metaphors or visual imagery to highlight themes that arise: "For just a moment, when you said those words, I couldn't help but imagine you as the hurt little boy you once described, the one who felt so lost and lonely.

And now those feelings of abandonment are so evident in your face and posture, as if you are reliving something from the past."

Taking Risks

If the goal is to become more creative in our relational work, this means experimenting and taking risks to a certain extent. Almost by definition, creative means trying something new, improvising, trying out something novel or different. With such attempts, there is increased probability that things might not work out as planned—sometimes because we aren't even sure where that will lead. This also means letting go of the familiar, time-tested recipes that have been honed over time.

In a review of ways that we might become more innovative in our work, Lawrence et al. (2015) advocated giving ourselves permission to operate in a more ambiguous, spontaneous, improvisational framework, a process that Gladding (2008) admitted does carry with it a degree of uncertainty. However, what we are all about is encouraging others to try new behaviors, take greater constructive risks, experiment with alternative ways of being, and that applies equally to ourselves, especially if we want to model those values and beliefs we teach to others.

Interpersonal Risk

Counseling relationships represent collaborations between and among all the participants. Although so much of the discussion in the literature is about earning the client's trust, we have discussed how this trust flows in *both* directions: If *we* don't feel safe in the relationship and fear criticism, manipulation, or some disastrous outcome, we are going to operate very cautiously and conservatively and are unlikely to do or say anything that may result in unpredictable responses. As such, the relationship is likely to remain relatively benign and, at best, lead to rather modest results. Deep relational engagement feels risky because it is. Once we enter into that space of realness, of authenticity, of honest disclosure of thoughts and feelings, true intimacy becomes possible. People get their feelings hurt. Misunderstandings are possible. Vulnerability is the norm. Even casualties are more likely once we have abandoned familiar structure. The kind of risking we are referring to does not put a client's safety in jeopardy, but it sometimes requires us to abandon the planned program or structure to engage the client in the moment.

When leading group or family sessions, a member may have difficulty seeing how his or her behavior affects others. This denial of responsibility can become a major impediment to progress. One creative technique, which may also involve risk, is for the counselor to encourage another member to "be a mirror." This can be done by saying to the other member, "If you were a mirror looking at this person in denial, what would you say and how would you behave?" The counselor encourages an interaction in which one person displays the behavior to another. Of course, the counselor has no idea what one member is going to say to the other and how the feedback will be taken, but we hope the counselor has enough insight to anticipate that this might work. Even if it doesn't work as expected, a solid relationship allows all the parties to deconstruct and debrief what happened and to discuss why the result was different from what was intended.

Intrapersonal Risk

The reality is that taking risks as a counselor can be pretty nerve racking, especially when you have little idea what the outcome might be. Interestingly, counselors' resistance to using creative interventions may be less related to their own perceptions about risk taking in counseling than to how they believe clients will respond. Perceived client rigidity may be a larger barrier to using creative interventions than the counselor's own preconditions for risk taking (Carson, Becker, Vance, & Forth, 2003). In other words, counselors may be more inclined to use creative interventions if they believed that their clients would be flexible enough to accept such a strategy—or at least demonstrate forgiveness and resilience if the result is unsatisfactory or even upsetting.

With that said, throughout history, during any era and in any discipline, creative breakthroughs tend to take place once we surrender to a position of not knowing and not understanding. This is a time to embrace and honor confusion, to tolerate ambiguity, and thus permit us to try something new, perhaps something we've never done before, but as long as we are convinced we know what is going on, we will remain comfortable with the status quo, whether it is working or not.

Systemic Risk

Unfortunately, another type of risk has less to do with the client and more to do with the system of care in which counselors work. When running an outpatient practice, I (Rick) was sent a workbook and a curriculum from a third-party payer who insisted that the client use the workbook to be reimbursed for services provided.

I remember thinking, "Really? This is what counseling has come to?" The process seemed insulting and demeaning, and there was no recognition that counseling was something far more than mere manualized techniques. This focus on manualized care by third-party payers and managed care companies has been identified as a genuine concern among clinicians and a significant barrier preventing the use of creative interventions (Carson et al., 2003). Efforts have been made to standardize treatment approaches as much as possible, making them replicable and reliable, so almost anyone can follow the clearly demarcated steps.

We tend to focus on and adopt processes that are expectations within the mental health system without ever challenging them or considering whether these practices are helpful to the client. If we accept the uniqueness of each client and situation, why is it that we insist that we sit down in our respective spaces in an office for a prescribed amount of time and believe that will work effectively for everyone? Why should sessions necessarily be 50 minutes long? Who says that counseling must take place in an office and involve conversation? What is the rationale behind labeling people before we even have the chance to get to know them? We take many assumptions for granted. Many are designed to protect either the client or ourselves, but others represent conventions that may be obsolete, unnecessary, or unwarranted for a particular client.

On the other hand, we have made a compelling case, with supporting evidence, that each relationship is unique and must be negotiated not only once in the beginning but multiple times throughout the process as needs change. If all of your clients, past and present, got together for a conference (wouldn't that be fun?) to compare notes on what their experiences were like with you, we hope they would have very different tales to tell. Some might find you warm and supportive, whereas others would say you were really tough on them. Some would say you talked a lot; others, not enough. Some would say all you seemed to care about was what happened in their families of origin, and others would report that you only wanted to delve into what was going on in the present. Of course, these differences reflect not only the particular client's issues and needs but also how *you* have evolved and changed over time.

Chapter 9

Boundaries and Barriers Within Counseling Relationships

Counseling relationships are structured to maximize the effects of our work while protecting the safety of clients. Certain traditions, policies, and procedures have evolved over time, such as the idea of the 50-minute hour or that our work takes place largely in conversation within an office setting, and they have become standardized throughout the profession. There are many other stipulations as well, such as avoiding physical contact, multiple relationships, or bartering. Many of these norms were developed as much for the counselor's convenience as they were thought to facilitate the therapeutic work.

Western forms of counseling and psychotherapy are the only healing tradition that has evolved in such a way with roles so carefully specified, specialized, prescribed, and compartmentalized. Within most indigenous cultures, for instance, community healers combine the roles of counselor, teacher, doctor, priest, coach, and teacher into a single job because sickness or emotional problems are usually considered to affect the mind, the body, and the spirit (Kottler, Carlson, & Keeney, 2004). As such, to truly have much lasting impact, healers significantly reduce the relational boundaries that limit therapeutic options. In many cultures, for example, it is usual and customary for the healer to move into the client's home until such time as a cure has resulted. It is also typical that therapeutic procedures would involve all kinds of integrated and varied activities that go *way* beyond mere conversations. Any self-respecting indigenous healer would likely avoid verbal conversation altogether and, instead, include music, dance, spiritual incantations, natural herbs, massage, public ceremonies, and other rituals, which are intended to affect the individual in a multitude of ways.

Counseling has evolved into a rather prescribed and structured healing practice within our own culture, and a number of consensual rules have been mandated by the various professional organizations. These "rules" help to set counseling relationships apart from other types of human connections, given their unique goals and focus. Many of these boundaries include standards for things such as where counseling should take place, its time parameters and enforcement, interpersonal space and physical contact, and counselor self-disclosure or acceptance of gifts; each of these boundaries may be honored, crossed, or violated, creating a certain amount of confusion (Barnett, 2014). This is especially true given the unique requirements of any given case, the ever-changing technological developments in the field, and the individual preferences of the participants.

As a point of clarification, "crossing" a boundary, such as shaking a client's hand, is not considered inappropriate or contraindicated, but "violating" a boundary implies the potential for exploitation, an ethical breach, and the possibility of causing significant harm, such as an unwanted physical touch that could be interpreted as sexual in nature (Smith & Fitzpatrick, 1995). There may be some debate regarding which behaviors cross a line and which do not, but there is general agreement that particular kinds of boundaries should never be crossed under any circumstances. Sexual contact is one example that is included in every ethics code and legal jurisdiction; the amount of time that must elapse after termination of the counseling relationship before a sexual relationship begins varies from 2 to 5 years according to various state laws and ethics codes. Flexible boundaries or multiple relationships can be harmful, neutral, or helpful. They can be inadvertent, avoidable, chosen, or mandated. They can occur in relationships that are low or high in emotional intensity and personal engagement. They can be classified as legal or illegal, ethical or unethical, and they are not always a matter of choice but rather of circumstances (Zur, 2014).

If you step back from the scene and consider how we operate and why we do so, it does seem a bit peculiar that counseling only takes place within the rigid parameters of a conversation with people sitting in chairs, 6 feet away from one another at all times, for exactly 50 minutes, at which time the conversation is declared over, regardless of what was taking place. As described by Homer

(2005), it is for this reason that the French psychoanalyst Jacques Lacan took pleasure in stirring up trouble among his colleagues by insisting there was nothing particularly sacrosanct, or even useful, about maintaining standardized sessions. It is as if a doctor would decide, even before she greeted patients, that she would spend exactly the same amount of time with each one, regardless of whether they needed a prescription for an antibiotic or neurosurgery. Lacan believed that some people might require only 10 minutes for a session, whereas others on a particular day might need 2 hours. He would not agree to schedule appointments but would require patients to just show up in his waiting room; then he would select candidates and decide how long their treatment required on that day. If he thought the patient wasn't sufficiently focused on the work, a session might last only a few seconds. It is for this reason that Albert Ellis, as well, reduced the amount of time he spent with clients to 25-minute sessions; he felt they could accomplish much more in whatever time was allotted.

Many prominent theorists in the field have challenged conventional wisdom (if it indeed can be called "wisdom" instead of tradition) related to the usual boundaries and barriers of counseling (or supervisory) relationships. When Carl Rogers had an emotional breakdown, teetering on the verge of a psychotic break, he chose to see one of his own doctoral students as his counselor to help him through the personal crisis. Carl Whitaker, Virginia Satir, Fritz Perls, and other early luminaries in the field experimented with all kinds of relational variations. Whitaker was known to have clients sit on his lap. Satir would twist families into sculpted pretzels. Arnold Lazarus (1994) has been an advocate for more flexible boundaries designed to help clients rather than to restrict therapeutic options. He has been known to take his clients on "field trips" to assist them in practicing new behaviors rather than just talking about them in session. Why, after all, would you only want to *discuss* what a client might want to do to overcome some problem rather than escorting him or her into the world to try it out?

Relationships Are Complicated

Boundary issues are an important aspect of counselor preparation, development, training, and practice, and much helpful information related to boundary issues can be found in the *ACA Code of Ethics* (American Counseling Association [ACA], 2014). An initial and important question we can ask related to boundary issues is,

"What the heck *is* a multiple relationship anyway, and why is it really a problem?" First of all, as Herlihy and Corey (2015) pointed out, such complex relationship configurations can be difficult to recognize when they are occurring. Boundary crossings can be quite subtle and incremental, starting out with the most benign gesture ("Sure, let's grab a cup of coffee before we get started") and escalating into something else that feels out of control. Second, such relationships are complicated, because there is no consensus about when they are necessarily harmful versus being neutral or helpful. Finally, multiple relationships aren't always avoidable, no matter how much we might prefer to maintain the strictest rules and structures.

In the good old days when the profession began, it seemed both realistic and desirable to insulate clients in such a way that the therapeutic work would take place in a sacred, secret, isolated space. The original psychotherapists arranged their offices so clients would enter and leave through separate doorways to preserve their privacy. Rules were put in place that defined the relationship in such a way that this rather intimate involvement would be protected and kept safe in the client's best interests. With the occurrence of sexual improprieties, exploitation, and abuses of power, professional organizations developed ethics codes designed to protect the welfare of clients. It was a matter of risk management for counselors and therapists to protect themselves from situations in which their roles and responsibilities, not to mention the already complex relationships, would be polluted or further eroded through any behavior or contact outside of the prescribed treatment.

The ethics codes of various organizations, including the American Counseling Association, American School Counseling Association, American Mental Health Counseling Association, American Psychological Association, American Association for Marital and Family Therapy, and the National Association of Social Workers, all say basically the same thing: Dual or multiple relationships should be avoided because they (a) compromise our objectivity, (b) risk the potential for harm, and (c) could lead to exploitation. There is no consensus that all multiple relationships are, in fact, harmful, nor whether some can indeed further therapeutic goals and lead to better outcomes. Of course, there are increased risks as a result of these "boundary crossings," but a more important question to ask is whether avoiding all options that could be in the client's best interests is really the optimal professional behavior. In fact, certain multiple relationships with some clients are not unethical, exploitative, or even inappropriate (Lazarus & Zur, 2002). This is especially the case in some rural and isolated regions, where the possibility of complete separation is virtually impossible to maintain (Kocet, 2006).

In some cases, such as in small or rural communities, multiple relationships with clients are absolutely unavoidable. I (Jeffrey) once worked in a small town in which I was the only licensed mental health professional in the community (besides an incompetent, somewhat erratic psychiatrist). This meant that I would regularly see my clients at all kinds of social events, walking down the street, and sometimes even attending my classes because I was teaching at the only university within 100 miles of the town. Zur (2014) makes the compelling point that "not all multiple relationships are created equal" (p. 15), a belief that is implicit in the ethics codes that recognize that some multiple relationships do not necessarily cause harm and may be initiated to further therapeutic objectives.

Furthermore, individuals often seek help within their own communities. When I (Rick) worked on a geriatric unit, on occasion, clients from the synagogue I attended were admitted to the unit. When I would meet with the family there, I often encountered expressions of immediate relief rather than reluctance. During one particular visit, I was introduced to "Pop" by the older man's son, who knew me from attending religious services. "Pop," he explained, "this is Rick who is going to help us. He's M.O.T." I had never heard that expression before. When the son saw my quizzical look, he explained with a smile, "member of the tribe!" This created an immediate connection between his father and me that wouldn't have been possible if I were just a stranger.

Multiple relationships exist in specific cultural, interpersonal, geographical, time and spatial contexts, some of which may be considered unnecessarily risky and inappropriate and others that are designed to better assist clients. Zur (2014) classified the various kinds of multiple relationships depending on whether they are considered helpful, neutral, or harmful. Consider, for example, some of the following options that probably would not be considered unethical or even inappropriate, although each does carry a certain risk that must be acknowledged:

- Conducting a home visit with a client who is critically ill and unable to arrange transportation to the office

- Accompanying a phobic client into an elevator, across a bridge, or to another terrifying situation to provide in vivo desensitization
- Going for a walk (or a run) with a client who is agoraphobic and fears any closed spaces
- Escorting a client to a doctor's appointment to provide support and encouragement
- Playing basketball, baseball, soccer, catch, or throwing a Frisbee with an adolescent client
- Having a client "like" a counselor's post on Facebook or other social media
- Mandated multiple relationships such as are commonly found in the court system, the military, and in prisons—and in graduate programs in counseling
- Attending a performance, dance recital, concert, or presentation given by a client
- Attending a client's wedding, bar/bat mitzvah, graduation, or quinceañera
- Loaning a client books or materials that may be of interest
- Developing a social relationship or friendship with an ex-client
- Counseling a neighbor or acquaintance or a "friend of a friend"
- Providing a client with a ride or transportation as an act of kindness
- Publically advocating on behalf of a controversial issue
- Exchanging small gifts as acts of appreciation and caring
- Sharing yourself and revealing a personal story
- Accepting payment for sessions in a form other than money (bartering)

It is important to distinguish between kinds of multiple relationships that are considered most risky and to be avoided and those that may potentially be helpful if they are carefully navigated. Although we talk about these categories as if they are clearly demarcated, one problem is that boundary issues are often unplanned, unexpected, and serendipitous. One example might be running into a client at coffee shop who then invites you to sit down and chat for a few minutes. Our response might not be as clear cut in the moment as we might anticipate, especially if it seems like it is more awkward to decline than to agree in a natural way.

The issue that concerns us, of course, is when the counseling relationship is somehow compromised as a result of the increased complexity. Whether that occurs or not depends on a host of factors: (a) Was it planned or spontaneous? (b) Did it cross the line of ethical behavior? (c) Was the nature of the contact emotionally mild or intense? (d) Was the context appropriate and suitable or awkward? and (e) Has it ultimately helped or harmed the client?

Boundary Crossings, Violations, and the Slippery Slope

Violating an established and consensually agreed-upon relational boundary almost always represents a betrayal of trust and fiduciary responsibility. Such behaviors are considered unethical, and sometimes also illegal, and they include sexual improprieties, fraud, forms of exploitation, and self-serving manipulation. Boundary *crossings*, however, simply mean that they deviate from the most stringent professional role and involve behaviors that are relatively commonplace, such as the counselor's use of appropriate self-disclosure or benign actions that are intended for the client's welfare.

Even the most orthodox counselors and therapists, those who swear fealty to the strictest standards of care, bend or break the rules on occasion when they believe the actions are both useful and minimize risk of harm. Freud was known to offer gifts to his clients or loan them money. In a few cases, he acted as matchmaker, provided legal advice, or invited clients to walk with him outside of his office.

The long-standing assumption is that almost any sort of boundary crossing is potentially risky and can easily lead to a "slippery slope" in which the small initial gesture of goodwill escalates into something else that can be quite dangerous (Gutheil & Gabbard, 1993). Typical of this attitude, one author advised, "In order to minimize the risk of sexual conduct, policies must prohibit a practitioner from having any contact with the client outside the treatment context and must preclude any type of dual relationships" (Woody, 1988, p. 188): an interesting theory, but one that is not supported by evidence.

It turns out that slippery-slope violations are actually pretty rare and not at all the likely consequence: The slope, when it exists at all, is usually neither steep nor slippery (Gottlieb & Younggren, 2009). There is little evidence to conclude that hugging a client will inevitably lead to some form of sexual exploitation or that going for a walk with a client will most certainly result in a breakdown of professionalism. It makes sense, however, that we would be more vigilant and cautious in any circumstance in which risk could be heightened. The fact that we live in a litigious society adds to the caution we implement with clients, and the reality for students and beginners is that it is highly advisable to be cautious and conservative when considering *any* departure whatsoever from a standard of care.

It is important to understand how different kinds of boundary crossings, such as a hug, self-disclosure, a walk in the park, or a gift, can be interpreted in different ways depending on the cultural context and the individual client. It is critical that any counselor accept full and complete responsibility for the choice to venture outside customary practices for the sake of a client's best interests. It helps to seek peer consultation on such matters, to carefully document the rationale for decisions and actions, and to remain clear about risk management issues. Protecting our clients from harm is our first and foremost responsibility, but we must also protect ourselves in a litigious climate in which certain behaviors can be misinterpreted. Nevertheless, we can do harm to clients not only by irresponsibly crossing relational boundaries but also by refusing to do so solely because we are unwilling to take constructive, needed actions that are outside the usual standards or policies currently in place. In addition, there is no compelling evidence to suggest that accepting small gifts from clients, touching them in nonsexual ways, conducting home visits, or sharing personal stories is necessarily harmful and, in many cases, it can have a significant positive effect on the counseling relationship (Zur, 2007).

In all cases, the question we should be asking is, "What does my client need most right now, and how can I be most helpful?" In other words, is a more nuanced, complex dual relationship indicated in a particular case? Ultimately, the decision is based on whether the benefits outweigh the possible risks, followed by a careful, cautious tracking of how the actions are affecting the relationship and the outcome of sessions.

Permeable, Fluid Boundaries

In a number of areas, relationship boundaries are more permeable than some counselors would prefer. In spite of guidance from ethics codes, the landscape of counseling practice is changing so quickly that it is difficult to sort out which boundaries should remain nonnegotiable and which ones can be stretched to better help clients.

Social Media

What are the rules with respect to when and how, and under what circumstances, clients and counselors communicate outside of sessions? Clients and counselors now routinely arrange and reschedule appointments via texts (example follows) or emails, but what about

Today, 9:20 AM

> Could we reschedule our appointment for Wednesday? I need to take my son to a meeting at school. I don't think I told you this but he got in trouble and now I'm missing work so I'm not sure if I can even afford our sessions. What do you think if we just skipped appointments for a few weeks and then I called you back Or else, maybe you think I'm just using this as an excuse because of what we talked about last time? Let me know. Oh yeah, I also forgot to tell you I'm pregnant.

when other questions are posed or reports are given or requests are made?

It has always been challenging for group leaders to control outside contact by members that could conceivably compromise or undermine work completed during sessions. These so-called parking lot groups often take place after the session has ended, with particular members continuing the discussion, sometimes retreating to a bar or a coffee shop afterward. This jeopardizes trust issues and confidentiality, but it also creates coalitions and sometimes even marginalizes members who are not included. In addition, because the counselor is not involved or privy to these conversations, critical information sometimes can be missing.

It is also impossible these days to partition oneself off from the digital grid. Group members often text one another or set up Facebook or other social media outlets for ongoing communication between group meetings. This can create problems, as well as lead to greater intimacy. The main problem is that such conversations are unmonitored and unsupervised by the counselor, creating a greater potential for misunderstandings or conflict. Imagine, for example, that one group member sends this text (left) to another person in the group and the potential problems that such outside contact could create for all the relationships involved.

Today, 1:48 PM

> So what did you think about what happened in group today? I can't believe that our esteemed leader actually fell for that crap. That guy is clueless so much of the time we could probably run the group better ourselves. Why don't we get together tonight and work out a plan together for the next session so we can stop this kind of thing happening before he turns things back on us?

Alternative Delivery Systems

Distance-based counseling is now the rage, and more and more practitioners are offering their services in forms other than face-to-face meetings. Counselors who use these modalities should be familiar with Section H of the *ACA Code of Ethics* (ACA, 2014). In spite of the thorny and challenging ethical, legal, jurisdictional, and procedural issues that have yet to be resolved, many counselors are seeing patients via Skype, FaceTime, and other video conferences. This is just another adaptation of the phone sessions that some professionals have been doing for years.

Some of the early reports and research seem to support the idea that these alternative delivery systems can be just as effective as traditional meetings; in some cases, they appear to offer additional advantages beyond mere convenience. This is especially the case for all kinds of people who would not ordinarily be able to access our services—those who are housebound, agoraphobic, seriously disabled, hospitalized, geographically isolated, and those who are elderly or economically deprived and don't have reliable transportation. We can even schedule family sessions when members are scattered around the world, but even if the relationships created and maintained are comparable to those in face-to-face sessions, they are certainly different in a number of ways.

One Romanian counselor of our acquaintance specializes in working with other Romanians living abroad who prefer to talk about personal problems in their native language. One of the biggest challenges she faces involves synchronizing time zones, because there might be a 10-hour time difference between locales. She has also learned to operate in a completely new way that was never part of her training. There is much greater informality in her relationships with clients, which she must take special care to manage well or the conversations can easily turn into chats about the old country instead of remaining focused on the personal issues at hand.

Despite consumer and public interest and the convenience and easy accessibility of this format, there are reasons to be cautious and hesitant (Marmarosh, 2015; Smith, 2015). There is something distinctly different about being in a room with someone and observing all the subtleties of their nonverbal behavior—their foot moving up and down, hands clenching, body posture—and viewing a portrait of the person's face. The sessions are likely not as private, they may not be taken as seriously, and there's something to be said for the journey itself to and from an office: In one sense, the session begins when clients first begin the commute, rehearsing in their heads what they want to say, and the session doesn't end until they arrive home as they review what transpired.

Alternative delivery systems such as video or Internet sessions might seem like an attractive option for clients who have intimacy issues and feel like they can better control the nature of the interaction in this kind of contact, but it may not help much in increasing the client's need and greater tolerance for close contact with others.

Some have predicted that conventional therapy, as we know it, is already obsolete. People will not want to schedule a 50-minute session at a predictable time of the week on a regular basis, preferring to schedule sessions at a time and specific length as needed. "Can I have 10 minutes to talk over an argument I just had with my wife?" "Can we schedule a quick 5-minute pep talk before I go in for the job interview?" "I'm having a panic attack right now and need you to talk me down off the ledge."

Because relational boundaries are essentially rules that govern interactions, it is important to be clear about issues related to confidentiality, scheduling, payments, cancellations, and gifts, even things related to physical proximity, clothing, language, and the way sessions are conducted. This is supposed to make interactions easier to predict and to manage behavior in the most appropriate and useful ways. Due to the nature of alternative delivery systems, things can quickly become far less formal, leading to flexible norms that can easily be changed and adjusted. What do you do when a client is nibbling on a snack or having a drink during the session? How about if the client gets up for a moment to answer the door or the phone? What if the client is lying in bed?

Practice guidelines have been developed for those who engage in counseling through alternative delivery systems (Drum & Littleton, 2014). Most of these are rather obvious but are still worth considering:

- Maintain the same degree of professionalism that you would in your office. This includes keeping the setting (visible on the camera) consistent, dressing appropriately, and enforcing consistent boundaries related to starting and ending on time.
- Manage communications carefully outside of sessions. Be clear about what sort of contact is acceptable and appropriate (e.g., only texts related to rescheduling) and provide responses in a timely way (within 24 hours).
- Protect privacy and confidentiality. This applies not only to the specific medium involved but also to the setting, which should be free of interruptions, intrusions, and others who may overhear conversations.

- Develop competence, if not mastery, in the unique aspects of this particular type of counseling service. Just as specialized training is required for group or family counseling, tele-counseling also requires a slightly different set of skills, which are rarely covered in graduate school.

While we are on the subject of technological innovations that affect the delivery of counseling services, one additional boundary issue is related to interruptions during session, either by the client or the counselor. Given that people routinely check their mobile devices as many as 220 times per day (Rucki, 2014), the likelihood of keeping an entire hour free from such distractions is quite a challenge. Every hour of every day, from the moment people awaken, they check their phones for weather and traffic reports, social media posts, texts, email, airplane schedules, and any other obscure information that impulsively seems important. Clients may be directed to avoid checking phones during sessions, but that doesn't stop the frequent buzzes we hear constantly. Some clients will carefully and lovingly place their phones beside them on the couch, and every time they hear a beep, a buzz, or feel a vibration, their eyes search downward automatically.

Despite how inappropriate this strikes us, some counselors do the same thing: constantly checking their phones after each new message, interrupting the flow of the session, and communicating the idea (as everyone else does throughout the day) that whatever is coming in, from whomever this might be, it is more important than whatever we are doing at this moment. So good luck making rules and trying to enforce boundaries related to electronic interruptions and distractions, especially with young people who are now so tethered to their devices that they often live inside the digital world more of the time than in the real world that surrounds them.

Location and Context

The context for where and how counseling takes place can have a huge effect on the relationship and how it unfolds. Counseling has many contextual features that depend on client characteristics (age, gender, culture, personality, preferences, presenting issues, social support), counselor characteristics (same as client), the type of counseling offered (theoretical orientation, modality, intensity, strategies), the amount of time and number of sessions allotted (frequency and length), where the treatment takes place (school, university, hospital, mental health clinic, group or solo private practice), and the geographical area (urban, rural). The type of relationship that is formed and negotiated also makes a difference: for instance, one that maximizes transference processes versus one that emphasizes authenticity, equality, and genuineness.

As we've mentioned previously, in some situations it might be advantageous to conduct the counseling outside of the usual office configuration, such as treating phobias or panic disorder, teaching assertiveness skills, or working with families in their homes. On some level, it seems limiting to merely talk about problems instead of figuring out ways to practice new behaviors in a safe, controlled environment with support, supervision, and mentoring available in real time.

One popular example of this alternative modality is adventure or travel-based therapeutic experiences; clients are placed in situations in which they are challenged to develop new personal resources and strengths when faced with physical or emotional challenges. Many institutions have built "ropes courses" and other outdoor and wilderness-based programs, which are designed to produce transformative experiences. Whether through Outward Bound or the National Outdoor Leadership School or another travel-based program, participants work together in teams to develop personal skills and greater emotional fortitude in the face of obstacles.

The counselor's role in such a therapeutic context, and the relationships that develop, are considerably more intense than could possibly be imagined in an office setting. I (Jeffrey) have been participating in and leading such travel-based programs for decades, often in the context of advocacy and service activities (Kottler, 1997; Kottler, Englar-Carlson, & Carlson, 2013; Kottler & Marriner, 2009). These have taken place as part of formal programs designed to enrich and stimulate the growth of university students as part of Semester at Sea or honors courses on social justice that involve field experiences staying in homeless shelters. They have also included supervised trips to Nepal to assist girls at risk of being trafficked into slavery or forced into early marriage, working with Syrian refugees crowded into Greek camps, mentoring children in isolated villages in Ghana, or teaching in orphanage schools in India. In each of these cases, the relationships that develop during so many weeks of intense interaction, difficult physical challenges, and emotional flooding often lead to the kinds of lasting personal changes that traditional counseling could never touch.

It so happens that when people get way, *way* outside their comfort zone, place themselves in novel environments, and have the necessary support, mentoring, and relational engagement to keep them safe, remarkable things can happen. When the structured activities involve altruistic acts of kindness and services, the effects can be further magnified.

Many therapeutic ingredients operate in adventure-based and service-based programs that mere talk can't begin to access. Clients are helped to face their fears instead of just talking about them. They encounter teachable moments in the real world that promote deep reflection and spirited conversations among all the participants, deepening their relationships. The high level of emotional arousal that accompanies these experiences is conducive to promoting new insights and experimenting with new ways of thinking. Because participants are insulated from their usual influences and familiar routines, they are more likely to try reinventing themselves in ways that would not be possible back home. Finally, the counselor's job in these therapeutic contexts is to help clients create meaning from the experience; to generalize aspects of their lives to others when they return home or perhaps reenter traditional counseling; and to make sense of all they have seen, felt, and lived.

Monet, a hospital administrator who traveled with me (Jeffrey) to provide medical and trauma assistance after the devastating earthquakes in Nepal, reflected on things she learned about herself, lessons that were possible only within the context of a caring, supportive group that helped her process all she witnessed and experienced.

"This trip has made me realize that I need deeper meaning in my life," Monet revealed. "I try to do my best every day at work and in everything else I do, but it just doesn't fulfill me. I question what difference I'm really making."

Monet is really good at her job, managing her own department and keeping the team running smoothly, but for a long time she felt that something was missing, something she couldn't put her finger on no matter how many conversations she had with others about her feelings.

"I am a control freak," she admits, "but this is not a new revelation. I want everything to be set up the best possible way so that we can have the greatest impact and therefore have the best possible outcome. When I get into 'go mode,' I sometimes lose sight of the human factor. I forget that there is also beauty in chaos."

While working with a medical team in Nepal, Monet had to surrender control because nothing unfolded as expected. Often, things did not fall into place as ideally as she might have preferred. Although she might have been inclined to take over responsibility so work would meet her exacting standards, with limited supplies and staff and resources, and the ever-present aftershocks of the earthquakes, that just wasn't possible.

Could these lessons have been learned in traditional counseling sessions? Perhaps, but certainly not as dramatically or in as powerful a way that has stuck with her ever since.

Zur (2007) mentioned several other examples of relational boundaries being stretched to better address the client's presenting issues in a way that transcends office conversation: Salvador Minuchin, the eminent family theorist, took anorexic clients out to lunch or arranged family meals with bulimic clients; Arnold Lazarus escorted a client to a bar to coach him on how to approach women because he was so painfully shy; and Albert Ellis encouraged his clients to engage in shame-attacking exercises by doing embarrassing things in public. Sports psychologists don't just sit with their athlete clients and provide advice; they spend time with them to coach them through emotional problems that are impeding their performance. Some counselors might accompany their clients to funerals because of their debilitating fears, and we can easily make a case that it is preferable to engage children and adolescents in some kind of activity rather than just sitting around talking.

Of course, these alternative methods aren't appropriate for every client, just as many counselors might not feel comfortable initiating them. Ultimately, for any counseling relationship to work, both (or all) the participants have to feel comfortable with the structure, setting, and format.

Incidental Encounters

You are walking along the sidewalk, lost in thought when, all of a sudden, someone calls out your name. You glance over your shoulder, and there is the smiling face of one of your clients. What do you do?

You would try to read the signals from this person and respond in a way congruent with who the client is and what your relationship with that person is like. Whether you would shake hands, offer a hug, or perhaps just give a brief wave and continue on your way would be shaped by your comfort level and what you anticipate would be most appropriate for this client.

For those counselors who work in school, university, military, or other institutional settings, running into a client outside of the office would not be unusual. These interactions are sometimes tests of a sort because if they feel awkward and unsatisfying, they can affect what happens when the next session resumes; so we try to balance a genuinely warm, affectionate manner with sensitivity and respect for the client's preferences related to privacy and confidentiality.

"I once showed up at a kid's birthday party with my own son," one counselor shared with us, "and I noticed that one of my clients was there with her own daughter of the same age. I walked up to her to say hello, and I immediately noticed her shrink in horror. I was so shocked, I just froze because I thought we had such a good relationship." The counselor shakes his head in remembrance, still dumbfounded by how awkward the encounter felt. "It was clear that she didn't want anyone there to know she was seeing me, and I completely blew it. It changed everything after that, and our relationship was never quite the same."

This example illustrates how important it is to allow the client to take the lead in determining what sort of greeting or interaction feels most comfortable. It also shows how boundaries can vary so much from one client to another. We can easily recall other examples in which we have been relatively reserved and cautious when running into a client in a social situation and noticed that he or she felt hurt because we appeared so formal and withholding.

Bartering and Compensation

True confession: Many of us have never been entirely comfortable collecting fees for counseling services. There are times, with some clients, when we might feel that there isn't enough money in the world to fairly compensate us for the aggravation or exhaustion we feel after a session. Other times, however, the ride is so much fun that we almost want to pay the client for sheer entertainment value. Sometimes, it doesn't feel right to extend a hand for cash or a check after finishing the most moving, intimate conversation about the most precious thing going on in someone's life.

There is no doubt that the counseling relationship is shaped significantly by the particular ways the counselor is compensated. A counselor in private practice thinks differently about a client who is leaving than does a professional on salary for a public agency or school with an interminable waiting list. The relationship also may feel different to participants who send in a check once per month as compared to those counting out 20 dollar bills in the room and handing them over. A counselor who is charging a fee for service might also feel different about a client who is paying the full fee versus someone who is paying a fraction of that on a sliding scale. A client who is paying out of pocket for services might feel different about the relationship than someone who is being subsidized by a relative or an insurance company.

There has been plenty of discussion about money issues in counseling over the years and how it influences the relationship in a variety of ways. What we find far more interesting and neglected is the use of bartering and the exchange of goods and services. Bartering has been a part of human culture for millennia as we struggled to find ways to fairly compensate individuals for their time, their effort, or the goods they provide. Bartering, as part of counseling relationships, has been a lot more controversial, even though it is common in some cultures. Most professional codes take the position that bartering should be avoided and discouraged whenever possible because of its unanticipated consequences. However, it is not specifically prohibited if (a) it is an accepted practice within that setting or community, (b) it is clinically appropriate and predicted not to compromise the therapeutic work, and (c) it does not disadvantage or exploit the client in any way.

We don't mean to gloss over or diminish the additional challenges of such an arrangement, nor do we mean to encourage bartering as an option. After all, there are all kinds of difficulties determining equivalent value in the exchange of services. There is also a difference in the kind of work or services that might be performed. Consider the difference, for example, between a counselor who negotiates with a client to perform 2 hours of community service or charitable work in exchange for a single session versus a client who does 2 hours of yard work at the counselor's home in exchange for a single session.

It helps to have a written record of what has been negotiated, with clear expectations of what has been agreed to and the terms of the contract. It is also advisable to minimize as much as possible any ways that the agreement could sabotage the work within the relationship. For instance, imagine a scenario in which the client, who works as a mechanic but has no reliable means to pay for counseling, agrees to do some work on the counselor's car. They work out an arrangement that fairly compensates both of them for their time, but what if the counselor is not satisfied with the results and continues to have difficulties with the vehicle after it has supposedly been repaired? Obviously, bartering presents additional complexities even if it may very well be the best arrangement within a specific cultural context. It is for this reason that this option should only be used in the most appropriate and cautious way.

A somewhat similar situation confronts the counselor when a client offers a gift. There is often a difference between what people say is the right thing to do and what they actually do in the real world. Approximately 90% of ACA members say it is wrong to accept a gift worth more than $25 from a client for any reason (Neukrug & Milliken, 2011), yet we'd be willing to go out on a limb and say that many more than 10% have accepted more valuable gifts for a host of reasons that have little to do with personal gain. A client brings a nice bottle of wine, or a painting that she created, or a couple of favorite books, all to show appreciation for a relationship that is about to end. We wonder how many counselors would really cross their arms and say they aren't able to accept the kind gesture.

A client may offer a gift to a counselor for a number of reasons, each having a special meaning. The underlying meaning and message that accompanies the offering must be assessed, not just the financial value. Consider, for example, a client who brings in a package of homemade cookies to share in a session because, during the previous conversation, they talked about the importance of developing new interests or hobbies. Another client brings in a baby gift for the counselor who is due to give birth a few months hence. Other gift offerings might not seem as benign, communicating very different meanings in the relationship. Imagine, for example, being offered an expensive watch as an expression of gratitude or an extra "tip" of $50 after an especially productive session. Again, context is everything, not only with regard to the symbolic meaning of the gesture but also in the context of the client's culture and the relationship that has been established.

Each of these aspects of boundaries within counseling relationships presents a separate set of challenges to be considered, negotiated, and managed effectively. They all can have a significant impact on the work that is attempted, for better or for worse. Counselors must be willing to discuss these issues openly with clients, not just as they are initially formulated but throughout the course of treatment to make sure that things are working out as anticipated.

Level of Personal Engagement

How much of yourself do you reveal in your counseling relationships? The answer to this question depends on a number of factors, including your theoretical preferences, personality, type and context of counseling, kind of supervisory oversight, and especially the individual client and situation.

Attitudes toward self-disclosure within the profession have evolved over time, beginning with the early psychoanalytic directives related to being as carefully opaque and impersonal as possible to maximize transference effects. During the early days of the humanistic movement, the pendulum swung in the other direction, not only permitting counselors to share themselves but encouraging them to be as authentic, genuine, and transparent as possible. This trend was reinforced by cultural shifts that have taken place on talk shows and social media where celebrities and hosts now confess all kinds of things in the most graphic and detailed way possible. We have recently struck a balance between these extremes: Counselor revelations are now permitted, perhaps even advisable in certain situations, but only when they are specifically for the client's benefit and clearly not an exercise in self-indulgence. In fact, the vast majority of counselors, approaching 90% of those surveyed, agree that sharing of oneself in session is not only ethical but useful at times (Neukrug & Milliken, 2011).

In Chapter 4, we discussed the uses of self-disclosure as a relational skill, but it is also an issue directly related to boundaries in the relationship. Ultimately, the true test of its appropriateness is related to addressing a few questions:

- Am I sharing this to meet my own needs or those of my client?
- Is there another way of getting this point across without putting the focus on me?
- How can I relate this example in such a way that it is most relevant and useful for the client?
- What are ways that I can encourage the client to apply what I'm sharing to his or her own life and situation?

With some clients, we would carefully restrict any personal sharing because it would not appear to be helpful or appropriate, and in some cases it could even potentially be harmful (to the counselor as well as to the client!). Certain clients who present so-called borderline features or other serious personality disorders might dig for personal details about their counselor to gain leverage and power that could be used manipulatively in the future. Other clients just don't particularly care to hear anything about the counselor other than what is on the agenda. You can see them looking at you with a cocked head and puzzled expression that seems to be saying,

"Why exactly are you telling me this now, and why do you think I care to know this about you?"

Let's Talk About Touching

Among all the relational boundaries in counseling, the subject of physical contact is most often mentioned when discussing the slippery slope into inappropriate sexual contact. "I remember one time," a counselor shared with us, "when I was saying good-bye to a client as our sessions were about to end. She was a very attractive woman," the man says with a wistful smile, "and I knew she also liked me a lot, so there was definitely a spark there." Even knowing that, when the woman asked for a hug to say good-bye, he could hardly resist. "There was a warning bell going off in my head, but if I'm honest, I have to admit that it felt really good to be within her embrace. But when I started to pull away, I could feel her hold on tighter, and then I knew I was in trouble."

This example shows the potential dangers of physical touch in a case when the warning signs were there all along. Realistically, we have each hugged literally thousands of clients, students, and supervisees without a single problem of the gesture being misconstrued. Nevertheless, there are some distinct cautions and potential difficulties if a well-intended action is misinterpreted, or worse yet, leads down that slippery slope.

Touch is one of the most important forms of human contact, perhaps the most powerful of all. It triggers all kinds of neurophysiological reactions that can reduce stress and offer comfort and support, depending on who is doing the touching and in what circumstances. In the context of counseling, all kinds of different forms of touch are possible, from a formal handshake or reassuring squeeze of a shoulder to a group session in which all members come together in a collective hug. Zur (2009) reviewed no less than 17 different kinds of touch that might be used in counseling, from the most traditional form of interaction to body therapies in which physical contact is the main form of intervention. There are "conversational markers" that might involve lightly touching a client's arm to emphasize a point. There are "consolatory" forms of touch that communicate support and caring. There are incidental types of touch, helping a client up out of a chair or touching him or her as the session ends. There are the deeper forms of physical contact, which seem to get the most attention in these discussions, such as holding and rocking a client for comfort or using body therapy techniques or deep massage to deal with internalized trauma or stress. And there is a tradition within our profession in which bioenergetics as well as Reichian and body practitioners routinely use physical touch as the cornerstone of their treatments.

Let's be absolutely clear about one thing: Touch can offer support, reassurance, and comfort, but it can also easily be misinterpreted in ways that are not intended. Many kinds of contextual features are involved in determining whether the choice to touch is indicated or not; these include age differences, feelings of sexual attraction, cultural factors, and simply whether or not the client responds appropriately to the way the gesture was intended.

"I simply would never hug a female client who is close to my own age, or a female adolescent client, because of the way it might be misunderstood," declared one male counselor. This as an inviolate rule that he says he would never break. Indeed, one's age, culture, background, gender, sexual orientation, and sexual feelings or romantic fantasies might very well come into play, combined with how these features might interact with those of a particular client. We do know when it feels safe and when it doesn't to reach out to a client in a physical way—and when we aren't sure, it's best to be cautious and conservative.

Cultural context certainly comes into play as well. Western culture in general, and American culture in particular, is somewhat inhibitive and restrictive regarding certain kinds of touch, but this is not the case in other cultural groups. In other parts of the world, people of the same gender routinely walk while holding hands or with their arms around each other without fear of sparking homophobic reactions.

Calmes, Piazza, and Laux (2013) considered the primary ethical principles that govern our ethics code and how they relate to touch. First and foremost, the decision to touch a client should do no harm and be grounded in a clear rationale for the client's best interests. Often, a counselor may offer a hug or a touch as much to alleviate his or her own discomfort or feelings of helplessness as because that is what would be most helpful to the client.

Bemak and Chung (2015) made the point that physical touch, self-disclosure, or any of the other boundary issues we have mentioned are embedded in a particular cultural context that may not apply to clients who come from non-Western backgrounds. In Asian, African, Latino, and indigenous cultures, multiple relationships and flexible boundaries within healing encounters are the norm rather than the exception. Especially when counselors take on advocacy roles on behalf of clients from marginalized groups, the roles that are adopted remain multifaceted. Self-disclosure is not only permitted in helping relationships but absolutely essential. Likewise, it would be incredibly offensive and disrespectful not to accept a gift or a hug offered by a client from many cultural groups. At times, we might function as an adviser, friend, mentor, healer, consultant, spiritual figure, teacher, doctor, or advocate, each requiring a different role that suggests not so much boundaries as expected responsibilities to fill.

Decision Making and Negotiations Related to Boundary Issues

When experienced counselors were asked how they handle difficult boundary issues in their relationships, it was clear that they didn't see themselves as rigidly rule bound but as guided by certain principles that emphasize client welfare (Frankel, Holland, & Currier, 2012). Most practitioners view everything as contextualized and individualized to each client, depending on what the client needs most to make the best progress in sessions. Regardless of their theoretical orientation, participants in the study shared similar beliefs about boundaries: They are important features of counseling but are not necessarily applied in the same ways to each case and situation. One counselor mentioned an example of differentiated responses that depend on the particular relationship: "So, when a bereaved mother reaches out for a hug at the end of a supportive session, that does not send shivers up my spine" (Frankel et al., 2012, p. 106). However, with a different client, this counselor would respond in quite a different way to such an overture. Just as a decision made to stretch boundaries has consequences, both positive and deleterious, so too does the choice not to adjust them according to what might be best for this particular client.

Several decision-making models have been constructed to help counselors make informed, ethical, and appropriate choices related to these relationship challenges (Calmes et al., 2013; Herlihy & Corey, 2015; Moleski & Kiselica, 2005; Younggren & Gottlieb, 2004; Zur, 2007). They all urge practitioners to consider a series of questions when sorting out how to respond to critical incidents related to multiple relationship issues.

1. First of all, what are the current laws, licensing mandates, and legal regulations related to the particular issue? There is clear guidance, for instance, related to any sexual contact whatsoever but much less guidance regarding multiple relationships in particular settings (military, prisons, universities, etc.).

2. Is this boundary crossing avoidable, desirable, or absolutely necessary? Some cultural groups may have different expectations and norms. Is the negotiated relationship consistent with professional standards of care in this context?

3. What is the relationship with the specific client like in terms of its intensity, frequency, quality, and particular norms and structure? Not all relationships are created equal or, in some cases, are even similar to one another because of the history, personality interactions, and level of intimacy.

4. What are the likely consequences of crossing a traditional relational boundary in terms of benefits versus risks? There almost always are some risks associated with departure from any consensual standard, and a decision must be made as to whether the potential rewards are worth any possible harm that could occur.

5. Who can I consult with to help me sort out the complexity of the issues raised and choose the best possible action? This is helpful when there is time (and there sometimes is not) to talk to a supervisor or trusted peer or to review literature about a relational decision.

6. Has accurate informed consent been provided to the client related to the risks and benefits of the choices being made? As with any other significant clinical decision, the rationale for the choices should be carefully documented.

7. What is the ultimate effect that has resulted from the choice to enter into a more flexible relationship with a client? As with every other aspect of counseling, the best predictor of a positive outcome is receiving continuous, accurate, and reliable information from the client, as well as objective observations, to determine whether the particular course of action is indeed constructive and helpful.

8. If it is determined that the relational complexities or flexibility is in any way compromising progress, what can be done to rectify the problems and right the ship, so to speak?

This last question is especially important because, realistically, miscalculations and mistakes are sometimes made regarding what we believe might work best in certain situations. We find out only after some new policy or structure has been implemented that progress is slowed or impaired in some way. As one example, a counselor was leading a relatively small counseling group (only six members) when one of the clients brought in donuts for the group. This seemed to be a lovely gesture that was greatly appreciated by everyone, including the counselor, given that the session occurred late in the afternoon. During the next meeting, however, several members brought in a whole smorgasbord of gastronomical treats. What had begun as a kindly action to build greater cohesion eventually interfered with the work being done because the tone of the group changed to much more of a social encounter. The counselor was forced to prohibit this action in the future so the group could focus on the business at hand.

All relationships have boundaries. Some have clearly demarcated rules, rituals, and norms, and others are far more flexible and contextual, depending on setting, mood, and circumstances. It is our job to negotiate and manage some degree of structure in our relationships with clients to maximize progress and protect and safeguard client welfare. As we discuss in the next chapter, it is important to arrange sessions in such a way that counselors also feel comfortable and protected.

Part 3
Relationships in the Counselor's Life

Chapter 10
Processing Disappointments and Failures

Whether some counselors are willing to admit it or not, it is perfectly normal for those in our profession, even experienced experts, to routinely feel a certain amount of doubt, confusion, insecurity, incompetence, and, at times, even failure (Kottler & Blau, 1989; O'Shea & O'Leary, 2009; Theriault & Gazzola, 2005). One reason is the incredible complexity, uncertainty, and emotional volatility that accompanies our work (McMahon, 2010), but other factors come into play, such as our own unrealistic expectations and misguided beliefs that we really do know what we are doing most of the time (Kottler & Carlson, 2002, 2015).

The reality is that sometimes we are less than certain about the course a case has taken and whether our choices were truly the best options. We have felt a certain amount of doubt and uncertainty throughout our careers, with varying degrees of safety at times to openly disclose these feelings publicly. The more we have learned and experienced, the less certain we sometimes are about what might really be going on. How is it possible to truly understand anyone else when we barely understand ourselves most of the time?

We often leave sessions flooded with questions about all the things we could have said—or perhaps should have done—much differently. "Should I have pressed so hard after his confession or perhaps backed off to provide more space?" "What did it really mean when he said he'd think about my suggestion?" "I couldn't tell whether he was agreeing with me or not when I mentioned his prior problems with authority figures." "What was that all about when he said he didn't remember what we talked about last time?" There are a dozen or more similar questions circling around and around inside our heads, with few definitive answers.

We have learned to embrace this confusion and remind ourselves that it is the client who is the expert on his or her own experience even if so much camouflage, distortion, and defensiveness is clouding the picture. Our relationship is very much like two uncertain explorers investigating relatively unknown territory; sometimes there will wrong turns, and one or both of us may feel lost.

How Do You Know When a Relationship Is Failing?

A client calls to cancel an appointment and says she will reschedule at a later time. What are we to make of that?

Clients decide not to return for all kinds of reasons, certainly the most obvious of which is that they aren't satisfied with how things have been going, but there are other possible explanations as well, such as the client just wants a break or is so happy with the progress that she doesn't feel the need to return. As we've mentioned previously, sometimes we can't trust what clients tell us because they don't want to hurt our feelings, or perhaps they aren't even sure themselves why they are doing what they're doing (or not doing).

There isn't much agreement in the literature about what constitutes a failure in counseling. Perhaps we could agree that if the client becomes significantly worse, that might clearly qualify, but even that becomes complicated considering that sometimes people do become worse before they get better. They are disoriented and experimenting with new behaviors that are not yet comfortable. They are sometimes reeling from new insights that are both disturbing and unfamiliar.

When Kottler and Carlson (2002) asked prominent theoreticians and practitioners in the field to supply examples of their worst counseling efforts, one of the interesting findings was how much they disagreed on what qualifies as a failure. Arnold Lazarus and Violet Oaklander, for example, defined failure as occurring when counselors follow their own agenda instead of listening to what their clients want and need. Michele Weiner-Davis and Jon Carlson were not troubled by making mistakes in their work but instead felt failure occurred only when you make the *same* mistakes over and over again. John Norcross, Peggy Papp, and Dick Stuart had a slightly different take, as they found failure most likely to occur when counselors are inflexible and unwilling to make needed adjustments.

Some contributors, such as Art Freeman, believed that negative outcomes are most likely to occur when counselors don't know exactly where they're going, yet Bill Glasser and Arnold Lazarus believed quite the opposite, that those are the times we are most often going to get into trouble through our own arrogance. Theorists such as Sam Gladding, Michael Hoyt, and Peggy Papp describe failure as an internal feeling of ineptitude, whereas Sue Johnson and others mentioned our familiar refrain about a ruptured relationship. Other definitions of failure were suggested as representing a loss of self-control (Pat Love, John Norcross), holding invalid assumptions (Francine Shapiro, Frank Pittman), or the simple description we mentioned earlier—negative outcomes for the client, regardless of what we do and how we do it.

Another reason it is challenging to define a failure is that some practitioners base the judgment on their own assessment, and others leave it in the hands of their clients to decide. Is counseling a success if the client insists that it was helpful even though you (and others) don't observe any noticeable changes? Is the relationship damaged because the client is noncompliant, or could this represent a streak of assertiveness and independence? Is failure more about the counselor's own feelings of ineptitude or the client's self-report about perceived progress? When the client doesn't return for sessions, is that because the relationship failed—or ultimately succeeded?

Nationally, roughly half of all scheduled client sessions end up as "no-shows" (DeFife, Conklin, Smith, & Poole, 2010). Perhaps not so surprising, community mental health agencies tend to have even higher rates of missed sessions than counselors in private practice. Given how relatively common these occurrences are, we are often left to make up our own reasons for what may be perceived as a lack of commitment on the part of some clients. One counselor at a community agency is expected to log 25 sessions each week but, given the rate of no-shows, has to schedule almost twice that number just to hit the desired target. Although he works with mostly indigent people, he has noticed that those most likely to take their sessions seriously and never miss an appointment are clients with whom he enjoys the closest, most trusting relationships.

Who Are the Difficult Clients Most Likely to Fail?

We may not all agree on the definition of a failure, but we can certainly reach consensus on those clients who have the worst prognoses. There is indeed a lot of discussion and literature about clients who, counselors report, are the most trouble and the least likely to improve. Intractable, long-standing personality disorders are often at the top of the list, along with chronic addictions, eating disorders, and psychotic disorders—in fact, almost any problem with "chronic" as a descriptor.

The extent to which practitioners might disagree about who are their most challenging cases is also interesting. Some counselors love working with belligerent adolescents, and others prefer working with heroin addicts, borderline personality disorders, or marital infidelity cases. Depending on our expertise and interests and our own life experiences, we may enjoy specializing in areas where most others fear to tread, even with the increased risk of failure, or at least rather modest improvement.

So-called difficult clients, or those with predicted poor outcomes, are often in the eye of the beholder. "I love the drama of working in the addiction field," one counselor explained. "I realize that the likelihood that my clients will relapse is quite high. They try to game me all the time. Some of them even show up to sessions high, even though that is specifically against the rules. They are just so wounded, so messed up, that everyone has given up hope. Except me. I guess I just love these lost causes and enjoy the challenge of working with people that nobody else will touch."

Like most other things in life, relative success or failure is judged primarily based on what is expected. If you believe that you are going to cure people of their troubles and do so in just a few sessions, there are going to be a fair number of disappointments. If, on the other hand, your clinical goals are more modest with some people, hoping just to get them on an even footing, then success is measured differently. This is especially true when working with clients who struggle with financial hardships and find it difficult just to manage basic daily tasks such as transportation, work, school, and child care. It is not so much that they may be resisting treatment as that they are unable to take care of practical daily tasks that we might take for granted.

How Failures Are Interpreted

It has been estimated that about one third of counseling failures are due either to poor motivation or to negative reactions to a somewhat tenuous and unsatisfactory relationship (DeFife et al., 2010). This can be the result of being involuntarily referred or blackmailed into attending sessions, or simply holding pessimistic attitudes toward counseling. Even if this was an initial posture, it only becomes worse when the client doesn't feel heard or understood, or believes he or she is being treated unfairly. In one study of premature termination among clients with eating disorders, they felt their relationships were unsatisfactory when the counselor didn't appear to individualize or personalize their treatment, relying on some kind of standard operating procedure that didn't address their stated needs (Oyer, O'Halloran, & Christoe-Frazier, 2016).

So-called ruptures or failures in counseling relationships are not nearly as uncommon as we might expect, especially considering how infrequently they are labeled as such. One estimate is that about one third of clients in counseling are not happy with how things are going, but the really interesting part is that, much of the time, the counselors are oblivious to the dissatisfaction, so they have no opportunity to address the rupture (Safran et al., 2011).

One of the intriguing aspects of this subject is the differential ways that counselors talk to themselves and interpret their disappointing outcomes. Some are inclined to blame their clients as "resistant," "noncompliant," "oppositional," "defiant," or otherwise unco-operative. In other words, it is the client's fault that things aren't proceeding according to plan. That could very well be a reasonable explanation for clients who are less than motivated or committed to the counseling, but it also lets us off the hook. When we don't accept at least some responsibility for the less-than-stellar results, there is little opportunity to learn from that experience and make adjustments accordingly.

One other way of looking at what might appear to be failure was described by an infectious disease specialist who was one of the first responders to the Ebola outbreak in Africa. In his first 2 months on the scene, Kent Brantly (2015) had only one patient out of dozens who survived. Clearly, his success rate was about as miserable as one could imagine, with a 95% mortality rate. He admits that it was incredibly difficult to stand by helplessly as so many of his patients suffered and died, but here's the really inspirational part of his story: "But it didn't make me feel like a failure as a physician, because I had learned that there's a lot more to being a physician than curing illness. In fact, that isn't even the most important thing we do. The most important thing we do is to enter into the suffering of others. And in the midst of what was becoming the worst Ebola epidemic in history, we were showing compassion to people during the most desperate and trying times of their lives." Even though he was insulated in a protective Tyvek suit and not one but *two* pairs of gloves, "we were able to hold the hands of people as they died, to offer dignity in the face of humiliating circumstances, to treat with respect the dying and the dead. And in my opinion, that made those weeks, those difficult weeks of my career a success." Could anyone in our own field have said this more poignantly?

That's the thing about failure—it is as much a state of mind as it is circumstances.

How Failure Helps

Once we accept that some of our relationships are, at times, doomed to fail, we can use these opportunities to our advantage, especially if the goal is to become better at what we do. When things go well, we usually nod our heads at what was expected and then move on, but it is during times of disappointment, mistakes, lapses, or perceived failure that we are often forced to reflect on what happened and why. The reality is that we spend more time thinking about things when they go wrong then when they go right. We are forced to consider what we might have done differently and to take constructive steps to plan for that in the future.

Another take on this subject is that failure doesn't actually exist in the world, that failure is just another name for new information. A negative or unexpected outcome is simply data on what didn't work very well, or at least didn't work as originally planned. It provides us with valuable feedback on the impact of any action, whether the results were as predicted or not. If we are paying close enough attention to this input, we are often provided with opportunities to make course corrections. This is especially true within a solid relationship in which mistakes and wrong turns are forgiven. Mistakes can become our greatest teachers if we are open to honestly acknowledging them and allowing them to help us become more flexible.

Some types of mistakes and failures most often lead to ineffective relationships, and several are worth considering if the goal is to learn from them (Duncan et al., 2010; Kottler & Carlson, 2002; Norcross & Wampold, 2011):

1. *Functioning in a counselor-centric style.* By this, we mean that certain assumptions are not grounded in the client's experience but rather in the counselor's preferences. When counselors do what they like, what is familiar and comfortable, what they believe might be helpful without confirming such beliefs, there are often problems.

2. *Rigidity and dogmatism.* We are most inclined to get into trouble not when we do something stupid or ill advised but rather when we *keep* doing the same thing over and over even though it isn't working or much appreciated, such as using a technique we like but that is just not effective with this client.
3. *Premature confrontation.* It is not a good idea to push the pace faster than clients can keep up with, sometimes discouraging or frightening them because of our own impatience.
4. *Pacing.* Just as moving too quickly can lead to premature dropouts, so too can proceeding too slowly and deliberately. How often has a counselor faced a client's impatience with complaints of frustration? In spite of explaining that counseling sometimes takes time, there are instances when clients are not sufficiently reassured to wait for desired results. Of course, there are other horror stories of clients who have been in counseling for years, if not decades, without much noticeable progress. It might be clear that there is a close (dependent?) relationship but one that may not be all that therapeutic.
5. *Countertransference.* This is a biggie. More often than not, a relationship breach occurs when personal feelings get in the way. Our projections, fantasies, feelings, and reactions toward particular clients often act as major obstacles to some semblance of mutual cooperation.
6. *Limitations of approach.* As much as we might value our favored counseling approach, any and every option has some limitations. No single model of counseling is appropriate for everyone and every situation. There are times when we must abandon what is most comfortable and familiar and experiment with alternatives that could produce very different results.
7. *Repeating the same mistakes over and over.* This occurs, first of all, when counselors fail to recognize and acknowledge their lapses and errors in the first place, but it is also common when they just become too attached to their favorite strategies in spite of recognizing that they aren't working.

Counselor: I think one reason you are having such difficulty is because you keep pushing him before he is ready.
Client: I'm not sure that's really . . .
Counselor: I notice even now that you are becoming argumentative, just like what occurs with him.
Client: Actually, I'm just trying to explain to you that . . .
Counselor: It's that type of explaining that often gets you in trouble.

In this extreme example, it's pretty clear that this client will not be returning.

Occasionally, we might attempt some intervention, perhaps a relatively benign interpretation or reflection, that the client doesn't respond to or perhaps just waves off. So then we try again, but this time more forcefully, or with a still deeper reflection, which puts the client off again. This is the same type of error in judgment that solution-focused counseling attempts to counteract by helping people to realize what they are doing that isn't working, to stop doing that, and to try something else. However, it is sometimes difficult to get counselors, like any other mortal beings, to cease behavior they are comfortable with, even when it is singularly ineffective.

Sometimes We Are Just Wrong

Counselor: I notice that you seem closed off right now, as if you are withdrawing from our connection because you feel threatened. I know that is a theme you've mentioned before in some of your relationships.

Client: [Looks quizzically] I'm not sure what you mean.

Counselor: Well, stop for a moment and look at yourself right now. Your arms are folded tightly across your chest, your hands hidden underneath. It's as if you are saying that you don't agree at all with what we've been talking about.

Client: Really? *That's* your conclusion about how you see me?

Counselor: Well, what else would you think your nonverbal behavior is saying right now?

Client: [Smiles sadly and shakes his head] I gotta tell you that right now I feel so judged by you and so misunderstood that I really wonder whether it is worth it for us to even continue with these sessions.

Counselor: All because I confronted you with the signs of your withdrawal? That seems awfully harsh.

Client: What would you say if you knew the reason my arms are crossed is not because I disagree with anything, or even feel the least bit, as you say, "closed off," but because of something entirely different.

Counselor: I don't know what you mean.

Client: I told you I have a chronic health condition, Reynaud's disease. I have poor circulation in my hands and feet, and they often feel cold. I often try to keep my hands warm by folding my arms like this so they are tucked in my armpits.

I'm surprised you never noticed. I'm also surprised how you could just make assumptions about me based on your own, I don't know, your own arrogance. It definitely makes me wonder about whether I can really trust you.

Sometimes we really do make interpretations or hold certain assumptions that are just not accurate. However, *that* really isn't the problem. Rather, the more significant difficulty is the unwillingness or inability to recognize when we are wrong, thus preventing the opportunity to do damage control.

Working Through Relationship Impasses

The first step, of course, is recognizing that there *is* a problem. This isn't quite as obvious as it may seem, considering how often counselors blithely continue with behavior that their clients don't find very helpful. The place to begin is to consider a rather objective assessment of signs that counseling may not be working as expected or hoped for. There could be all kinds of reasons for this, some of them lodged in the client, some in the counselor, and some in an interactive effect within the relationship.

Sometimes the problem is defined in a way that it can't be resolved, and until such a time as it is reframed, most efforts will prove futile. The client may be enjoying "secondary gains" as a result of remaining stuck: As long as the impasse continues, the client has a ready excuse for maintaining the status quo instead of investing the hard work needed to make changes. Feeling stuck has other advantages as well. The client can blame external factors outside of his or her control: "I've just had some bad breaks." "It's not my fault the economy turned." "Maybe if you pushed me a little harder in the first place we wouldn't even be having this conversation."

It often helps to do a systematic review (often with a colleague or supervisor) of what has been most and least helpful so far. Instead of focusing on what the client isn't doing, or how he or she isn't responding, what's the good news? What has been effective thus far and managed to get through to the client? What strategies, interventions, or responses have produced the most favorable results?

During this assessment process, it also helps to consider outside and external influences that may be compromising, or even sabotaging, progress. Who has a vested interest in making sure that counseling does not succeed? Who might be most threatened by the changes that are being made? What is missing in terms of a constructive support system in the client's life that can reinforce the progress that has been accomplished?

Our own growth edge from such challenging experiences with difficult or failing clients is often the result of courageous self-scrutiny to consider what in *you* might be getting in the way of being more effective. This includes far more than countertransference reactions and encompasses any personal limitations, weaknesses, or things that you may have overlooked. In other words, what can you learn from this case that will help you grow?

Failures in Supervisory Relationships

One of the ways that we attempt to deal with disappointments and professional challenges is by seeking consultations with peers and supervisors. Unfortunately, some of the problematic relationships in a counselor's life are not necessarily with clients but with colleagues. It is a strange phenomenon indeed that members of our profession can sometimes prove to be so annoying, troublesome, and even toxic in our daily lives. Although we might expect a high degree of compassion, support, and empathy from colleagues in a profession devoted to caring, the number of loose cannons who leave swaths of destruction in their path never ceases to amaze us. It is for this reason that our relationships in our role associated with supervision is so critically important.

For counselors who are actively engaged in supervision and mentoring others, certain feelings of ineptitude are sometimes a way of life. Ladany (2014) listed some of the common ways supervisors sabotage or undermine their relationships with those they are helping, most often because our training focused more on what *not* to do rather than on what might be most effective. In the tradition of Haley's (1969) or Schwartz and Flowers's (2010) essays on how to guarantee you will fail as a therapist, Ladany (2014) humorously and incisively described the clearest pathways to disaster, beginning with counterproductive attitudes that denigrate the value of the supervisory relationship in the first place. When supervisors mistakenly and arrogantly believe that it is only their words of wisdom, expert advice, and instructive lessons that make all the difference, minimizing the importance of empathic resonance and support, their supervisees may feel even more insecure and less than appreciative. This relates to a second common error: supervisors who think that the best way to teach counselors how to diagnose rampant narcissism is by personal examples of self-aggrandizement.

They chronically and persistently tell story after story about how wonderful and brilliant they are; how unappreciated they might be; and how, if only the supervisee would walk carefully in the counselor's footsteps, the supervisee might someday turn out to be almost as accomplished.

Just as multicultural incompetence is evident in counseling relationships, so too do supervisors sometimes overgeneralize or fail to adapt their style and relational patterns to better match the needs of those they are helping. Most commonly, power imbalances become problematic, blind biases and microaggressions become inadvertently evident, and supervisors are awkward or insensitive in the ways they acknowledge and address cultural identities and feelings of marginalization based on age, race, gender, ethnicity, or sexual orientation.

One additional way supervisory relationships are compromised relates to how evaluation takes place. There is often a fairly obvious and uncomfortable dual (or multiple) relationship in supervision because of the different roles the supervisor is assigned: both to support learning and growth and to monitor and evaluate progress. How are counselors supposed to honestly and openly confide their areas of greatest weakness and confusion when their ongoing competence is assessed during these meetings? The evaluative functions are among the most important functions that supervision serves, especially when supervision provides constructive, supportive feedback that can immediately be incorporated into cases. It is definitely counterproductive when unreliable and inappropriate instruments are used during this process (Bernard & Goodyear, 2014).

Another consequence of treating supervisees as "objects" that are evaluated to determine whether they are worthy, and "good enough" to remain in the guild is that inequalities in power are emphasized over collaboration. Constantly feeling critically judged often results in feelings of shame and complete deference in the relationship. We can all recall relationships from the past when it did not feel safe at all to disagree, much less argue, with someone in an authoritarian role. The experience was much less about learning than about surviving without excessive humiliation.

Clearly, a supervisor's job is complex and multifaceted, balancing the roles of advocate and gatekeeper. Very few of us were specifically prepared to handle both aspects of the job in such a way that we remain supportive and ultimately helpful. Ladany (2014) concluded his list with the provocative statement that because many supervisors are so poorly trained and marginally skilled in this complicated relational specialty, the whole enterprise is mostly a waste of time in 90% of cases. To prove his point, he asks counselors to consider their own experiences in supervision in the past, comparing lousy relationships to those that were exceptional. He has found that almost all of us have unfortunately encountered all three varieties, in large part because supervisors are rarely held accountable for their own level of expertise and competence.

Although we have offered an initial exploration into some of the personal relationships in a counselor's life, we continue this discussion in much greater depth in the two chapters that follow. Our goal is to emphasize the ways that our relational skills can serve us equally well, whether we are with clients or loved ones.

Chapter 11

Conflicts and Struggles in a Counselor's Personal Relationships

The counseling relationship, whether in individual or group milieus, establishes a unique bond between client and counselor. It is a relationship in which counselors are the authorities and experts; we control the pace and rhythm and hone in on the content we feel is most advantageous for the client. Counselors have the power, even when we claim that clients are the ones in charge.

A good counseling relationship allows for a level of authenticity and vulnerability that people might not otherwise explore. As a matter of fact, client resistance is often a function of unrehearsed behaviors, because the client has not been in a situation in which authenticity is valued or warranted. When people reveal too much of themselves in daily conversations, they are often viewed as needy or self-centered. Being completely transparent and forthcoming at all times would be exhausting as well as off-putting.

We fully expect clients to be cautious and withholding, even resistant at first, to protect and defend themselves against perceived attacks. Counselors normalize these fears and reluctance as perfectly legitimate responses: "Sometimes it is difficult to talk about issues that you find shameful and uncomfortable, so it makes sense that you would want to be cautious and take your time."

Client resistance also can be a function of the counselor's own behavior, especially when misunderstandings or miscommunications take place (Nelson & Neufeldt, 1996; Tannen & Daniels, 2010). When the timing or pace is off; when we push too far, too fast; or when we confront prematurely or interpret awkwardly, resistance is the appropriate reaction. That is one reason we offer such interventions tentatively, carefully, and matched to what we believe the client can truly take in and handle.

Coordination and collaboration within the relationship mean everything, because we are talking about an interpersonal process in which each participant leads and follows the other. Both the client and the counselor decide, independently as well as together, to what extent their conversations will be open and truly honest (Tannen & Daniels, 2010). The convergence of two independent people simultaneously deciding to be authentic is generally seen in the early stage of the working alliance. At this time, client and counselor are feeling each other out with respect to verbal and nonverbal communications. In the best-case scenario, this results in an authentic engagement that grows into an interpersonal dynamic. Hence, presence is both a conscious decision made by the counselor and the client and an unconscious or subconscious manifestation flowing from that decision. It is through this spontaneous and rather creative interchange that healing can occur.

Contagious Effects of the Client's Experience and Influence

When Sigmund Freud was first developing his therapeutic method, he became aware of being affected by his patients' tales of trauma and suffering in a very different way than when he was functioning in his capacity as a neurologist and a physician. It was for this reason that he first conceived of the idea that his work would take place with his patients lying on a couch, out of his visual field. This was suggested as much to focus his own attention and protect himself from vicarious pain as it was to isolate transference reactions. Freud readily acknowledged that therapeutic practitioners carried major burdens trying to manage their own strong personal reactions to their clients. This goes beyond countertransference reactions and projective distortions and also includes what has become recognized as vicarious or secondary trauma.

Charles Figley (1995) documented the kinds of chronic stress conditions and conflicts that are commonly associated with helping trauma survivors. Doctors, nurses, other health professionals, and counselors and therapists all may suffer from what he called "compassion fatigue," a much kinder and gentler term for the insidious exhaustion, anxiety, and despair that can accompany treating those who have suffered tragedies, disasters, devastation, terrorism, war, or abuse. The symptoms may parallel those of their clients and often result from prolonged exposure to the disturbing stories presented in sessions (American Counseling Association, 2011; Mailloux, 2014; Mathieu, 2012). Here are some of the common counselor complaints among those who are struggling:

- Depression and sadness
- Chronic anxiety and stress
- Hopelessness and despair
- Insomnia and restlessness
- Reduced job satisfaction
- Intrusive thoughts and disturbing memories
- Low energy and motivation
- Irritability and annoyances
- Cynicism and reduced empathy
- Withdrawal and isolation
- Apathy and loss of interest
- Somatization and physical complaints
- Impaired decisions
- Self-medication

Each of us has heard stories during our careers that will haunt us for the rest of our lives. Through listening to our clients' stories as active partners in their process, we have been exposed to horrors and brutality and senseless violence that may never quite leave us. We have our own flashbacks to images that we re-created in our own minds and hearts. We have felt the collateral damage that may result when exposed, even vicariously, to others' intense agony. We resonate with their sense of helplessness and vulnerability. We literally feel their pain, no matter how carefully we attempt to remain perfectly neutral and detached.

After I (Jeffrey) had spent several weeks doing trauma counseling in Nepal after the earthquakes, I returned somewhat of a wreck. "My heart still hurts," I wrote in my journal. "I can barely sleep. I've lost ten pounds and my clothes no longer fit. It feels like I can't get comfortable in my body."

I was well aware that I was suffering from my own primary and secondary trauma, but that knowledge didn't seem to offer much reassurance. "I know it is the result of working insane hours and seeing so many people compressed in a day. I know it is the result of seeing so much devastation and despair, so much sickness. I know that what we have done is just a drop in the bucket compared to the millions of people who still need help, need tents and food and water, need support. But after a life devoted to service, a life dedicated to teaching and helping others, I am certain that everything I have ever done, everything I have ever prepared for, was to be here now," I wrote in my journal.

There is a price to be paid for this sort of work for sure, one that affects our relationships with colleagues, clients, and loved ones, but whether working in disaster recovery or in the comfort of a well-appointed office, we are subjected to the most horrifying tales of fate, maltreatment, and self-harm. Our ability to recover and metabolize these "contagious" experiences from our clients is related to our own attention to self-care (Abendroth & Figley, 2011). Specifically, this means being clear and honest with ourselves about the extent to which we were affected by the work that we do. It means carefully monitoring our own stress levels, modulating the ways we commiserate and empathize with clients, but most important, it means taking care of ourselves in whatever ways are most helpful and supportive. Often, this involves applying in our own lives exactly the same kinds of practices we are advocating for in our clients' lives: engaging in regular physical exercise; maintaining a positive attitude; challenging dysfunctional thinking; engaging in stress reduction activities; increasing social support; or seeking counsel with friends, colleagues, supervisors, or our own counselor.

Compassion fatigue and vicarious trauma, along with other related conditions, such as countertransference and co-dependence, may compromise client care and lead to both internal and interpersonal conflicts with others, but just because you choose to be a counselor, that does not mean that you will respond to emotional and traumatic events from clients in maladaptive ways. Although counselors may be more vulnerable to collateral damage when working with clients who suffer from extreme circumstances and traumatic events, not all counselors fall victim to compassion fatigue, vicarious trauma, burnout, or relational conflicts. Măirean and Turliuc (2013) examined the relationship between personality and vicarious trauma among medical staff and found that workers who identified as less extroverted, less conscientious, and more neurotic were more likely to experience dysfunctional beliefs associated with vicarious trauma. As a professional counselor, you might look at this finding with some relief, as we tend to be the opposite of what was found in this study. Studies that identify trends in counselor personalities are quite limited, but we tend to be more conscientious than the general population and to adopt healthier lifestyles (Măirean & Turliuc, 2013; Williams, Helm, & Clemens, 2012). In addition, other protective factors many include workplace support, access to supervision, and a perception of our work as being empowering and noble (Slattery & Goodman, 2009).

Aside from personality characteristics, another reason that some counselors are more vulnerable to symptoms is due to their own personal histories. Counselors who experienced their own childhood trauma are at greater risk, although this can be moderated by adopting wellness attitudes (Williams et al., 2012). Even though it's the case that many of us found this profession in the first place as a way to work through our own unresolved issues, we might still have some work left to do in this realm.

Despite the inherent obstacles facing counselors who work with clients after traumatic events, these close connections with clients provide opportunities for us to grow and learn along with them. Unfortunately, the focus of research has concentrated on the hardships that come with the practice of counseling; very little attention has been directed toward the joys and gifts we receive as a result of this work (Kottler, 2017; Kottler & Carlson, 2006; Kottler & Marriner, 2009).

Internal Conflicts and Personal Relationships

Perhaps there is no greater impediment to the client–counselor relationship than the counselor's own personal difficulties. We are trained to overcome clients' resistance, but when our own stuff gets in the way, the development and maintenance of a meaningful counseling relationship is often compromised. It isn't surprising that, like most other mortals, when we have a bad day at the office there is often spillover once we arrive home. Likewise, when we face some personal difficulty, whether with respect to love, money, or health, it can affect our ability and performance on the job, especially if we do not practice sound habits of physical, emotional, and spiritual wellness.

The good news is that, as a professional group, counselors tend to be healthier than the general population, at least with regard to standard measures of wellness (Lawson & Myers, 2011). In one survey of practitioners, more than 80% reported a high degree of both job and life satisfaction, and they were more willing to seek counseling themselves during times of difficulty (Lawson, 2007).

Although we are taught to prioritize wellness in our clients and in ourselves, we may forget that feeling impaired is sometimes a normal response. That is one reason we hope counselors are taught early in their careers how to metabolize the painful and difficult conversations they may be forced to endure. It is indeed the stuff of nightmares.

One means by which counselors manage to maintain their equanimity is through the process of *bracketing*, a deliberate separation of self from others (Kocet & Herlihy, 2014; Lee & Prior, 2013). This means practicing deep listening without lapsing into indulgent or distracted thoughts and feelings. It means intentionally separating our own values and beliefs from those of the client, as well as keeping our own personal issues on the shelf, not allowing them to become triggered by what clients say or do.

Obviously, self-awareness is the key to being able to manage the effects our own interpersonal conflicts can have on clients. For example, when working in unhealthy or distressing relationships, identifying the expectations prior to engaging with the individual and considering what is likely to occur within the context of the interaction can be helpful in alleviating concerns when interpersonal conflicts lead to unmet expectations. In other words, being aware of our buttons and knowing they are likely to get pressed can help minimize the impact when they do in fact get pressed.

Addressing blind spots is more difficult, as these are often situations that catch us off guard. This is where bracketing is probably the most difficult, as described by one professional counselor:

> My hardest day at the office was when my father texted me with four words, "I believe it's time." My family clearly is not the best communicators and do not handle delivering bad news with much thought or care. Knowing my favorite uncle was ill, I assumed he was about to die or has died. Which one, I had no clue. I was in the middle of my workday with five more clients remaining on the schedule when I saw this text.
>
> At that moment, I had to make a choice: End the day or continue on to meet with clients in crisis. I assessed what I felt in the moment, what I needed, and the pros and cons for myself and my clients by cancelling the day. I also consulted with a longtime supervisor. Within a few minutes, I decided to push through.
>
> My charge for the remainder of the day was to be professional, focused, and in tune with my clients in front of me instead of my family life. I took each moment as it came and kept my mind from wandering. It was a difficult day. However, I was able to make it through and provide the level of care my clients deserved.
>
> For myself, I took time off the following days to attend services and be present with family. There are only so many days off I can be

away from my clients for their care. Also, financially, I can only take a limited number of days off from the practice. I had a hard choice to make. However, I made the best choice for everyone involved that fit for me.

In this commentary, you can see components of self-awareness, bracketing, self-care, and the need to attend to clients. In addition, the counselor is pressed with the reality of not just working with clients but also managing her practice. Cancelling clients is not so simple, as many of the clients we see may be dealing with their own crises. In addition, there is the reality that this is part of a counselor's livelihood—how a counselor earns a living. This counselor was able to bracket her emotional concerns and to attend to her clients in a way that was meaningful and productive.

Taking Better Care of Ourselves

One of the main challenges counselors may face is being prepared with self-care strategies to work through the difficulties that result from personal crises or relational challenges that can interfere with our professional effectiveness. Whether this involves peer consultation, initiating healthy lifestyle activities such as physical exercise or better sleep habits, or even seeking the services of another counselor for support, it is absolutely critical that we do for ourselves what we would do for others.

Most of the research on self-care has focused on the stressors for graduate students and beginning practitioners, whose problems may be different from those of far more experienced counselors. Table 11.1 identifies some of the most common strategies of counselor self-care (and their sources) and addresses both relational and personal components.

Supervision and Consultation

Certainly, the most direct and accessible option for self-care is the one that is usually already in place; that is, consulting with a supervisor or a colleague to talk through what is most bothersome. Whether this is part of regularly scheduled group or individual sessions or initiated informally, the idea is to reach out for relational support as much as for any specific feedback or advice.

"I noticed that I was avoiding our staff meetings whenever I could make up some excuse," one agency counselor admitted. "There's this one woman on our team who drives me crazy. She just talks incessantly and never listens to anyone else. Our supervisor never does or says

TABLE 11.1

Concepts and Strategies of Counselor Self-Care

Concept and Strategy	Authors
Supervision Consultation, formal supervision	Cummins, Massey, & Jones, 2007; Neswald-Potter, Blackburn, & Noel, 2013; Venart, Vassos, & Pitcher-Heft, 2007
Hardiness Extent to which we feel in control and committed to our work	Cummins et al., 2007; King, King, Fairbank, Keane, & Adams, 1998
Physical health Balance, breathing and movement, nutrition	Cummins et al., 2007; Davis, Balkin, & Juhnke, 2014; Venart et al., 2007
Self-assessment Awareness of personal and professional strengths and challenges	Cummins et al., 2007; Skovholt, 2001; Stebnicki, 2007; Venart et al., 2007
Personal and professional maintenance Managing workload, recreation, continued learning, personal counseling	Cummins et al., 2007; Neswald-Potter et al., 2013; Stebnicki, 2007; Venart et al., 2007
Self-concept Self-belief in competency and skill as a professional counselor	Neswald-Potter et al., 2013
Compassionate spirit An empathic understanding for those who may be wounded or vulnerable	Stebnicki, 2007
Interpersonal relationships Engagement with others, expressing emotions, celebrating victories	Neswald-Potter et al., 2013; Venart et al., 2007

anything, so we all just sit around and check out. It's been destroying morale, at least for me, and lately I've been thinking of leaving."

Rather than just bailing on the conflict, the counselor decided to talk to one of his trusted colleagues. Rather than just being a sympathetic listener, the counselor was surprised when his friend confronted him on his own behavior. "Look, she can be a little annoying," the friend agreed, but he refused to let things get into a bitch session and instead challenged the counselor to consider his own "pouting" as part of the ongoing problem. This led the counselor to stop the blaming and externalized complaints and to stop using the woman as an excuse. Instead, he focused on what he might do differently to restore his enthusiasm.

Seeking the help of a trusted friend or a more experienced colleague is the most obvious self-care strategy, but it is not relied on nearly as much as we might imagine. This is especially true for those in private practice who don't necessarily have the same accessibility to consultations as do counselors who work in public agencies or schools (Lawson, 2007). Every organization or practice has its own culture and relational configuration, and some can be rather isolated environments that don't provide many opportunities for unscheduled personal contact.

It is relatively commonplace to approach a supervisor or a colleague with the opening, "I'm having trouble with a client right now. Could we talk about what's going on?" It is much less comfortable to ask for help about a personal issue or a relational conflict that has been activated by our clinical work or one that has arisen in our personal life, yet the connections between our personal and professional domains are inextricably bound.

Personal and Professional Maintenance

Personal counseling is certainly a form of self-advocacy and also provides for personal and professional maintenance. There is considerable evidence that the vast majority of counselors and therapists not only are open to seeking personal counseling but have already done so at some time during their careers (Norcross & Guy, 2007). However, there are myriad reasons why counselors might resist seeking personal counseling. Some of the most frequent excuses are already familiar to us from what we hear from clients:

- "I just don't have the time right now. Maybe later, when I can catch my breath."
- "I just don't want to spend the money. I've got enough financial pressure in my life as it is."
- "It's kind of embarrassing for me to admit I can't take care of this myself. What kind of counselor does that really make me?"
- "I just don't think I could ever find a professional who is really good enough to help me."

Yes, being unwilling to seek precisely those services we are selling to others *does* make us hypocrites. For those who have pushed themselves to seek a professional's help when they most needed it, such choices are often reported as having been both seminal and transformative experiences in their lives and careers.

"Okay," one counselor reluctantly disclosed, "I resisted and resisted getting help for the longest time. I just didn't think I needed it. . . . No, that's a lie. I *knew* that I needed help, but I just kept telling myself I could handle things on my own. By the time I got into sessions, I had made such a mess of my life I was at first reluctant to even tell my counselor everything that was going on. It's weird to have to admit to a colleague that I just couldn't take care of myself and it was affecting my work with clients."

We admit that counselors can be quite a handful once we sit in the other chair. We play games. We stall and distract. We launch filibusters to hide. We constantly analyze what the counselor is doing and wonder what we would do differently. We often act as spectators to the performance rather than as participants in the proceedings. However, as we will readily attest, being a client in counseling, especially during times of difficulty, is likely the single most courageous and helpful professional development effort possible. We learn more about how and why counseling works when it is applied to real circumstances in our own lives.

A Counselor's Personal Traits

Just as our clients have certain characteristics that predispose them to be vulnerable to conflict or troubles, so too do counselors have more or less immunity to similar difficulties. Those among us who are stubborn, highly anxious, prone to negative attitudes, or have unresolved issues from the past are going to be at higher risk for impairment than those who exhibit hardiness and resilience in the face of crises (Cummins, Massey, & Jones, 2007).

Sometimes it isn't so much a personal trait as it is a habit that can lead to problems, such as counselors who don't control their schedules according to reasonable standards. For those in private practice, it is really hard to turn down a new referral, even when the person wants to come late at night or during a day off. Those who work in schools, agencies, or organizations with overwhelming caseloads may have limited options for setting their own time commitments. Nevertheless, there is probably no other circumstance that sucks the fun and satisfaction out of our work more than a series of intense and successive sessions, one after the other, without a break. This is what often compromises our compassionate spirit (Stebnicki, 2007).

Counselor traits such as exhibiting hardiness, possessing a spirit of compassion, or demonstrating the ability to bracket our own stressors when working with others are crucial if we are truly to flourish over time (Neswald-Potter, Blackburn, & Noel, 2013). One key appears to be related to an accurate and honest self-assessment of functioning on an ongoing basis: "How am I doing right now? How am I *really* doing?" This means being able to recognize when relational or other stressors are starting to take a toll and compromise our effectiveness (Cummins et al., 2007; Skovholt, 2001; Stebnicki, 2007; Venart, Vassos, & Pitcher-Heft, 2007). It also means having a clear idea of our personal strengths and weaknesses, which can act as both a buffer and an impediment to seeking help when we need it the most.

Although our relationships with clients sometimes act as an impetus, if not a trigger, for setting off internal fireworks that disrupt our own sense of personal efficacy and professional effectiveness, such intimate connections also can be the cure. As much as we might like to bracket or compartmentalize our professional lives from our personal domain, the two will always be connected in a multitude of ways, both potentially distracting and enhancing.

Our relationships with clients can feel depleting and lead to empathic emptiness or compassion fatigue, but they can also invigorate our sense of caring toward everyone in our lives. We only have to consider the focused concentration, the unwavering attention, and the extreme responsiveness we devote to our clients to wonder why we don't offer these same attributes to our loved ones who matter most. This is what our clients can, and do, teach us—the commitment to nurture and to prize *all* of our relationships, whether with our colleagues, friends, or family.

Chapter 12

A Way of Being
in All Relationships

It isn't just what we *do* but who we *are* as human beings that forms the essence of our relationships. The truth is that much of what we do as relationship specialists is still very much a mystery and not even close to being fully understood. After describing several of his most memorable and seminal cases, Yalom (2015) confessed that he would be deluding himself if he claimed to believe that some specific intervention or strategy made all the difference with these clients. "The most important thing I, or any other therapist, can do is offer an authentic healing relationship from which patients can draw whatever they need" (p. 209). What clients need can range tremendously from reassurance and support to direct confrontation and reality testing.

Ending Relationships

It is both ironic and peculiar that the ultimate goal of any counseling relationship is to work toward ending it as efficiently as possible. We suppose the same could be said for any helping relationship if the goal is to avoid unhealthy dependence on a mentor for continued progress to occur. Throughout the process, we continuously comment on the work clients are doing and the ultimate responsibility they have for their own growth and development.

The subject of ending counseling relationships spawns all kinds of interesting questions, such as when the process actually begins, who is primarily responsible for initiating the sequence of steps, and how it is best accomplished. Most of the time, it doesn't exactly look like an orderly and deliberate decision as it is happening in the moment. Only after the process has been completed can the participants look back and identify the hints and clear signs of an ending that was emerging (Rabu, Binder, & Haavind, 2013). The conversation about closure thus often starts with a series of small, incremental "feelers" that test the water, so to speak, to see whether the conditions are ripe for these discussions.

From this point further, the proposal is on the table, perhaps initiating an ongoing discussion to prepare for the final work to be completed. Of course, there may be considerable negotiation regarding when and how to end, and there may be a difference of opinion about goals left to reach. In their study on how clients and counselors end their relationships, Rabu et al. (2013) found that it was important to both parties that the other felt okay about the arrangement, that there was relative agreement about the timing. In any intimate relationship, personal or professional, nobody wants to feel like they are being pushed out the door without some say in the matter.

Although "termination" is the usual term used to describe the ending of a counseling relationship, we much prefer "closure" or "ending" to an image of turning off someone's life support system. In theory, this is supposed to be a planned and carefully scripted process. However, the relationship often ends when the client just doesn't return, which occurs roughly half the time (Reis & Brown, 2006). In addition, one third of those who show up for a first or second session never return, and 90% never complete 6 months of treatment (Vasquez, Bingham, & Barnett, 2008). These so-called premature terminations, or "dropouts," occur for all kinds of reasons:

- Financial problems
- Transportation difficulties
- Physical or health problems that compromise functioning
- Managed care restrictions on type or timing of sessions
- Change in job responsibilities or time availability
- Perceived mismatch with counselor's personality or values
- Lack of consensus on therapeutic goals
- Insufficient progress in sessions
- Boredom or inertia
- Pace of sessions is too fast or too slow
- Avoidance of clinically significant but painful material

- Unwillingness to go where counselor is leading
- Outside toxic influences (peer group, family, friends)
- Already met desired goals and are satisfied with results

We have both a moral and an ethical responsibility to make sure that counseling ends appropriately, with opportunities for clients to make sense of their experience and plan for ongoing future growth and continued progress. More often than not these days, the choice regarding when to end sessions is prescribed or mandated by insurance companies or agency policies. Ending poorly can undo much of what has already been done, leading to feelings of betrayal and abandonment as well as serious relapses (Vasquez et al., 2008). It is also not unusual for the end of counseling to trigger a reexperiencing of previous episodes of abandonment and loss (Joyce, Piper, Ogrodniczuk, & Klein, 2007). We don't want to overemphasize these potential losses, however, because the vast majority of clients, over two thirds, do want to talk about endings before they quit. Most clients talk about all their positive feelings associated with the tradition, including pride and a sense of accomplishment (Hardy & Woodhouse, 2008).

Ideally, the process of ending the relationship includes a series of important features, although realistically there is sometimes not enough time or opportunity to accomplish all of these goals as fully as we might prefer. Often, counseling comes to a close when the client simply announces that he or she isn't coming back because (fill in the blank): "I lost my job." "I'm moving to another part of town." "My dad won't let me come anymore." "My insurance just ran out." "I don't think I need it anymore." We might try to negotiate in these circumstances, adjust the fee, schedule sessions less frequently, or brainstorm other options, but often it is already a done deal. It is not uncommon for a client to cancel an appointment and never reschedule it, leaving us to wonder what happened and why. We prefer to think that the client already got what he or she hoped for and saw no need to return, even to share the good news, but that is often just optimistic thinking.

When a client leaves a message on voicemail saying something like "I need to cancel my next appointment, but I'll call you to reschedule," so many questions are left unanswered, mostly related to what happened and why. We second-guess ourselves and make up reasons to explain the abrupt departure, most of which are couched in optimistic terms.

In the best circumstances, ending is negotiated over a period of time in such a way that clients are not pressured into continuing if that is not what they really want to do. Sometimes counselors use their influence and power as leverage to push an agenda, both because it might be in the client's best interests and because *we* are the ones unwilling to let go. From the beginning of the relationship, we hope, counselors have discussed that it is best not to stop sessions abruptly, to give us sufficient notice (at least a few sessions) to bring things toward smooth closure.

All kinds of different metaphors have been introduced to clients as a way to think about the relationship coming to a close, perhaps the most common of which is that the journey together is coming to the end of the road (Rabu, Haavind, & Binder, 2013). Others frequently used include the image of cleaning up a mess or tying up loose ends, a fortification of resources and strengths, gifts that were received in the form of new insights, and being repositioned on more solid, stable ground. In each case, it appears to work best when the preferred metaphor has been co-created with shared language that represents both the client's and the counselor's experience.

Ending Relationships Smoothly

One theme of this book, and particularly this chapter, is that relationships in counseling reflect the participants' unique ways of being, not only during sessions but also as we each walk through life. When we do have the chance to systematically plan and implement a perfect, ideal ending to the relationship, the following objectives are part of the structure.

Explore the meaning of the loss and ending. The client may appear all joyful and excited about "graduation" from counseling, but this is also a time to acknowledge and talk about feelings associated with saying good-bye and moving on. Anyone (including the counselor) who denies that this is a bittersweet moment filled with ambivalence is likely in denial or lying.

Review the initial goals. Goals and priorities change over time, especially considering that what clients initially bring to the first session is not necessarily what they need help with the most. Nevertheless, it is useful to review the beginning point and to track the path that delivered the client to the present state of affairs: "You might remember when you first came to see me you said you wanted to be in a healthier relationship with your partner. Over time, you've come to realize that this goal just isn't possible without her consent and active participation." Of course, it is far better to ask the client for this summary.

Assess progress that has been made. There is sometimes a difference of opinion about what has been successfully achieved and what is left to do. There may also be some disagreement regarding whether this is the best time to end. A client may be ready to end sessions even though the counselor feels like there is still much left to do, or the counselor may be pushing the client out the door even though the client is showing considerable reluctance. Regardless of the reasons and circumstances, it is important to systematically determine what has been accomplished and to provide space for sharing mutual feedback. This is the time when clients might talk about things they liked, and those that they weren't that pleased with. It is also an opportunity for the counselor to provide final input and feedback framed in direct and hopeful language. This is, in a sense, a summary of the relationship.

Although this assessment process is an important part of closure, perhaps the most important aspect, it is nevertheless challenging for two reasons. First of all, how clients behave in sessions, or report how they are doing outside, may not necessarily reflect what is really happening. Second, it sometimes takes a while before the results become fully realized; there could be a delayed reaction.

Generalize results. Based on what was learned in sessions, and the issues that were addressed, the next area for exploration focuses on how clients can apply their new skills and ways of thinking to other areas of their lives.

One client, Alberto, talked a lot about his shame related to early sexual abuse, which he mostly had buried. "In my culture [Mexican] we just don't talk about things like this. [Laughs nervously] I'd never hear the end of it. My family would somehow blame me for what my uncle did, even though I don't think I was more than 6 years old at the time."

Alberto had done some fabulous work on himself in counseling, mostly focusing on shame attacking strategies and self-acceptance; yet even though the relationship was ending, he still had some lingering discomfort about other aspects of his past about which he felt some regret. In the second-to-last session, some time was devoted to talking about ways he could continue to challenge his thinking by utilizing strategies that had worked for him previously.

Acknowledge unfinished business. It's inevitable that there are going to be some lingering issues that can't possibly be covered during the limited time available. It is important to identify the work left to do, if for no other reason than to help clients plan for their ongoing growth and development. "Yes, we have accomplished so much in our time together. You have managed to renew a far more positive relationship with your father, as well as to extricate yourself from the usual conflicts that occur at home. But as we've discussed, this is only a temporary truce: at one point, likely in the near future, you are going to have to move out on your own. And that is going to present a whole new set of challenges, not so much related to functioning with greater independence, which you will be quite skilled at, but rather what this will mean for your relationship with your mother who so completely depends on you."

Develop a remediation plan for the future. In Alberto's case, he had also struggled with parenting issues related to his adult son, who was having his own troubles, and drove his father crazy. In addition, Alberto was in the throes of a major life transition as he approached age 50, wondering what he wanted to do with the rest of his life. These subjects were mentioned during sessions, but they were not seen as urgent enough to take priority over some other problems.

Plan for relapses. Most of all, clients fear that once the counseling ends they will backslide and revert to old dysfunctional patterns. Motivational interviewing (Miller & Rollnick, 2012; Moyers, 2014) constructs the kind of relationship in which systematic steps are included to help clients plan for inevitable slips and then recover effectively. This begins with identifying high-risk situations that might occur in the future, such as an upcoming invitation to a party in which there will be a lot of drugs and drinking. Next, the likely triggers are reviewed; in this case, the availability of drugs and alcohol everywhere with pressure from others to indulge. Coping skills are developed in counseling that can be rehearsed and applied to the anticipated challenge: self-talk, distraction, avoidance, and choosing other people with whom to socialize. Scenarios might be role-played in which the counselor pretends to offer the client a drink or a smoke, and the client practices declining. Finally, there is some attention paid to becoming resilient and adaptable if a mistake is made. The standard mantra to be repeated is, "Just because I made one mistake doesn't mean I can't recover quickly and get back on track."

Recruit an ongoing support system. Once counseling ends, whether in individual, group, or family modalities, so too does the weekly accountability. It helps a lot if clients are able to make the kinds of lifestyle changes that limit their exposure to the kinds of temptations that might lead to relapses. This means making wise decisions regarding where, how, and with whom to spend one's time.

Schedule follow-up sessions as needed. This is one of those tasks we are "supposed" to do but that frequently just doesn't work out as planned. We make promises to one another to stay in touch, but that rarely happens. We might think about one another, but ongoing contact is rare. With that said, if the goal really is to make changes last, then it is highly advisable to make occasional follow-up sessions a regular part of our operation, even if scheduled a month or a half-year later just to check in and continue being accountable.

Say good-bye in a meaningful way. This is a time to honor the relationship and all that has been accomplished, not just in terms of presenting issues but also to recognize the deep connection that has been forged. Some counselors are quite creative in structuring memorable rituals that have been customized for a given client.

Reflect on the experience. Once the client walks out the door for (maybe) the last time, we are left sitting in the empty office to think about our own feelings and reactions to the ending. We review all that happened, and all that *didn't* happen, and consider what we could have done differently. We reflect on the seminal events in the relationship, the breakthroughs, the mistakes and miscalculations, what worked best, and what didn't seem to work well at all. We settle on a few things we learned from the encounter, perhaps lessons that will better inform our practice in the future.

If we truly care about our clients, and it is not an act or disingenuous performance, then it is likely that we will also feel some degree of disappointment, loss, and even grief when a counseling relationship ends. We have spent hours immersed in the most intimate conversations about the most sacred aspects of a person's life. We have figuratively (and sometimes literally) held someone for weeks or months or even years on end. We have been privy to their most precious secrets, innermost thoughts, and deepest feelings. We have heard heart-wrenching stories that feature incredible suffering and resilience. We have laughed with them, sometimes cried with them, and when they leave to go out on their own, it is both a time of triumph and a time of sadness.

How often do you think about clients who have been gone for months, if not years? We still wonder how some of them are doing; others, we worry about in spite of efforts to let them go and move on. Some clients' stories will haunt us until the end of our days because they were so tragic or poignant. Some clients touched us with deep love (not the romantic kind), feelings that were reciprocated. Just because they moved on doesn't mean they still don't inhabit our thoughts and memories.

We live with uncertainty related to never really knowing the ends of the stories after clients leave. Sometimes we get follow-up reports, but far more often they just leave, say good-bye, *sayonara, au revoir, adios, ciao*. We may have our fantasies about the next chapters of their lives, but we never really know nearly enough about the lasting effects of our encounters with them. We just pretend that they lived happily ever after.

The Counselor's Experience of Ending

One premise of this book is that the counseling relationship is the single most important aspect that determines the best counseling outcomes for the client—but what about the counselor?

The struggle to let go and say good-bye to clients to whom we have become attached has been a long-standing issue from the inception of our profession (Goodyear, 1981). In fact, we can look back at the issue of counselors' feelings related to termination and see ties to Freudian ideas of countertransference—the idea that our feelings about clients are usually obstacles to our clients' well-being. This is, of course, antithetical to the idea that we have been discussing in this book—that the counseling relationship is based on mutuality and collaboration. It is normal to feel some loss after helping someone through difficult times or promoting a sense of growth and personal empowerment. When we are making a meaningful contribution to someone's life, of course we will feel both a sense of pride and accomplishment and loss when the relationship ends.

As sessions come to an end, there is a lot of uncertainty. Clients worry about whether their changes and progress will stick, and counselors spend a lot of time going forward wondering how they are doing. We continue to have concerns about their welfare, and we reflect on the relationship and what it meant to both of us.

Ending Our Relationship

The relationship that develops between authors and readers is both interesting and strange. We talk to one another; at times you may even argue points that might not fit with your experience. We imagine dialogues between us, conversations that continue beyond the discussion on the pages. Through the time we've spent together, we consider what happens next.

Do you just resell this book and move on to the next ones? Maybe stick it on your bookshelf somewhere, warehoused with so many others? What do you keep with you? What sticks in your mind? What ideas might you have integrated into your own way of being? When you put this book down and move on to the next best thing, our relationship, at least in this dimension, abruptly ends—although we suppose you can go back any time you want to and rekindle some favorite part of our dialogue together.

The greatest challenge with any helping relationship, whether in the context of counseling, teaching, parenting, coaching, or engagement through a book, is how to keep the momentum going after the regular contact ends. No matter how intimate, productive, and satisfying a relationship might feel with a counselor, supervisor, mentor, or author, what ultimate use is the time together if the effects and influence don't last?

We have been talking about the ways that counseling relationships eventually end, but as Solomon (2010) pointed out, there's been a lot of practice along the way, because every session has a beginning and an ending, a kind of "snapshot" of how the participants manage these transitions on a weekly basis. A pattern thus emerges that provides a unique way of understanding how each of the participants experience endings. How does it feel when the meeting ends and client and counselor go their own way?

As counselors, it is part of our job to continually separate, to let go and move on, at times surrendering to the process. We say goodbye to people all day long, every hour. We are constantly leaving and being left, and now we are about to leave one another as well. During this journey together as authors, we have forged a new and deeper friendship directed by the work to be completed. It is, after all, a reality of our lives (perhaps yours as well) that limited time is partitioned to those tasks that take priority. We have communicated with one another almost every week, not only about the job we are doing together but also talking about our own relationship and the way we function with one another. Now that abruptly ends, and in spite of promises we might make to stay in touch, we will likely revert to the previous pattern of seeing and saying hello to one another at annual conferences.

Just as likely, you will direct your attention to establishing relationships with new and different authors, realigning your loyalties, and perhaps what happened between us will become a distant memory. If there is indeed one idea, one theme, that we hope you hold onto as dearly as we treasure it ourselves, it is that counselors walk through life as relationship specialists. We are privileged to belong to a profession that heals others through the engagement of intimacy and trust, creating a space in which it feels safe to talk about anything without fear of judgment, and yet counseling is far more than just a job or a profession; it is truly a way of being, a way of treating everyone in our lives, whether clients, friends, family, colleagues, neighbors, or strangers, with the kind of dignity, respect, and caring that we have infused in our daily work.

References

Abendroth, M., & Figley, C. (2011). Vicarious trauma and the therapeutic relationship. In J. C. Norcross (Ed.), *Psychotherapy relationships that work* (pp. 111–125). New York, NY: Oxford University Press.

Aboraya, A. (2007). The reliability of psychiatric diagnoses: Point—Our psychiatric diagnoses are still unreliable. *Psychiatry (Edgmont), 4*(1), 22–25.

American Counseling Association. (2011). *Vicarious trauma: Fact sheet #9*. Alexandria, VA: Author.

American Counseling Association. (2014). *ACA code of ethics*. Alexandria, VA: Author.

American Psychiatric Association. (1952). *Diagnostic and statistical manual: Mental disorders*. Washington, DC: Author.

American Psychiatric Association. (2013). *Diagnostic and statistical manual of mental disorders* (5th ed.). Arlington, VA: Author.

Appel, M. (2008). Fictional narratives cultivate just-world beliefs. *Journal of Communication, 58*, 62–83.

Appel, M., & Richter, T. (2007). Persuasive effects of fictional narratives increase over time. *Media Psychology, 10*, 113–134.

Audet, C. T. (2011). Client perspectives of therapist self-disclosure: Violating boundaries or removing barriers? *Counselling Psychology Quarterly, 24*(2), 85–100.

Bachi, K. (2012). Equine-facilitated psychotherapy: The gap between practice and knowledge. *Society & Animals, 20*(4), 364–380. doi:10.1163/15685306-12341242

Balkin, R. S., & Juhnke, G. A. (2014). *Theory and practice of assessment in counseling.* Columbus, OH: Pearson.

Barnett, J. E. (2011). Psychotherapist self-disclosure: Ethical and clinical considerations. *Psychotherapy, 48*(4), 315–321.

Barnett, J. E. (2014). Sexual feelings and behaviors in the psychotherapy relationship: An ethics perspective. *Journal of Clinical Psychology, 70*(2), 170–181.

Bateson, G. (1972). *Steps to an ecology of mind.* New York, NY: Ballantine Books.

Baum, N. (2010). Shared traumatic reality in communal disasters: Toward a conceptualization. *Psychotherapy: Theory, Research, Practice, Training, 47*(2), 249–259. doi:10.1037/a0019784

Bemak, F., & Chung, C. Y. (2015). Cultural boundaries, cultural norms: Multicultural and social justice perspectives. In B. Herlihy & G. Corey (Eds.), *Boundary issues in counseling: Multiple roles and responsibilities* (3rd ed., pp. 84–92). Alexandria, VA: American Counseling Association.

Bernard, J., & Goodyear, R. (2014). *Fundamentals of clinical supervision* (5th ed.). Boston, MA: Pearson.

Binder, P., Holgersen, H., & Nielsen, G. H. (2009). Why did I change when I went to therapy? A qualitative analysis of former patients' conceptions of successful psychotherapy. *Counselling and Psychotherapy, 9*(4), 250–256.

Bloomgarden, A., & Mennuti, R. B. (Eds.). (2009). *Psychotherapist revealed: Therapists speak about self-disclosure in psychotherapy.* New York, NY: Routledge.

Bohart, A., & Tallman, K. (1999). *How clients make therapy work: The process of active self-healing.* Washington, DC: American Psychological Association.

Booker, C. (2004). *The seven basic plots: Why we tell stories.* London, UK: Continuum.

Bordin, E. S. (1979). The generalizability of the psychoanalytic concept of the working alliance. *Psychotherapy, 16,* 252–260.

Boudewyns, P. A., & Hyer, L. (1990). Physiological response to combat memories and preliminary treatment outcome in Vietnam veteran PTSD patients treated with direct therapeutic exposure. *Behavior Therapy, 21,* 63–87.

Bowlby, J. (1978). Attachment theory and its therapeutic implications. *Adolescent Psychiatry, 6,* 5–33.

Brantly, K. (2015, May 17). *Ebola doctor to grads: Enter the suffering of others.* National Public Radio. Retrieved from http://www.npr.org/2015/05/17/407447354/ebola-doctor-to-grads-enter-the-suffering-of-others

Burlingame, G., McClendon, D., & Alonso, J. (2011). Cohesion in group psychotherapy. In J. C. Norcross (Ed.), *Psychotherapy relationships that work* (2nd ed., pp. 110–131). New York, NY: Oxford University Press.

Burns, G. W. (2001). *101 healing stories: Using metaphors in therapy.* New York, NY: Wiley.

Burns, S. T. (2008). Utilizing fictional stories when counseling adults. *Journal of Creativity in Mental Health, 3*, 441–454.

Butler-Barnes, S. T., Estrada-Martinez, L., Colin, R. J., & Jones, B. D. (2015). School and peer influences on the academic outcomes of African American adolescents. *Journal of Adolescence, 44*, 168–181. doi:10.1016/j.adolescence.2015.07.007

Calhoun, L. G., & Tedeschi, R. G. (2013). *Posttraumatic growth in clinical practice.* New York, NY: Brunner Routledge.

Calmes, S. A., Piazza, N. J., & Laux, J. M. (2013). The use of touch in counseling: An ethical decision-making model. *Counseling and Values, 58*, 59–68. doi:10.1002/j.2161-007X.2013.00025.x

Campbell, J. (1988). *The power of myth.* New York, NY: Doubleday.

Carson, D. K., Becker, K. W., Vance, K. E., & Forth, N. L. (2003). The role of creativity in marriage and family therapy practice: A national online study. *Contemporary Family Therapy, 25*, 89–109.

Cashwell, C. S., Shcherbakova, J., & Cashwell, T. H. (2003). Effect of client and counselor ethnicity on preference for counselor disclosure. *Journal of Counseling & Development, 81*, 196–201.

Chandler, C. K. (2006). Animal assisted therapy in counseling. *Anthrozoos, 19*(3), 285–286.

Chandler, C. K., Portrie-Bethke, T. L., Barrio Minton, C. A., Fernando, D. M., & O'Callaghan, D. M. (2010). Matching animal-assisted therapy techniques and intentions with counseling guiding theories. *Journal of Mental Health Counseling, 32*, 354–374.

Chandler, N., Balkin, R. S., & Perepiczka, M. (2011). Perceived self-efficacy of licensed counselors to provide substance abuse counseling. *Journal of Addictions & Offender Counseling, 32*, 29–42.

Cloitre, M., Koenen, K. C., Cohen, L. R., & Han, H. (2002). Skills training in affective and interpersonal regulation followed by exposure: A phase-based treatment for PTSD related to childhood abuse. *Journal of Consulting and Clinical Psychology, 70*, 1067–1074. doi: 10.1037//0022-006X.70.5.1067

Cohen, J. A., Deblinger, E., Mannarino, A. P., & Steer, R. A. (2004). A multisite randomized controlled trial for children with sexual abuse-related PTSD symptoms. *Journal of the American Academy of Child & Adolescent Psychiatry, 43*, 393–402.

Cohen, S. (2004). Social relationships and health. *American Psychologist, 59,* 676–684.

Combs, A. W., Avila, D. L., & Purkey, W. W. (1971). *Helping relationships.* Boston, MA: Allyn and Bacon.

Conroy, P. (1986). *The prince of tides.* Boston, MA: Houghton Mifflin Harcourt.

Cooper, M. (2005). Therapists' experiences of relational depth: A qualitative interview study. *Counselling and Psychotherapy Research, 5*(2), 87–95.

Cooper, M. (2013). Experiencing relational depth in therapy: What we know so far. In R. Knox, D. Murphy, S. Wiggins, & M. Cooper (Eds.), *Relational depth: New perspectives and developments* (pp. 62–76). New York, NY: Palgrave Macmillan.

Coppock, T. E., Owen, J. J., Zagarskas, E., & Schmidt, M. (2010). The relationship between therapist and client hope with therapy outcomes. *Psychotherapy Research, 20*(6), 619–626. doi:10.1080/10503307.2010.497508

Corey, M. S., Corey, G., & Corey, C. (2016). *Groups: Process and practice* (10th ed.). Belmont, CA: Cengage Learning.

Courtois, C. A., & Ford, J. D. (2013). *Treatment of complex trauma: A sequenced, relationship-based approach.* New York, NY: Guilford Press.

Cozolino, L. (2006). *The neuroscience of psychotherapy.* New York, NY: W. W. Norton.

Cummins, P. N., Massey, L., & Jones, A. (2007). Keeping ourselves well: Strategies for promoting and maintaining counselor wellness. *Journal of Humanistic Counseling, Education and Development, 46,* 35–49.

Davidson, P. R., & Parker, K. C. H. (2001). Eye movement desensitization and reprocessing (EMDR): A meta-analysis. *Journal of Consulting and Clinical Psychology, 69*(2), 305–316. Retrieved from http://dx.doi.org/10.1037/0022-006X.69.2.305

Davis, R. J., Balkin, R. S., & Juhnke, G. A. (2014). Validation of the Juhnke-Balkin Life Balance Inventory. *Measurement and Evaluation in Counseling and Development, 47,* 181–198. doi: 10.1177/0748175614531796

de Shazer, S. (1985). *Keys to solutions in brief therapy.* New York, NY: W. W. Norton.

DeFife, J. A., Conklin, C. Z., Smith, J. M., & Poole, J. (2010). Psychotherapy appointment no-shows. Rates and reasons. *Psychotherapy, 47,* 413–417. doi: 10.1037/a0021168

DeFife, J. A., Hilsenroth, M. J., & Gold, J. R. (2008). Patient ratings of psychodynamic psychotherapy session activities and their relation to outcome. *Journal of Nervous and Mental Disease, 196*(7), 538–546.

Dewell, J. A., & Owen, J. (2015). Addressing mental health disparities with Asian American clients: Examining the generalizability of the common factors model. *Journal of Counseling & Development, 93*, 80–87. doi:10.1002/j.1556-6676.2015.00183.x

Diener, M. J., & Monroe, J. M. (2011). The relationship between adult attachment style and therapeutic alliance in individual psychotherapy: A meta-analytic review. *Psychotherapy, 48*, 237–248.

Dorris, M. (1987). *Yellow raft in blue water.* New York, NY: Henry Holt.

Drum, K. B., & Littleton, H. L. (2014). Therapeutic boundaries in telepsychology: Unique issues and best practice recommendations. *Professional Psychology: Research and Practice, 45*(5), 309–315.

Duarte, N. (2010). *Resonate: Present visual stories that transform audiences.* New York, NY: Wiley.

Duffey, T., & Haberstroh, S. (2013). Deepening empathy in men using a musical chronology and the emerging life song. *Journal of Counseling & Development, 91*, 442–450. doi:10.1002/j.1556-6676.2013.00116.x

Duffey, T., Haberstroh, S., & Trepal, H. (2009). A grounded theory of relational competencies and creativity in counseling: Beginning the dialogue. *Journal of Creativity in Mental Health, 4*, 89–112.

Duncan, B., & Miller, S. (2000). The client's theory of change: Consulting the client in the integrative process. *Journal of Psychotherapy Integration, 10*, 169–187.

Duncan, B. L. (2010). *On becoming a better therapist.* Washington, DC: American Psychological Association.

Duncan, B. L. (2014). The person of the therapist: One therapist's journey to relationship. In K. Schneider, J. F. Pierson, & J. F. T. Bugental (Eds.), *Handbook of humanistic psychology* (2nd ed., pp. 457–472). Thousand Oaks, CA: Sage.

Duncan, B. L., Miller, S. D., Wampold, B. E., & Hubble, M. A. (2010). *The heart and soul of change: Delivering what works in psychotherapy* (2nd ed.). Washington, DC: American Psychological Association.

Eamon, M. K., & Altshuler, S. J. (2004). Can we predict disruptive school behavior? *Children & Schools, 26*(1), 23–37.

Efran, J., & Fauber, R. (2015, March/April). Spitting in the client's soup: Don't overthink your interventions. *Psychotherapy Networker*, 31–37.

Elad-Strenger, J., & Littman-Ovadia, H. (2012). The contribution of the counselor–client working alliance to career exploration. *Journal of Career Assessment, 20*, 140–153. doi: 10.1177/1069072711420850

Elliott, R., Bohart, A. C., Watson, J. C., & Greenberg, L. S. (2011). Empathy. In J. C. Norcross (Ed.), *Psychotherapy relationships that work* (pp. 132–152). New York, NY: Oxford University Press.

Farber, B. A. (2006). *Self-disclosure in psychotherapy*. New York, NY: Guilford Press.

Figley, C. (Ed.). (1995). *Compassion fatigue: Coping with secondary traumatic stress disorder in those who treat the traumatized*. New York, NY: Routledge.

Fisher, J. (2014, May/June). Putting the pieces together: 25 years of learning trauma treatment. *Psychotherapy Networker, 38*(3). Retrieved from https://www.psychotherapynetworker.org/magazine/article/108/putting-the-pieces-together

Fitts, W. H. (1965). *The experiences of psychotherapy: What it's like for clients and therapists*. Princeton, NJ: Van Nostrand Reinhold.

Ford, J. D., & Russo, E. (2006). Trauma-focused, present-centered, emotional self-regulation approach to integrated treatment for posttraumatic stress and addiction: Trauma adaptive recovery group education and therapy (TARGET). *American Journal of Psychotherapy, 60*, 335–355.

Frank, J. D. (1971). Therapeutic factors in psychotherapy. *American Journal of Psychotherapy, 25*(3), 350–361.

Frankel, Z., Holland, J. M., & Currier, J. M. (2012). Encounters with boundary challenges: A preliminary model of experienced psychotherapists' working strategies. *Journal of Contemporary Psychotherapy, 42*, 101–112.

Frankl, V. E. (1984). *Man's search for meaning: An introduction to logotherapy*. New York, NY: Simon & Schuster.

Freud, A., & Burlingham, D. T. (1943). *War and children*. New York, NY: New York University Press.

Freud, S. (1933). New introductory lectures on psychoanalysis. In J. Strackey (Ed. & Trans). *The standard edition of the complete psychological works of Sigmund Freud* (Vol. 22, pp. 1–182). London: Vintage Press. (original work published 1916–1917).

Frey, J. (2003). *A million little pieces*. London, England: John Murray.

Gallo, C. (2014). *Talk like TED*. New York, NY: St. Martin's Press.

Gass, M. A., & Gillis, H. L. (2010). Clinical supervision in adventure therapy: Enhancing the field through an active experiential model. *Journal of Experiential Education, 33*(1), 72–89. doi:10.5193/JEE.33.1.72

Geller, S. M., & Greenberg, L. S. (2012). *Therapeutic presence: A mindful approach to effective therapy*. Washington, DC: American Psychological Association.

Geller, S. M., & Porges, S. W. (2014). Therapeutic presence: Neurophysiological mechanisms mediating feeling safe in therapeutic relationships. *Journal of Psychotherapy Integration, 24*(3), 178–192.

Gelso, C. J., & Bhatia, A. (2012). Crossing theoretical lines: The role and effect of transference in nonanalytic psychotherapies. *Psychotherapy, 49*, 384–390.

Gianakis, M., & Carey, T. A. (2008). A review of the experience and explanation of psychological change. *Counselling Psychology Review, 23*(3), 27–38.

Gillis, H. L., Gass, M. A., & Russell, K. C. (2008). The effectiveness of Project Adventure's behavior management programs for male offenders in residential treatment. *Residential Treatment for Children & Youth, 25*(3), 227–247. doi:10.1080/08865710802429689

Gillis, H. L., & Simpson, C. (1991). Project choices: Adventure-based residential drug treatment for court-referred youth. *Journal of Addictions & Offender Counseling, 12*, 12–27.

Gladding, S. T. (2008). The impact of creativity in counseling. *Journal of creativity in mental health, 3*, 97–104. doi: 10.1080/15401380802226679

Gladding, S. T. (2015). *Groups: A counseling specialty* (7th ed.). Boston, MA: Pearson.

Goldsmith, R., Barlow, M., & Freyd, J. (2004). Knowing and not knowing about trauma: Implications for therapy. *Psychotherapy: Theory, Research, Practice, Training, 41*, 448–463.

Goodyear, R. K. (1981). Termination as a loss experience for the counselor. *The Personnel and Guidance Journal, 59*, 347–350. doi: 10.1002/j.2164-4918.1981.tb00565.x

Gottlieb, M. C., & Younggren, J. N. (2009). Is there a slippery slope? Considerations regarding multiple relationships and risk management. *Professional Psychology: Research and Practice, 40*(6), 564–571.

Gottschall, J. (2012). *The storytelling animal: How stories make us human.* New York, NY: Houghton Mifflin.

Greenberg, J. (1964). *I never promised you a rose garden.* New York, NY: Holt.

Greenberg, L. (2014). The therapeutic relationship in emotion-focused therapy. *Psychotherapy, 51*(3), 350–357.

Greenberg, L., & Johnson, S. M. (2010). *Emotionally focused therapy for couples.* New York, NY: Guilford Press.

Grencavage, L. M., & Norcross, J. C. (1990). Where are the commonalities among the therapeutic common factors? *Professional Psychology: Research and Practice, 21*(5), 372–378.

Gutheil, T. G., & Gabbard, G. O. (1993). The concept of boundaries in clinical practice: Theoretical and risk-management decisions. *American Journal of Psychiatry, 150*, 188–196.

Haddon, M. (2003). *The curious incident of the dog in the nighttime.* London, England: Jonathan Cape.

Haley, J. (1963). *Strategies of psychotherapy.* New York, NY: Grune & Stratton.

Haley, J. (1969). The art of being a failure as a therapist. *American Journal of Orthopsychiatry, 39*(4), 691–695.

Hansen, J. T., Speciale, M., & Lemberger, M. E. (2014). Humanism: The foundation and future of professional counseling. *Journal of Humanistic Counseling, 53,* 170–190. doi: 10.1002/j.2161-1939.2014.00055.x

Hanson, J. (2005). Should your lips be zipped? How therapist self-disclosure and non-disclosure affects clients. *Counselling and Psychotherapy Research, 5*(2), 96–104.

Hardy, J. A., & Woodhouse, S. S. (2008, April). How we say goodbye: Research on psychotherapy termination. *Society for the Advancement of Psychotherapy.* Retrieved from http://societyforpsychotherapy. org/say-goodbye-research-psychotherapy-termination/

Harrison, C., Jones, R., & Huws, J. C. (2012). "We're people who don't touch": Exploring clinical psychologists' perspectives on their use of touch in therapy. *Counselling Psychology Quarterly, 25*(3), 277–287.

Hatcher, R., & Gillaspy, J. A. (2006). Development and validation of a revised short version of the Working Alliance Inventory. *Psychotherapy Research, 16*(1), 12–25. doi:10.1080/10503300500352500

Hayes, S. C., Strosahl, K. D., & Wilson, K. G. (2012). *Acceptance and commitment therapy* (2nd ed.). New York, NY: Guilford Press.

Hayes, S. C., Villatte, M., Levin, M., & Hildebrandt, M. (2011). Open, aware, and active: Contextual approaches as an emerging trend in the behavioral and cognitive therapies. *Annual Review of Clinical Psychology, 7*(1), 141–168. doi:10.1146/annurev-clinpsy-032210-104449. PMID 21219193

Hendricks, C. B., & Bradley, L. J. (2005). Interpersonal theory and music techniques: A case study for a family with a depressed adolescent. *Family Journal, 13,* 400–405. doi:10.1177/1066480705278469

Herlihy, B., & Corey, G. (2015). *Boundary issues in counseling: Multiple issues in counseling* (3rd ed.). Alexandria, VA: American Counseling Association.

Hess, M. (2012). Mirror neurons, the development of empathy and digital storytelling. *Religious Education, 107*(4), 401–414.

Higginson, S., & Mansell, W. (2008). What is the mechanism of psychological change? *Psychology and Psychotherapy: Theory, Research, and Practice, 81,* 309–328.

Hill, C. E. (2014). *Helping skills: Facilitating exploration, insight, and action* (4th ed.). Washington, DC: American Psychological Association.

Hirai, M., & Clum, G. A. (2006). A meta-analytic study of self-help interventions for anxiety problems. *Behavior Therapy, 37*, 99–111.

Hodgetts, A., & Wright, J. (2007). Researching clients' experiences: A review of qualitative studies. *Clinical Psychology and Psychotherapy, 14*, 157–163.

Hoglend, P. (2014). Exploration of the patient–therapist relationship in psychotherapy. *American Journal of Psychiatry, 171*(10), 1056–1066.

Homer, S. (2005). *Jacques Lacan*. New York, NY: Routledge.

Hovarth, A. O., Del Re, A. C., Fluckiger, C., & Symonds, D. (2011). Alliance in individual psychotherapy. In J. C. Norcross (Ed.), *Psychotherapy relationships that work* (pp. 25–69). New York, NY: Oxford University Press.

Horvath, A. O., & Greenberg, L. S. (1989). Development and validation of the Working Alliance Inventory. *Journal of Counseling Psychology, 36*, 223–233.

Howe, D. (1993). *On being a client: Understanding the processes of counselling and psychotherapy*. London, UK: Sage.

Howe, D. (2013). *Empathy: What it is and why it matters*. New York, NY: Palgrave.

Hsu, J. (2008). The secrets of storytelling: Our love for telling tales reveals the workings of the mind. *Scientific American Mind, 19*(4), 46–51.

Iacoboni, M. (2008). *Mirroring people: The new science of how we connect with others*. New York, NY: Farrar, Straus & Giroux.

Ickes, W. (1997). *Empathic accuracy*. New York, NY: Guilford Press.

Ingemark, C. A. (Ed.). (2013). *Therapeutic uses of storytelling*. Lund, Sweden: Nordic Academic Press.

Jack, S., & Ronan, K. (2008). Bibliotherapy: Practice and research. *School Psychology International, 29*(2), 161–182.

Jamison, K. R. (1995). *An unquiet mind*. New York, NY: Alfred A. Knopf.

Johnson, D. R., & Lubin, H. (2015). *Principles and techniques of trauma-centered psychotherapy*. Arlington, VA: American Psychiatric Publications.

Joseph, S. (2011). *What doesn't kill us: The new psychology of posttraumatic growth*. New York, NY: Basic Books.

Josselson, R. (2003). On becoming the narrator of one's own life. In A. Lieblich, D. P. McAdams, & R. Josselson (Eds.), *Healing plots: The narrative basis of psychotherapy* (pp. 111–127). Washington, DC: American Psychological Association.

Joyce, A. S., Piper, W. E., Ogrodniczuk, J. S., & Klein, R. H. (2007). *Termination in psychotherapy: A psychodynamic model of processes and outcomes.* Washington, DC: American Psychological Association.

King, L. A., King, D. W., Fairbank, J. A., Keane, T. M., & Adams, G. A. (1998). Resilience–recovery factors in posttraumatic stress disorder among female and male Vietnam veterans: Hardiness, postwar support, and additional stressful life events. *Journal of Personality and Social Psychology, 74,* 420–434.

Knox, R. (2013). Relational depth from the client's perspective. In R. Knox, D. Murphy, S. Wiggins, & M. Cooper (Eds.), *Relational depth: New perspectives and developments* (pp. 21–35). New York, NY: Palgrave Macmillan.

Knox, S., & Hill, C. E. (2003). Therapist self-disclosure: Research-based suggestions for practitioners. *Journal of Clinical Psychology, 59,* 529–539.

Kocet, M. M. (2006). Ethical challenges in a complex world: Highlights of the 2005 *ACA Code of Ethics. Journal of Counseling & Development, 84,* 228–234.

Kocet, M. M., & Herlihy, B. J. (2014). Addressing value-based conflicts within the counseling relationship: A decision-making model. *Journal of Counseling & Development, 92,* 180–186. doi:10.1002/j.1556-6676.2014.00146.x

Kohut, H. (1977). *The restoration of the self.* New York, NY: International Universities Press.

Kottler, J., & Blau, D. (1989). *The imperfect therapist: Learning from failure in therapeutic practice.* San Francisco, CA: Jossey-Bass.

Kottler, J., Sexton, T., & Whiston, S. (1994). *Heart of healing: Relationships in therapy.* San Francisco, CA: Jossey-Bass.

Kottler, J. A. (1991). *The compleat therapist.* San Francisco, CA: Jossey-Bass.

Kottler, J. A. (1992). *Compassionate therapy: Working with difficult clients.* San Francisco, CA: Jossey-Bass.

Kottler, J. A. (1997). *Travel that can change your life.* San Francisco, CA: Jossey-Bass.

Kottler, J. A. (2014). *Stories we've heard, stories we've told: Life-changing narratives in therapy and everyday life.* New York, NY: Oxford University Press.

Kottler, J. A. (2017). *On being a therapist* (5th ed.). New York, NY: Oxford University Press.

Kottler, J. A., & Carlson, J. (2002). *Bad therapy: Master therapists share their worst failures.* New York, NY: Brunner/Routledge.

Kottler, J. A., & Carlson, J. (2006). *The client who changed me: Stories of therapist personal transformation.* New York, NY: Brunner/Routledge.

Kottler, J. A., & Carlson, J. (2015). *On being a master therapist: Practicing what we preach.* New York, NY: Wiley.

Kottler, J. A., Carlson, J., & Keeney, B. (2004). *An American shaman: An odyssey of ancient healing traditions.* New York, NY: Brunner/Routledge.

Kottler, J. A., & Englar-Carlson, M. (2015). *Learning group leadership* (3rd ed.). Thousand Oaks, CA: Sage.

Kottler, J. A., Englar-Carlson, M., & Carlson, J. (Eds.). (2013). *Helping beyond the 50 minute hour: Therapists involved in meaningful social action.* New York, NY: Routledge.

Kottler, J. A., & Marriner, M. (2009). *Changing people's lives while transforming your own: Paths to social justice and global human rights.* New York, NY: Wiley.

Krakow, B., & Zadra, A. (2006). Clinical management of chronic nightmares: Imagery rehearsal therapy. *Behavioral Sleep Medicine, 4*(1), 45–70.

Krupnick, J. L. (2013). Therapeutic alliance in working with trauma survivors. In D. Murphy & S. Joseph (Eds.), *Trauma and the therapeutic relationship: Approaches to process and practice* (pp. 25–43). New York, NY: Palgrave.

Ladany, N. (2014). The ingredients of supervisor failure. *Journal of Clinical Psychology, 70*(11), 1094–1103. doi: 10.1002/jclp.22130

Lambert, M. J. (1986). Implications of psychotherapy outcome research for eclectic psychotherapy. In J. C. Norcross (Ed.), *Handbook of eclectic psychotherapy* (pp. 436–462). New York, NY: Brunner/Mazel.

Lambert, M. J. (Ed.). (2013). *Bergin and Garfield's handbook of psychotherapy and behavior change* (6th ed.). New York, NY: Wiley.

Lambert, M. J., & Shimokawa, K. (2011). Collecting client feedback. *Psychotherapy, 48*(1), 72–79.

Landreth, G. L. (2012). *Play therapy: The art of the relationship* (3rd ed.). New York, NY: Taylor & Francis Group.

Lankton, C. H., & Lankton, S. R. (1989). *Tales of enchantment: Goal-oriented metaphors for adults and children in therapy.* New York, NY: Routledge.

Larsen, D., Edey, W., & LeMay, L. (2007). Understanding the role of hope in counselling: Exploring the intentional uses of hope. *Counselling Psychology Quarterly, 20*, 401–416.

Larsen, D. J., & Stege, R. (2012). Client accounts of hope in early counseling sessions: A qualitative study. *Journal of Counseling & Development, 90*, 45–54.

Laska, K. M., Gurman, A. S., & Wampold, B. E. (2014). Expanding the lens of evidence-based practice in psychotherapy: A common factor perspective. *Psychotherapy, 51*(4), 467–481. doi: 10.1037/a0034332

Lawrence, C., Foster, V. A., & Tieso, C. L. (2015). Creating creative clinicians: Incorporating creativity into counselor education. *Journal of Creativity in Mental Health, 10*, 166–180.

Lawson, G. (2007). Wellness and impairment: A national survey. *Journal of Humanistic Counseling, Education and Development, 46*, 20–35.

Lawson, G., & Myers, J. E. (2011). Wellness, professional quality of life, and career-sustaining behaviors: What keeps us well? *Journal of Counseling & Development, 89*(2), 163–171.

Lazarus, A. A. (1994). How certain boundaries and ethics diminish therapeutic effectiveness. *Ethics and Behavior, 4*, 255–261.

Lazarus, A. A., & Zur, O. (2002). *Dual relationships and psychotherapy.* New York, NY: Springer.

Lee, B., & Prior, S. (2013). Developing therapeutic listening. *British Journal of Guidance & Counselling, 41*, 91–104. doi:10.1080/0306 9885.2012.705816

Levers, L. L. (2012). *Trauma counseling: Theories and interventions.* New York, NY: Springer.

Levine, M. (2004, June 1). Tell your doctor all your problems, but keep it less than a minute. *New York Times.* Retrieved from http://www.nytimes.com/2004/06/01/health/tell-the-doctor-all-your-problems-but-keep-it-to-less-than-a-minute.html?pagewanted=all&src=pm

Levitt, H. M., Rattanasampan, W., Chaidaroon, S. S., Stanley, C., & Robinson, T. (2009). The process of personal change through reading fictional narratives: Implications for psychotherapy practice and theory. *The Humanistic Psychologist, 37*, 326–352.

Ligiero, D. P., & Gelso, C. (2002). Countertransference, attachment, and the working alliance: The therapist's contribution. *Psychotherapy: Theory, Research, and Practice, 39*, 3–11.

Luborsky, L. (1976). Helping alliances in psychotherapy. In J. L. Cleghhorn (Ed.), *Successful psychotherapy* (pp. 92–116). New York, NY: Routledge.

Lynn, D. J., & Vaillant, G. E. (1998). Anonymity, neutrality, and confidentiality in the actual methods of Sigmund Freud: A review of 43 cases, 1907–1939. *American Journal of Psychiatry, 155*, 163–171.

Magai, C., & Haviland-Jones, J. (2002). *The hidden genius of emotion.* Cambridge, UK: Cambridge University Press.

Maguire, J. (1998). *The power of personal storytelling: Spinning tales to connect with others.* New York, NY: Jeremy Tarcher.

Mailloux, S. L. (2014). The ethical imperative: Special considerations in the trauma counseling process. *Traumatology, 20*(1), 50–56.

Măirean, C., & Turliuc, M. N. (2013). Predictors of vicarious trauma beliefs among medical staff. *Journal of Loss & Trauma, 18*(5), 414–428. doi:10.1080/15325024.2012.714200

Manthei, R. J. (2005). What can clients tell us about seeking counselling and their experience of it? *International Journal for the Advancement of Counselling, 4,* 541–555.

Marmarosh, C. L. (2015). Emphasizing the complexity of the relationship: The next decade of attachment-based psychotherapy research. *Psychotherapy, 52*(1), 12–18.

Maroda, K. J. (2012). *Psychodynamic techniques: Working with emotion in the therapeutic relationship.* New York, NY: Guilford Press.

Mathieu, F. (2012). *Compassion fatigue workbook.* New York, NY: Routledge.

McKee, R. (2003, June). Storytelling that moves people. *Harvard Business Review,* 51–55.

McMahon, L. (2010). Long-term complex relationships. In D. Tumey (Ed.), *Relationship-based social work: Getting to the heart of practice* (pp. 148–163). London, England: Jessica Kingsley.

McMillan, M., & McLeod, J. (2006). Letting go: The client's experience of relational depth. *Person-Centered and Experiential Therapies, 5*(4), 277–292.

Meichenbaum, D. (2013). The therapeutic relationship as a common factor: Implications for trauma therapy. In D. Murphy & S. Joseph (Eds.), *Trauma and the therapeutic relationship: Approaches to process and practice* (pp. 2–24). New York, NY: Palgrave.

Meichenbaum, D., & Cameron, R. (1989). Stress inoculation training. In D. Meichenbaum & M. E. Jaremko (Eds.), *Stress reduction and prevention* (pp. 115–154). New York, NY: Springer.

Miller, S., & Hubble, M. (2011, March/April). The road to mastery. *Psychotherapy Networker,* 22–31.

Miller, W. R., & Rollnick, S. (2012). *Motivational interviewing: Helping people change* (3rd ed.). New York, NY: Guilford Press.

Minuchin, S. (1974). *Families and family therapy.* Cambridge, MA: Harvard University Press.

Moleski, S. M., & Kiselica, M. S. (2005). Dual relationships: A continuum ranging from destructive to therapeutic. *Journal of Counseling & Development, 83*, 3–11.

Moyers, T. B. (2014). The relationship in motivational interviewing. *Psychotherapy, 51*(3), 358–363.

Mozdzierz, G. J., Peluso, P. R., & Lisiecki, J. (2014). *Advanced principles of counseling and psychotherapy: Learning, integrating, and consolidating the nonlinear thinking of master practitioners.* New York, NY: Routledge.

Murphy, D., & Joseph, S. (Eds.). (2013). Putting the relationship at the heart of trauma therapy. In *Trauma and the therapeutic relationship: Approaches to process and practice* (pp. 1–11). New York, NY: Palgrave.

Nakash, O., Nagar, M., & Kanat-Maymon, Y. (2015). "What should we talk about?" The association between the information exchanged during the mental health intake and the quality of the working alliance. *Journal of Counseling Psychology, 62*, 514–520. doi: 10.1037/cou0000074

Neimeyer, R. (Ed.). (2001). *Meaning reconstruction and the experience of loss.* Washington, DC: American Psychological Association.

Neimeyer, R. (2012). *Techniques of grief therapy.* New York, NY: Routledge.

Nelson, M. L., & Neufeldt, S. A. (1996). Building on an empirical foundation: Strategies to enhance good practice. *Journal of Counseling & Development, 74*, 609–615.

Neswald-Potter, R. E., Blackburn, S. A., & Noel, J. J. (2013). Revealing the power of practitioner relationships: An action-driven inquiry of counselor wellness. *Journal of Humanistic Counseling, 52*, 177–190. doi:10.1002/j.2161-1939.2013.00041.x

Neukrug, E., Bayne, H., Dean-Nganga, L., & Pusateri, C. (2013). Creative and novel approaches to empathy: A neo-Rogerian perspective. *Journal of Mental Health Counseling, 35*, 29–42.

Neukrug, E., & Milliken, T. (2011). Counselors' perceptions of ethical behaviors. *Journal of Counseling & Development, 89*, 206–216.

Nolan, P. (2012). *Therapist and client: A relational approach to psychotherapy.* New York, NY: Wiley.

Norcross, J. C. (Ed.). (2011). *Psychotherapy relationships that work* (2nd ed.). New York, NY: Oxford University Press.

Norcross, J. C., & Guy, J. D. (2007). *Leaving it at the office: A guide to psychotherapist self-care.* New York, NY: Guilford Press.

Norcross, J. C., & Lambert, M. J. (2011). Evidence-based therapy relationships. In J. C. Norcross (Ed.), *Psychotherapy relationships that work* (pp. 3–21). New York, NY: Oxford University Press.

Norcross, J. C., & Wampold, B. E. (2011). Evidence-based therapy relationships: Research conclusions and clinical practices. In J. C. Norcross (Ed.), *Psychotherapy relationships that work* (pp. 423–430). New York, NY: Oxford University Press.

O'Callaghan, D. M., & Chandler, C. K. (2011). An exploratory study of animal-assisted interventions utilized by mental health professionals. *Journal of Creativity in Mental Health, 6,* 90–104. doi:10.1 080/15401383.2011.579862

Oddli, H. W., & Ronnestad, M. H. (2012). How experienced therapists introduce the technical aspects in the initial alliance formation: Powerful decision makers supporting clients' agency. *Psychotherapy Research, 22,* 176–193.

O'Shea, E., & O'Leary, E. (2009). Counsellor anxiety in working with clients: A qualitative study. *The Irish Psychologist, 36,* 13–22.

Oyer, L., O'Halloran, M. S., & Christoe-Frazier, L. (2016). Understanding the working alliance with clients diagnosed with anorexia nervosa. *Eating Disorders, 24*(2), 121–137. doi: 10.1080/10640266.2015.1034050

Palacio, R. J. (2012). *Wonder.* New York, NY: Alfred A. Knopf.

Park, C. L., & Ai, A. L. (2006). Meaning-making and growth: New direction for research on survivors of trauma. *Journal of Loss and Trauma, 11,* 389–407.

Paul, A. M. (2012, March 17). Your brain on fiction. *New York Times.* Retrieved from http://www.nytimes.com/2012/03/18/opinion/sunday/the-neuroscience-of-your-brain-on-fiction.html?pagewanted=all&_r=0

Paul, S., & Charura, D. (2014a). The relationship in group therapy. In D. Charura & S. Paul (Eds.), *The therapeutic relationship handbook: Theory and practice* (pp. 131–145). Berkshire, UK: Open University Press.

Paul, S., & Charura, D. (2014b). The therapeutic relationship in counselling and psychotherapy. In D. Charura & S. Paul (Eds.), *The therapeutic relationship handbook: Theory and practice* (pp. 3–17). Berkshire, UK: Open University Press.

Peluso, P. R., Liebovitch, L., Gottman, J. M., Norman, M. D., & Su, J. (2012). A mathematical model of psychotherapy: An investigation using dynamic non-linear equations to model the therapeutic relationship. *Psychotherapy Research, 22*(1), 40–55. doi: 10.1080/10503307.2011.622314

Perryman, K. L., & Keller, E. A. (2009). Floratherapy as a creative arts intervention with women in a retirement home. *Journal of Creativity in Mental Health, 4*, 334–342. doi:10.1080/15401380903372653

Phelps, A., Lloyd, D. Creamer, M., & Forbes, D. (2009). Caring for carers in the aftermath of trauma. *Journal of Aggression, Maltreatment and Trauma, 18*, 133–330.

Plath, S. (1963). *The bell jar.* London, England: Heinemann.

Prochaska, J. O., & DiClemente, C. C. (1982). Transtheoretical therapy: Toward a more integrative model of change. *Psychotherapy: Theory, Research and Practice, 19*, 276–288.

Prochaska, J. O., & DiClemente, C. C. (1984). *The transtheoretical approach: Crossing traditional boundaries of therapy.* Homewook, IL: Dow Jones/Irwin.

Prochaska, J. O., & DiClemente, C. C. (1986). Toward a comprehensive model of change. In W. R. Miller & N. Heather (Eds.), *Treating addictive behaviors: Processes of change* (pp. 3–27). New York, NY: Plenum Press.

Prochaska, J. O., & Norcross, J. C. (2013). *Systems of psychotherapy: A transtheoretical analysis* (8th ed.). Belmont, CA: Wadsworth.

Rabu, M., Binder, P. E., & Haavind, H. (2013). Negotiating ending: A qualitative study of the process of ending psychotherapy. *European Journal of Psychotherapy and Counselling, 15*(3), 274–295.

Rabu, M., Haavind, H., & Binder, P. E. (2013). We have traveled a long distance and sorted out the mess in the drawers: Metaphors for moving towards the end in psychotherapy. *British Journal of Counselling and Psychotherapy, 13*(1), 71–80.

Ratts, M. J., Singh, A. A., Nassar-McMillan, S., Butler, S. K., & McCullough, J. R. (2015). Multicultural and Social Justice Counseling Competencies: Guidelines for the counseling profession. *Journal of Multicultural Counseling and Development, 44*, 28–48. doi:10.1002/jmcd.12035

Ray, D. C. (2011). *Advanced play therapy: Essential conditions, knowledge, and skills for child practice.* New York, NY: Taylor & Francis Group.

Razzaque, R., Okoro, E., & Wood, L. (2015). Mindfulness in clinician therapeutic relationships. *Mindfulness, 6*, 170–174.

Reese, R. J., Toland, M. D., & Slone, N. C. (2010). Effect of client feedback on couple psychotherapy outcomes. *Psychotherapy: Theory, Research, Practice, and Training, 47*(4), 616–630.

Reis, B. F., & Brown, L. G. (2006). Preventing therapy dropouts in the real world: The clinical utility of videotape preparation and client estimate of treatment duration. *Professional Psychology: Research and Practice, 37*, 311–316.

Reynolds, A. L. (2008). Universalism. In F. T. L. Leong, E. Altmaier, M. G. Constantine, H. E. A. Tinsley, & B. Walsh (Eds.), *Encyclopedia of counseling* (Vol. 4: Cross-Cultural Counseling, pp. 1359–1361). Thousand Oaks, CA: Sage.

Reynolds, G. (2012). *Presentation Zen: Simple ideas on presentation design and delivery.* Berkeley, CA: New Riders.

Rizzolatti, G., & Craighero, L. (2004). The mirror-neuron system. *Annual Review of Neuroscience, 27*, 169–192.

Rogers, C. (1957). The necessary and sufficient conditions of therapeutic personality change. *Journal of Consulting Psychology, 21*, 95–103.

Rogers, C. (1980). *A way of being.* Boston, MA: Houghton Mifflin.

Rosenthal, H. (2011). When therapists lie to promote their own agendas. In J. Kottler & J. Carlson (Eds.), *Duped: Lies and deception in psychotherapy* (pp. 39–46). New York, NY: Routledge.

Rucki, A. (2014, October 7). Average smartphone user checks device 221 times a day, according to research. *London Evening Standard.* Retrieved from http://www.standard.co.uk/news/techandgadgets/average-smartphone-user-checks-device-221-times-a-day-according-to-research-9780810.html

Safran, J. D., Muran, J. C., & Eubanks-Carter, C. (2011). Repairing alliance ruptures. In J. C. Norcross (Ed.), *Psychotherapy relationships that work* (pp. 224–238). New York, NY: Oxford University Press.

Satir, V. (1983). *Conjoint family therapy* (3rd ed.). Palo Alto, CA: Science and Behavior Books.

Schroder, D. (2004). *Little windows into art therapy: Small openings for beginning therapists.* Philadelphia, PA: Jessica Kingsley.

Schwartz, B., & Flowers, J. (2010). *How to fail as a therapist: 50+ ways to lose or damage your patients* (2nd ed.). Atascadero, CA: Impact.

Shapiro, S. L. (2009). The integration of mindfulness and psychology. *Journal of Clinical Psychology, 65*(6), 555–560.

Siegel, D. J. (2012). *The developing mind: How relationships and the brain interact to shape who we are.* New York, NY: Guilford Press.

Simmons, A. (2006). *The story factor: Inspiration, influence, and persuasion through the art of storytelling.* New York, NY: Basic Books.

Skovholt, T. M. (2001). *The resilient practitioner: Burnout prevention and self-care strategies for counselors, therapists, teachers, and health professionals.* Needham Heights, MA: Allyn & Bacon.

Slattery, S. M., & Goodman, L. A. (2009). Secondary traumatic stress among domestic violence advocates: Workplace risk and protective factors. *Violence Against Women, 15*(11), 1358–1379. doi: 10.1177/1077801209347469

Smith, D., & Fitzpatrick, M. (1995). Patient–therapist boundary issues: An integrative review of theory and research. *Professional Psychology: Research and Practice, 26*(5), 499–506.

Smith, K. (2015, March/April). The rise of distance therapy. *Psychotherapy Networker*, pp. 11–12.

Solomon, G. (2001). *Reel therapy: How movies inspire you to overcome life's problems.* New York, NY: Lebhar-Friedman Books.

Solomon, R. (2010). Working with endings in relationship-based practice. In D. Tumey (Ed.), *Relationship-based social work: Getting to the heart of practice* (pp. 164–179). London, UK: Jessica Kingsley.

Spaulding, A. E. (2011). *The art of storytelling: Telling truths through telling stories.* Lanham, MD: Scarecrow Press.

Staemmler, F. M. (2012). *Empathy in psychotherapy: How therapists and clients understand each other.* New York, NY: Springer.

Stebnicki, M. A. (2007). Empathy fatigue: Healing the mind, body, and spirit of professional counselors. *American Journal of Psychiatric Rehabilitation, 10*(4), 317–338. doi:10.1080/15487760701680570

Stewart, L. A., Chang, C. Y., & Rice, R. (2013). Emergent theory and model of practice in animal-assisted therapy in counseling. *Journal of Creativity in Mental Health, 8,* 329–348. doi:10.1080/15401383.2013.844657

Stinson, D. W. (2011). When the "Burden of Acting White" is not a burden: School success and African American male students. *The Urban Review, 43*(1), 43–65. doi:10.1007/s11256-009-0145-y

Strong, T., & Nielsen, K. (2008). Constructive conversations: Revisiting selected developments with clients and counsellors. *Counselling and Psychotherapy Research, 8*(4), 253–260.

Swift, B. K., Callahan, J. L., & Vollmer, B. M. (2011). Preferences. In J. C. Norcross (Ed.), *Psychotherapy relationships that work* (pp. 301–315). New York, NY: Oxford University Press.

Tannen, T., & Daniels, M. H. (2010). Counsellor presence: Bridging the gap between wisdom and new knowledge. *British Journal of Guidance and Counseling, 38*(1), 1–15.

Tedeschi, R. G., & Calhoun, L. G. (1995). *Trauma and transformation: Growing in the aftermath of suffering.* Thousand Oaks, CA: Sage.

Teyber, E., & Teyber, F. M. (2014). Working with the process dimension in relational therapies: Guidelines for clinical training. *Psychotherapy, 51*(3), 334–341.

Theriault, A., & Gazzola, N. (2005). Feelings of inadequacy, insecurity, and incompetence among experienced therapists. *Counselling and Psychotherapy Research, 5,* 15–26.

Tryon, G. S., & Winograd, G. (2011). Goal consensus and collaboration. In J. C. Norcross (Ed.), *Psychotherapy relationships that work* (pp. 153–167). New York, NY: Oxford University Press.

Ulus, F. (2003). *Movie therapy, moving therapy! The healing power of film clips in therapeutic settings.* New Bern, NC: Trafford.

van der Kolk, B. (2014). *The body keeps score: Brain, mind, and body in the healing of trauma.* New York, NY: Viking.

van Emmerik, A. A. P., Kamphuis, J. H., Hulsbosch, A. M., & Emmelkamp, P. M. G. (2002). Single session debriefing after psychological trauma: A meta-analysis. *The Lancet, 360,* 766–771. doi:10.1016/S0140-6736(02)09897-5

Vanheule, S., Desmet, M., Meganck, R., Inslegers, R., Willemsen, J., De Schryver, M., & Devisch, I. (2014) Reliability in psychiatric diagnosis with the DSM: Old wine in new barrels. *Psychotherapy and Psychosomatics, 83,* 313–314. doi: 10.1159/000358809

Vasquez, M. J. T., Bingham, R. P., & Barnett, J. E. (2008). Psychotherapy termination: Clinical and ethical responsibilities. *Journal of Clinical Psychology, 64*(5), 653–665.

Vega, D., Moore, J. L., III, & Miranda, A. H. (2015). In their own words: Perceived barriers to achievement by African American and Latino high school students. *American Secondary Education, 43*(3), 36–59.

Venart, E., Vassos, S., & Pitcher-Heft, H. (2007). What individual counselors can do to sustain wellness. *Journal of Humanistic Counseling, Education and Development, 46,* 50–65.

Walker, A. (1982). *The color purple.* San Diego, CA: Harcourt Brace Jovanovich.

Wampold, B. E. (2001). *The great psychotherapy debate: Models, methods, and findings.* Mahwah, NJ: Erlbaum.

Weinrach, S. G., & Thomas, K. R. (2004). The AMCD Multicultural Counseling Competencies: A critically flawed initiative. *Journal of Mental Health Counseling, 26,* 81–93.

Werdel, M. B., & Wicks, R. J. (2012). *Primer on posttraumatic growth.* New York, NY: Wiley.

White, M., & Epston, D. (1994). *Narrative means to therapeutic ends.* New York, NY: W. W. Norton.

Williams, A. M., Helm, H. M., & Clemens, E. V. (2012). The effect of childhood trauma, personal wellness, supervisory working alliance, and organizational factors on vicarious traumatization. *Journal of Mental Health Counseling, 34,* 133–153.

Wooder, B. (2008). *Movie therapy: How it changes lives.* UK: Rideau Lakes.

Woody, R. H. (1988). *Protecting your mental health practice: How to minimize legal and financial risk.* San Francisco, CA: Jossey-Bass.

Yalçın, İ., & Malkoç, A. (2015). The relationship between meaning in life and subjective well-being: Forgiveness and hope as mediators. *Journal of Happiness Studies, 16*(4), 915–929. doi:10.1007/s10902-014-9540-5

Yalom, I. D. (1975). *The theory and practice of group psychotherapy.* New York, NY: Basic Books.

Yalom, I. D. (2005). *Schopenhauer's cure.* New York, NY: HarperCollins.

Yalom, I. D. (2015). *Creatures of a day and other tales of psychotherapy.* New York, NY: Basic Books.

Yashinsky, D. (2004). *Suddenly they heard footsteps: Storytelling for the twenty-first century.* Jackson, MS: University Press of Mississippi.

Younggren, J. N., & Gottlieb, M. C. (2004). Managing risk when contemplating multiple relationships. *Professional Psychology: Research and Practice, 35*(3), 255–260.

Zipes, J. (2006). *Why fairy tales stick.* New York, NY: Routledge.

Ziv-Beiman, S. (2013). Therapist self-disclosure as an integrative intervention. *Journal of Psychotherapy Integration, 23*(1), 59–74.

Zur, O. (2007). *Boundaries in psychotherapy: Ethical and clinical explorations.* Washington, DC: American Psychological Association.

Zur, O. (2009). Therapist self-disclosure: Standard of care, ethical considerations, and therapeutic context. In A. Bloomgarden & R. B. Mennuti (Eds.), *Psychotherapist revealed: Therapists speak about self-disclosure in psychotherapy* (pp. 31–51). New York, NY: Routledge.

Zur, O. (2014). Not all multiple relationships are created equal: Mapping the maze of 26 types of multiple relationships. *Independent Practitioner, 34*(1), 15–22.

Index

Tables are indicated by "t" following page numbers.

power of, 94
relationships with stories, 100–102
self-disclosures as. *See* Self-disclosures
stories as coded packages, 98–100
story recommendations outside of
sessions, 100–102
Strategic counseling, 104
Strategies and interventions
for boundaries and barriers in
counseling relationships, 121–144.
See also Boundaries and barriers
customizing relationships, 63–78. *See
also* Customized relationships
for enhancing counseling relationships,
17, 107–119. *See also* Enhancement
of relational effects
for promotion of relationships, 45–61.
See also Promotion of relationships
for storytelling, 93–106. *See also*
Storytelling
for trauma counseling, 79–91. *See also*
Trauma counseling
Strength-based approach to counseling, 113
Strong, T., 77, 78
Stuart, D., 148
Stuck, feelings of being, 16–18, 47
Substance abuse
book recommendations for clients
on, 101
difficult patients and, 150
motivational interviewing and, 31,
65, 176
relapse plans for, 176
Supervisory relationships, 156–158
Support systems and groups, 38–39,
79–80, 176
Symonds, D., 77
Sympathy, 33
Systemic counseling. *See* Family counseling
Systemic model of diagnoses, 20
Systemic risks, 118–119

T

Tedeschi, R. G., 88
Television, recommendations for clients
as counseling, 101
Terminating counseling. *See* Ending
counseling relationships
Theory selection, vi, 8, 15–18
Three Approaches to Psychotherapy (film), 29
Time periods
for client sessions, 122–123
for enhancing relationships, 109
for trauma counseling, 109
Touching
boundaries for, 36, 39, 122, 127–128,
140–142
as healing method, 82–84

Transcendent empathy, 30–31, 36
Transference reaction
in group settings, 66
interventions, 47–50
in trauma counseling, 85
Transformation and transition, stories
of, 103
Trauma counseling, 79–91
approaches to, 80–82, 81*t*
book recommendations for clients
on, 101
compassion fatigue in, 160–163
customizable relationships with, 64
further treatments for, 86–88
language choice for empowering
clients, 113
overview, 79–80
posttraumatic growth for, 88–91
presence and touch healing for, 82–84
relationship construction recommendations for, 84–86
transference in, 48
Travel-based therapeutic experiences,
133–134
Trust. *See also* Deep work and
engagement
development of, 109, 114, 117
issues with, 46, 72, 85
as relationship component, 28, 30–31,
39, 90
self-disclosure and, 53
in trauma counseling, 85–87
violations of, 127–128
Turliuc, M. N., 162

U

Unique outcomes technique, 17
Universality, 70–71
An Unquiet Mind (Jamison), 101

V

Validation
in group sessions, 69
during trauma recovery, 79–80
Vanheule, S., 19
Vertical cohesion in group therapy, 68
Vicarious learning, 68
Vicarious (secondary) trauma, 160–163
Violating vs. crossing boundaries, 122,
124–125, 127–128, 142–144
Vulnerability
client resistance and, 159–160
of deep engagement, 55
as interpersonal risk, 117–118
in trauma counseling (client), 85–87
(Continued)